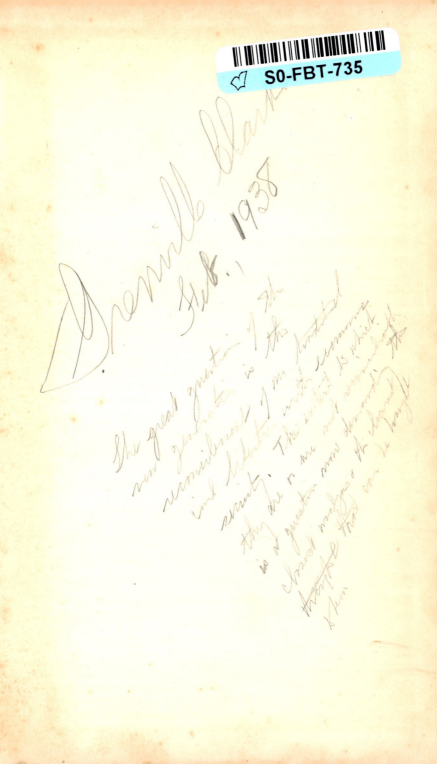

Dremile Clark

Feb. 1938

The great question of the new generation is the nonexistence of our frustrated and fulfilled with expression security. The world is what they are & are and animate, is a question man to humanity toward making to though thought that can be brought Dean

COMMUNISM, FASCISM, OR DEMOCRACY?

COMMUNISM

FASCISM

OR DEMOCRACY?

By EDUARD HEIMANN

*Formerly Professor, University of Hamburg, now Member of
Graduate Faculty, New School for Social Research*

W · W · NORTON & COMPANY · INC · PUBLISHERS
NEW YORK

This book is dedicated to
ELISABETH HEIMANN,
most German of Germans,
and to
ALVIN JOHNSON,
most American of Americans,
the two persons to whom the author owes
the continuance of his work

PREFACE

As these lines are being written, the plan for this book is in its eighth year. It was conceived in 1930 and tentatively drafted in varying forms; parts were first presented in Germany in a series of articles and a number of lectures continuing down to 1933. Enriched by a vast amount of new material and experience, it was transferred to the United States and gradually reshaped in academic and public lectures. In the meantime it received much encouragement from the rise of reformed democratic movements in various countries, such as it had tried to anticipate. Although it met defeat in 1933—or rather in the preceding years—it has been confirmed in its validity and is now presented in systematic form. It is hoped that the book may have profited by the test through which it has passed, and that its original concentration upon European points of view may have given way to the world outlook imposed upon the author by the study of conditions in America.

What the book tries to expound is the working of the various political principles. Its data are derived from the experience of the countries where the principles have been put to the test of actual application, but its results are easily adaptable to other countries as well. It strongly maintains the general validity of these principles, and at the same time recognizes the necessity of adapting and reshaping them in order to make them applicable to any individual country. It does not presume to teach the Americans what they should do, but it hopes to offer them material relevant for their decisions.

There are many to whom the author is deeply indebted for their help. Besides Alvin Johnson, the protector and mentor of all his undertakings, he wishes first to mention Professor Willard Earl Atkins, New York University, who first invited him to lecture in his department on these problems and thereby greatly furthered the final formation of the ideas. The author is under profound obligation to Mrs. Minette Kuhn, who volunteered in the war against the formidable alliance between the innumerable intellectual and linguistic Teutonisms of the first draft and the author's obstinacy. When she had to leave the task unfinished, Mr. Sidney Ratner took it up and completed it; he rewrote certain sections of the first two chapters, and whatever merit there may be in the present English form of the book must be entirely credited to him. Hans Simons was the first to read and criticize the manuscript; all his points were found to be worth heeding, which led to far-reaching changes and enlargements. Gerhard Colm, Adolf Löwe, and Paul Tillich contributed their helpful criticisms too.

Eduard Heimann.

NEW SCHOOL FOR SOCIAL RESEARCH,
OCTOBER, 1937.

CONTENTS

COMMUNISM, FASCISM, OR DEMOCRACY?

INTRODUCTION: THE PROBLEM

IN ANY discussion of political principles today the true meaning of the word democracy is a major point of controversy. Capitalism, communism, and fascism are clear-cut concepts in contrast to the vague associations that democracy evokes. Capitalism and democracy have personal and civil liberties in common, and owing to their history of association, they seem to some people to be necessarily dependent upon one another. But they are not identical. Historically, capitalism has arisen and developed under undemocratic forms of government, and today it is being attacked in behalf of democratic principles. An uncapitalistic democracy is logically possible: Jefferson clearly envisaged such an order, and the ideal order that Karl Marx contemplated was similar in spirit although very different in conditions and institutions.

The world is apparently drifting away from democracy. But while communism and fascism deride democratic liberty as a bourgeois prejudice, they both claim to be in line with the true democratic tradition, even though the means they use to attain their aims seem to be contrary to it. From this confusion only one thing stands out as clear and certain: democracy has a moral authority that cannot be ignored even by those who may be opposed to it; they are forced to invoke the magic of its name while they rally their forces to destroy it.

To dispel a confusion that has been deepened by most

contemporary discussion, we must analyze the nature and history of modern democracy. Conflicting political movements of our day, like the rival churches that emerged from original Christianity, have a common historical origin; each feels it has the true doctrine, and each has had its development affected by interaction with the others. They all start from a period in modern history when people believed in the idea of democracy and its realization seemed to be assured owing to relatively simple conditions. Since then conditions have changed and the institutions of democracy have not achieved their original goals. The reform and revolutionary currents of the present are due to men's quest for an even partly democratic order that would operate under the modern conditions which the early prophets of democracy could not have foreseen.

The democratic liberalism of Adam Smith and Thomas Jefferson, the classical socialism of Marx and Engels, the communism of Lenin and Stalin, the fascist dictatorships headed by Mussolini and Hitler, and the capitalistic system to which they all are somehow related, do not necessarily exhaust the range of political programs men have to choose from. The vehemence of the conflict today suggests that a more constructive, more comprehensive solution must be sought, a solution that wields sufficient spiritual force to dispense with the excessive use or threat of physical force. Unless we have a clear understanding of the principles underlying the various possible systems of life, our choice may be a tragic mistake. This book attempts to trace the development of capitalism and of democracy in the modern world and to furnish criteria by which we may judge the proper direction that democratic movements should take and the way in which the democratic ideal of peace through justice may be applied under changing conditions.

I

CAPITALISM *and* DEMOCRACY

A. Capitalist Monopolies and the Absolute State

CAPITALISM dominates the modern world. In the economic sphere it stresses the idea of rational business: the organization of industry and commerce on the principle of minimum costs and maximum profits. Although this idea was not unknown in ancient and medieval times, it was confined to such speculative activities as war-financing, piracy, and foreign trade. Only with the breakdown of feudalism and the guilds did rational business succeed in controlling everyday production and trade. As its power grew, large-scale industry and big business corporations rose on the ruined fortunes of the small manufacturers and businessmen they had undersold.

With the rich bourgeoisie's rule over economic affairs came social prestige and political influence. High society and high finance gradually became one after long centuries of struggle. The old regime of landowning nobility, military and political officers, and priests, was forced to give way before the new oligarchy of big business owners and managers. They and their families became the patrons of art and learning, the arbiters of fashion and taste, from the Medicis of the Italian Renaissance to the Morgans of our own day. On them the laboring classes depended for employment, the government for financial support, and the political parties for campaign contributions. The empire of the capitalists was based on their system of production and distribution, but its sway extended over society and politics. As a result, wealth became the primary criterion of social position, and all other standards were secondary. A new social pattern replaced the old.

The rise of the bourgeoisie was joined to that of the modern state, first in western Europe, later in the other European countries. Powerful princes and ministers needed the technological and financial support of the bourgeoisie in their drive toward supremacy in foreign affairs and authority at home over the nobles. Their desire for absolutism in politics made them eager to foster capitalism, commercial and industrial. This new system would free the masses from the bonds of feudalism by opening up new avenues of employment. Its productivity would enable the population to expand rapidly without starving, and would thereby furnish industry itself with more workers, the army with more soldiers, and the treasury with greater revenue. It also would supply the gunpowder and deadly firearms that were necessary for subjecting the knights and for defending and aggrandizing the state.

Capitalism in turn drew strength from the protection and encouragement given by the state. A strong monarchy like that of the Tudors in England was the bulwark of the bourgeoisie against the oppressive feudal privileges, exploitation, and exemption from taxation of the nobles. The dynastic state created from the fifteenth century onwards the necessary conditions for the expansion of the trade market: a single unified political control over wide areas of territory, a centralized legal system (the king's justice), better roads and bridges (the king's highway), security in traveling, and reduction in the number and amount of tolls. It substituted for the local coinage of towns and feudal lords a sound and widely accepted state currency and thereby created an integrated national market. It also sent out explorers to discover new worlds, chartered great trading and colonizing corporations like the British, Dutch, and French East India Companies, and acquired colonial empires in America, Asia, and Africa.

Quite as important to the bourgeoisie was the eagerness of the rulers to lavish their patronage and financial aid on industry, to erect tariffs, and to pass navigation acts like the noted ones of Cecil, Cromwell, and Colbert, so designed as to give a monopoly over shipping and commerce to the subjects of the state against all foreign rivals. State authorities supervised the source and quality of the manufactured products, gave special training to business executives in state schools and to workers in public work houses; they caught the paupers and rented them out to industrialists. The climax of regimentation was reached in German mining because the state alone could provide for the safety of the mine and the miners. The graduates of the state-operated training schools were forced upon the private mines as managers; the miners were under direct state protection. Down to this day this is symbolized by ancient customs; a group of miners on the first of every January goes to Berlin to greet the head of the state and be regaled by him. Direct state ownership in mines has always remained very large and has survived the liberal era in Germany, especially in the Saar Basin and in Upper Silesia. The English mine "royalties" spring from the same source. As late as 1769 a decree in Glatz (Silesia) provided: when a private mine is established, the mining authority "has immediately to take care of it, to regulate production, to hire the necessary workers and foremen, and to impose contributions in order to cover the cost."

A large merchant marine was carefully built up in order

to aid the naval defense in time of war and to increase the national wealth in time of peace by winning a favorable balance of trade through its foreign commerce. England's early naval policy proves that it promoted business to increase its power in international affairs. It could not yet afford a special naval fleet for the emergency of war; it relied instead for safety and victory on arming a large merchant fleet and therefore encouraged the maritime trade of its citizens and the building of merchant vessels.

This policy of governmental regulation of industry and trade for the glory, wealth, unity, and strength of the state is known as mercantilism. It reached its greatest heights in France under Colbert, Louis XIV's minister of finance, in England under Cecil and Cromwell, in Sweden under Gustavus Vasa, in Prussia only under Frederick the Great, and in Austria under Maria Theresa's husband, Francis I, and their son, Joseph II. These men were the true pioneers of modern business and were responsible for many enterprises having been started and succeeding. In Germany and Austria this was usually done through state management, but with private citizens holding shares of the stock; an example is the Preussische Seehandlung, later state bank of Prussia. In countries further west the state conferred political privileges on certain corporations that were financed mainly by private capital. Companies like the British East India Company, defined in its state-regulated charter as a "body politic and corporate," had their own armies, navies, and colonial jurisdiction, all granted to them by the state.

This system represented state-regulated capitalism in full bloom; constant supervision everywhere was the price of its success. Strange as it may now seem, even intelligent and energetic business people did not welcome the new economic system just because it offered higher profits. The

sanctity of tradition, the power of custom, were too great to be overcome easily. A mercantilist writer once remarked that the improvement of manufacture depends on the innovations introduced through the shrewdness, planning, and bounty of the state: "the merchant however keeps to what he has learned and is familiar with."

Higher profits alone could not have broken the crust of business custom and overcome the inertia of the people. New social ideas had to take the place of the old before capitalism could triumph. In our own day factory workers will often prefer greater leisure to higher income and will take advantage of increases of their wages for piece work either by slowing down their pace or by shortening the working day. The entrepreneurs of early capitalism similarly, after some success in the new field, were often content to settle down into positions they regarded as satisfactory and refused to strive for still greater profits. In England they aspired to enter the ranks of the landed gentry; in France they tried to become public officials and to fill positions that would give them an entrée to the nobility. As late as the American Revolution Frederick of Prussia had to warn the weavers of Silesia that unless they made more money through improved methods of production, he would harass them with taxes and military conscription. "The plebs," he said, "will not keep from the humdrum tune unless you drag them to their profit by their noses and ears." The "enlightened" state took upon itself the duty of enlightening the bourgeoisie as to their true interests.

But even a despot could not substitute capitalism at one stroke for the older forms of production and commerce. This new way of life, of earning a livelihood, could be forced upon the people only gradually. Meanwhile life, society, and the state itself followed the traditional pattern, the normal one compared with the deviant pioneering experiments in capitalistic production. Since manufacture and trade were organized within the framework of the feudal hierarchy and the conservative guilds, no legal form at first existed for the new enterprises. But a way was soon found: they were granted special legal exemptions from the traditional regulations. In addition, the same charter gave them positive privileges and favors such as the reservations of special markets, financial aid, and state-trained staffs. Mercantilism, the first phase of capitalism, was a system of franchises, privileges, and legal monopolies, given to favored individuals and groups by the state, in order to bring into being rational business: it meant the encouragement of timid investors and the dragging of conservative businessmen "to their profit by their noses and ears."

B. Economic Freedom: Its Original Democratic Meaning

From the state of paternalism free (laissez-faire) capitalism emerged when the time was ripe. The progress that mercantilism had brought about resulted finally in its destruction. Those who had prospered through government regulation and subsidies came to resent the bureaucratic supervision as their business transactions increased in number, volume, and complexity. Their principal spokesmen were Adam Smith in England and the group of Quesnay and Turgot in France; it is these who coined the slogan *laissez faire, laissez passer,* the program of the emancipation of production and trade from state interference. That principle had partly been anticipated by the English rebellion of 1640 and the Glorious Revolution of 1688; it underlay the American and French revolutions and even the English reforms of 1832. The bourgeoisie had come of age, declared their independence of the bureaucracy, and made themselves master of the state they had formerly been beholden to.

A new society had ripened in the womb of the old. Monopolistic mercantilism had given birth to laissez-faire capitalism, absolute monarchy to representative government. Representative government expressed the political supremacy of the bourgeoisie and was the logical consequence and completion of their self-rule in their businesses. For all political events and measures may have a bearing on business and cannot, therefore, be abandoned to the control of the bureaucracy once the bourgeoisie seizes the control of business. In the social realm the rule of the middle class meant the continuance of the class cleavages and inequalities that the mercantilistic state had developed through its monopolies. Big enterprises that had been actively supported by the old regime continued to flourish under the new one. An economic oligarchy owned and controlled industry and used the propertyless laboring masses to operate it. All this seems logical and simple, and it is the usual interpretation of that revolutionary period.[1]

Yet the victory of free bourgeois capitalism over state-controlled capitalism was not won without using a program of economic and social equality to get the support of the masses for the bourgeoisie. The leading thinkers of the revolutionary epoch, men as different as Rousseau, Adam Smith, Jefferson, and Fichte, expressed these democratic aspirations powerfully, although not always aware of the ultimate conclusions. Rousseau denounced the prevailing contrast of opulence and destitution and proclaimed that the ends to be striven for in society were universal liberty,

[1] A recent brilliant example of this traditional historiography is Harold J. Laski, *The Rise of Liberalism*, 1936.

equality, and fraternity. Adam Smith scolded those who "love to reap where they never sowed" and predicted that a rise of wages far in excess of profits would promote equality as society and industry progressed. He ignored the economic power and productive efficiency of accumulated capital so completely that he regarded the seemingly unwieldy joint stock companies as unfit to organize industry. The trend of his thought was anti-"monopolistic," that is, opposed to big business as he knew it, because in his opinion monopoly was "a great enemy to good management," was supported by unjust and cruel laws, and was injurious to the people at large. Fichte went beyond Smith when at the dawn of the nineteenth century he predicted that the champions of economic freedom would live to see "the remarkable spectacle of land and property yielding returns in inverse proportion to their size." And Jefferson, most consistently of all, expressed the philosophy of a new land and people, with its faith in human nature, its economic individualism, its conviction that through the instrumentality of political democracy the lot of the common man should be made better. His primary principle was that "the care of human life and happiness, and not their destruction, is the first and only legitimate object of good government." His hope was to establish a true democracy safe from the domination of Hamiltonian big business rule and protectionism.

The aim of these spokesmen for the people was not the liberation of big business from bureaucratic control, but its destruction, although they would have differed among themselves on how far to go in this direction. This raises the question: how could such keen thinkers believe in a tendency toward equality and democracy when forces were at work that soon wrecked their hopes and started opposite currents flowing? The answer is that scientific technology was only beginning to revolutionize production and build up industry when these prophets of liberalism were working out their plans for a pre-industrial society. No wonder they failed to appreciate the power and sweep of this movement and could not see how it would affect their program. Even Smith assumed, when describing the function of capital as a factor of production, that it must strengthen the position of labor since it requires labor for its operation: an increase in capital must result in greater demand for labor and raise wages. This view of capital as represented by the tool of the laborer is in sharp contrast with the type of capital described by Marx who anticipated technological unemployment as an outcome of labor-saving machines. The pre-industrial, pre-technological conditions under which Smith wrote were the basis for his optimistic belief that the free market would result in harmony and that the accumulation of capital would benefit the workers in the main. The notable series of inventions that made Whitehead call the nineteenth century the age of the invention of the method of invention began after Smith's *Wealth of Nations* had been published.[2]

[2] Much controversy in recent years has centered on the origin of the Industrial Revolution. Historical investigation has revealed many technological innovations, several of considerable importance, from the sixteenth century on, especially in England. The entire movement, however, slackened down and seemed to approach exhaustion in the second half of the eighteenth century. The literature of this era is dominated by the overshadowing fear of what might become of mankind after the exhaustion of the forests. Wood was the only fuel and almost the only material for tools and buildings; its consumption grew with the number and the buying power of the people. The sudden rise of technical innovations may be due to the pressure of this fear and the need for finding a substitute for the exhausted stock of wood. Only when coal was introduced as fuel and iron and steel as building material for machines, ships, bridges, and houses, could technical thinking and economic progress develop without handicap. It is this unpredicted and unforeseeable coincidence of the technical revolution with the social and political emancipation achieved through the

If one is to grasp the full meaning of liberalism as first conceived, and is to realize what its wreckage implies, one must dismiss the prevalent notions on the free market and think of it as unaffected by modern technological developments. Survival and success in business today depend on the power of capital, in the sense of productive machinery, because it alone secures technological superiority. Within certain limits the larger and more expensive machinery is, the greater its efficiency and the cheaper its product. If this decisive factor were eliminated, the small shop where owner and laborer are one and have a personal interest in its efficiency and success would triumph over the big plant with its indifferent or refractory workers. The monopolies of Smith's day owed their prosperity not to their size, which was a psychological handicap, but to their legal privileges and the restrictions placed upon their competitors.

The first vision of economic democracy that inspired the common man was of a world swarming with small independent producers. The program of economic liberty was not proclaimed in behalf of those in business, but of those who were excluded from business. Admission to business was under the monopolistic system an exclusive legal privilege, as admission to the guilds had become a privilege in the extra-capitalistic sphere of society. Severe legal penalties kept down the workers of the "monopolies," the lifelong journeymen of the degenerating guilds, and the bondsmen of the feudal estates, and prevented any escaping from this hopeless condition. Consequently, personal freedom, with an emphasis on economic freedom and the abolition of all privileges, appeared as the one

American and French revolutions that forms the starting point of our analysis. This coincidence explains why the original liberal ideas were conceived as pre-technical and pre-industrial.

remedy that would make every able man independent in his own field of work. The best example down to this day of the type of existence aimed at by original democracy is that agrarian reform which substitutes a number of independent small units for a few big ones and expects them to be self-sustaining. In original democracy this plan would have applied to all branches of economic life. Liberalism was democratic because it promised to lead to universal independence and equality.

The desire of the rich bourgeoisie for a government representative of their interests was paralleled by the desire of the independent workers for self-government. They could have applied the logic of the bourgeoisie to their own advantage and could have shown that economic and political democracy complemented one another and that both were necessary to bring into existence a true community of the free and equal. That implied a society composed of small, independent farmers, manufacturers, and businessmen, all more or less equal in wealth and united in common administration of their common affairs.

This ideal was not realized, however, in industry, owing to the rise of scientific technology. Large plants commanded enough capital to secure the new techniques with which they surpassed the small shops in competition. Their technological superiority outweighed the psychological advantage of the small shops. Victory depended on funds sufficient to buy the new machines. The old monopoly corporations, despite the deprivation of their privileges, had the necessary capital for winning in the race of free competition. As science and industrialism progressed, the financial and technological advantages of the capitalistic enterprises sealed the doom of the small shops, made independent craftsmen propertyless workers for big concerns, and crushed the former serfs struggling to gain independence. Big business lost the support of legal monopolism only to gain a monopoly in high-powered industrial techniques.

Within the short span of a hundred years capitalism multiplied its output and succeeded in adding a surprising amount to the real incomes of even the meanest citizens, though population grew apace. Average life expectancy rose by many years; infant mortality was reduced to a small percentage. All this was due to the tremendous increase and refinement in goods made possible by capitalistic production. It is true that the work of scientific laboratories in medicine and chemistry must also be credited with a significant contribution to the fortunate result. These sciences, however, do not only spring from the same source as pioneering technology but entirely depend on the precision of the instruments and measurements provided by modern industry. The positive function of capitalism, which Marx has discovered, becomes particularly clear when contrasted with the modest idea of progress implicit in the Utopian democratic scheme. This scheme had attempted to overcome the inertia of the old order and attain progress through an appeal to individual self-interest. But pre-industrial conditions restricted progress to the limits of personal skill and knowledge attainable under the handicraft system, and had to give way to large-scale industry on the basis of capitalism.

Economic liberty had been designed to destroy the rule of big business by exposing the corporations to the competition of the newly admitted small shops, but in practice it achieved the opposite.

C. Cleavages in Capitalistic Society and Social Philosophy

Modern technology gradually transformed the principle of the freedom of business and of competition into an instrument of industrial and financial control. The democracy of the small producer and trader was superior in productivity to the bureaucratic monopolies and feudal estates, but the big industrial plants grew in resources and efficiency and overshadowed their small competitors. This had varying effects on different classes. The capitalists became the staunchest defenders of the freedom of business because they benefited most from a system that had the halo of liberalism about it. The victims of capitalism, workers and ruined businessmen, became confused and somewhat skeptical of a liberty that did not lead to real independence and prosperity. Even those independent workmen and small owners who managed to get along felt unsafe and were in danger of being misled into betraying their liberal heritage.

The forms of representative government that might have complemented a true democracy as originally envisioned became the means by which the great industrialists and financiers through their economic power, social prestige, and moral repute erected and maintained big business rule. The most striking instance of the way a new social structure has arisen, modeled on the lines of the feudal hierarchy with its fixed social status for all individuals and groups, is modern England. There the new business aristocracy and the old knightly aristocracy have gradually merged through common business ventures, a common world outlook, and family alliances. They have won an unusual political success by building up a generally recognized standard of behavior to which everybody seeks to live up, irrespective of political allegiance. The English gentleman, representing all that is admired by the English people, has been confirmed in his position of leadership time and again under the freest elections in the world. Political power has been kept through a wise restriction of class rule and many concessions to popular demands, as for example in social and labor legislation. Those in power realize the paradox that a genuine conservative must be a progressive and must adapt capitalism to a changing world if he is to succeed in keeping the system together and retaining control of it. The English system is not a rational one; it is a stratified traditional society based on the philosophy of the "free play of forces" and on the civil and political liberties of democracy.

The belief in the freedom of the natural forces as the primary source of social welfare had its roots in the hostility of the bourgeoisie to bureaucratic regimentation and went beyond the desire for freedom of business enterprise and economic innovations to that of one's personal life. This includes choice of one's mate, occupation, and residence, and the civil liberties of free citizenship. Dynamic business required a flexible society. New industrial projects often drew the masses to new manufacturing centers and forced laborers to acquire new skills. Unlimited freedom, complete mobility for all individuals, were necessary if the great opportunities of new inventions, discoveries, lands, industries, occupations, and jobs were to be realized. The enthusiasm of the bourgeoisie for progress and freedom was not confined to the economic realm; it animated science, philosophy, and art, and found fervent expression notably in England and America in a championship of the civil liberties: free speech, press, and religion, trial by jury, equality before the law.

Those who belittle these liberties by denouncing political democracy as a disguise for a capitalist dictatorship are as misleading as those who deny that democratic forms are often a façade for the plutocracy in control. In case of violent social conflict the ruling class may try to annul the liberties. If, however, the ruling class in the past had to grant the liberties to prevent a revolution, as some have argued, that would prove that the rulers could not revoke them without being overthrown. If, on the other hand, they were not forced to grant these rights, but gave them freely to the people because they themselves had fought for the principle of liberty, then these rights had become an integral part of their being and hence could not easily be abolished. Suppose, however, that the ruling class in England or America abandons the tradition of democracy in a desperate effort to retain its privileges. That does not mean that the liberties in existence up to this crucial moment have been of no value and are to be lightly dismissed today by those working for a new social order. Those liberties have been and still are very far from being identical with class rule even though they had an origin favorable to the present ruling class; otherwise they would not try to abolish them. And why have tyrants and oligarchies in other countries refused to grant them if this were not so? The history of the Prussian Junkers testifies to that domineering caste's hatred of all liberties as a potential threat to their supremacy. In short, civil liberties are more than an instrument of the capitalist regime, they represent human values other than the economic. Even the Communist Internationale, which in previous years had ridiculed their defense as a "bourgeois prejudice," was forced by the fascist experiences to acknowledge officially that the positive significance of the liberties transcends class interests.

Capitalism and democratic government, as they exist in

America and England, are not one, nor are they completely opposed. They form a highly complex system, subject to great stress and strain, yet operating at high-powered speed. The survival of the system depends upon two conditions. First, it has to prove its efficiency and adaptability by coping with the technical difficulties inherent in it, especially the economic crisis. For the time being England has succeeded in doing so without, however, any guarantee or definite program for the future. Second, the system has to maintain intact its moral standards and retain the faith and desire of the people to uphold it.[3] Recent sensational events culminating in the abdication of a king have shown how watchful the English are in this respect and how relentlessly they strike at any deviation, not hesitating at great sacrifices for the sake of preserving their social and moral structure. Seldom in history have the imponderables of social cohesion been so clearly understood, so wisely built up, and so shrewdly defended.

In the United States capitalism lacks the sanctions of morality and tradition, notwithstanding some minor approximations to it in the East. The popularity of President Roosevelt is certainly enhanced by the combination of his democratic and humane qualities with his distinctly aristocratic family background. In the main, however, the American people admire and emulate their rulers not for their moral or aesthetic standards but for their success. As long as the masses can or will believe in inexhaustible prospects for everybody in a country rich in resources and still needing men, capitalism will be upheld by democratic vote. Generally as this is accepted, many do not understand that the hope for opportunity rests on the possibility

[3] For a detailed and penetrating analysis *cf*. Adolf Löwe, *The Price of Liberty*, Day-to-Day Pamphlets, ed. by Leonard and Virginia Wolff, No. 36, London, 1937.

of an escape from capitalist domination into a genuine economic democracy, the nearest American approach to which is among the farmers of the West, although they may be under the pressure of debts to eastern capitalists. No better evidence of the force of the original democratic ideas could be given than that the democratic masses of the United States think of their present form of capitalism as a transitional stage to the time when everybody will enjoy the latent opportunities for property and independence. The "American dream" remains that of a Jeffersonian democracy of the free and equal. Capitalistic domination and inequality are only tolerated by the people; they are not accepted as a final stage.

This tense working relationship between capitalism and democracy is of course uniquely American; it is no model for the European countries where capitalism leaves practically no outlet open. In those countries the democratic reaction is against capitalism. If capitalism can no longer command faith as a halfway station on the road to renewed democratic independence, those in quest of this ideal must seek new stations.

The capitalists are content with the forms of democracy, but the democratic masses want the substance. The system of "natural liberty"—small-scale production, individual ownership for each worker, a free market—has proved impossible in an era of large-scale industry and monopoly capitalism. A new social system must be built on the basis of modern technology to reconcile economic efficiency and the essence of the eighteenth-century ideal: each man's independence in his work. Since large-scale production requires the organized, disciplined co-operation of many workmen in the same plant, the work cannot be broken up on an individualistic pattern, but has to be treated as an integrated whole, a collective enterprise. Each man's independence in his work cannot be attained directly through individual ownership, but it can be achieved indirectly through a collective independence based on collective ownership. Changing conditions force men to invent new techniques, new social institutions to realize old ideals in a revised form. This is the starting point of the socialist opposition to capitalism on behalf of democracy.

Not all the equalitarian conditions and institutions of the pre-industrial age, however, have disappeared. They still persist in important fields. The small farmers in Continental Europe, for instance, show a tendency to progress at the expense of the big estates of feudal origin and traditions. This is an important deviation from the prevailing capitalistic character of modern society. The independent producers, small farmers and businessmen, constitute a powerful and decisive element in our society, no matter how great the difference of opinion may be in regard to their future. Of course, the present crisis of capitalism has affected them, especially those who specialize in certain products and are therefore dependent on sales in the market. They have become indebted to financiers for loans covering rationalization and specialization and now feel the pressure of their debts. They face the danger of becoming bankrupt additions to the vast army of the proletariat, as millions of other once independent people before them. Can they recapture and defend their independence? That is their problem.

In a society containing sharply conflicting groups, they occupy a halfway position. They are workers, but not proletarian wage-laborers; small property-owners, but not capitalists. The two main parties in the capitalistic class struggle were formed predominantly by the Industrial Revolution, to which one credits its position of power and control and the other its degradation for the present and its expectations for the future. Both are progressive-minded and intellectual. Progress through intellectual achievement has been the pride of the bourgeoisie, progress of a more radical and far-reaching character the hope of the laborer. The intermediate lower-middle-class group, however, is in a world that antedates and is to a certain extent outside the capitalistic system. Its members are unfamiliar with the dynamic atmosphere of intellectual criticism and progress, which touches only the periphery of their pattern of life. This pattern has changed in part owing to the change in society from the static eighteenth-century economy to dynamic capitalism. The small producers do not hold the key position in economic and political life they once thought they would. But the pivot of their existence, their mode of work, still endures. What distinguishes them from other classes is the uninterrupted tradition of their pattern of work and life. Tradition is not identical with unchanging rigidity, either in technique or human experience. It allows for and includes such gradual steady development and modification as is consistent with people's sense of historical continuity in institutions and symbols. Whether serf or free man, the European peasant, for instance, plows the same field as his ancestors and resides in the shadow of the trees planted by them. An infinite number of things, big and small, important and trivial, connect his daily life with the past and with a future conceived of in similar terms. That is the reason for the tension between the independent producer and the industrial world, with its alien ways and new modes of life.

D. Freedom Versus Organization

The conflicts of society arise from the clashing interests and ideals of different social groups. Each group feels that its rights are precious, but limited by the rights of others. In a rapidly changing world, however, the traditional lines of demarcation become inadequate guides to justice; men grow alarmed about possible invasions of their rights, and new groups arise and raise their claims. All fear the suppression of the things they hold dear, all feel that they cannot submit to tyranny, and dread the cost of conflict in lives and suffering. Can some way be found to reconcile the claims of the different groups to their rights? This is the question of life or death.

The answer depends in part on understanding exactly what one means by rights and interests. A right is a claim to the recognition of a human value or set of values capable of being realized in the daily life of men on this earth, and includes the satisfaction of their economic needs. The "economic interest" of a group is in earning a livelihood that is the basis, and a major part, of the pattern of life it is striving to create. Too often writers (not Marx) have failed to see that money is only one phase of the economic interest, at least in somewhat normal times, and that the conditions under which the money is earned—the type of work, the kind of boss and fellow workers, the relations to other people, the social standing of one's position, and so on—are of as great or greater importance. All these experiences are the basis on which a group builds its program for its pattern of life, the incorporation of its values.

Not all conceivable human values, however, can be fulfilled simultaneously in a limited universe: every pattern, individual and social, is restricted in scope. There is a wide range of human possibilities as such, and of social institutions through which they may be realized. But although different societies may emphasize different traits and values, each society has to select those qualities and institutions that will fit its pattern of values, or at least not counteract it. For the functioning of society is the continuance of life itself, and no society can incorporate opposite values if it is to function and flourish as a whole. Some standard of behavior, some principle of selection, some criterion of preference has to be used. The greater the need for organization and conformity to some accepted scale of values, however, the greater the danger of conflict and the political responsibility. Modern capitalism presents a striking example of a powerful, dynamic system that has achieved so much but only at the price of crushing out other ways of life. The present economic and spiritual crisis that threatens the unity of society represents a need for new integration. Diversity versus conformity, freedom versus organization—that is the great and formidable problem of political life. We shall discuss it in the light of the various solutions that have been proposed from the time of Adam Smith and Jefferson to the present crisis.

II

INDIVIDUALISTIC DEMOCRACY

A. Liberty and Equality

THE LIBERTY and the equality that the pioneers of liberalism dreamed of were never completely realized anywhere, even in the United States during the administrations of Jefferson and Jackson. The course of history swerved from the path of small-scale industry and trade to that of modern capitalism. Nevertheless, the principles underlying the pre-capitalistic democracy that Adam Smith and other "Utopians" strove for are still of crucial importance. They dominate those engaged in the sections of production not conquered by big business and have left their impress on all the past and current efforts to build under changed conditions a true democracy free from economic domination. That is why we must fully understand them in order to comprehend the true purport of modern democracy in the countries of Western civilization.

 Liberty, in modern democracy, is meant to encompass and permeate the whole of life. It centers, therefore, on the sphere of work because that fills the main part of life. In the sense of man's independence in his work, liberty is the core of the modern democratic idea, with all the consequences for self-government at large that follow. In this sense liberty and democracy are identical. The ways of realizing democracy will vary under different conditions, but they all are realizations of the same democratic impulse. In the frame of this book we cannot inquire why ancient democracy was not connected with the organization of work and why this impulse has arisen only in the modern world. The desire for self-government and independence stands out as one of the distinguishing features of modern civilization. It is not, however, a fixed, invariant phase of human nature as the rise of fascism in Italy and Germany definitely proves. That does not affect the worth of democracy. It only indicates that modern democracy sprang from a definite historical milieu, that it needs a definite historical type of man. This will be discussed later.

The desire for independence originates in the sufferings from serfdom or bondage of any sort. In the Europe preceding the liberal era, the serfs on the manorial estates, the lifelong journeymen of the guild masters, the workers assigned to monopolistic corporations by the police and the poor-house authorities, all felt that their labor was not their own, but their lord's, master's, and corporation's. The German Peasants' Revolts of 1524-25, which were choked in streams of blood by the nobles, still had sprung only from the desire of the peasants to restore genuine feudal morality and responsibility by the nobles for their protection against abuse and exploitation. But Luther's belief in authority as the only possible safeguard of social cohesion was so strong that he denounced the rebellious men as "poisonous, pernicious, and devilish." Similar uprisings occurred in England, and the feeling of the insurgents found expression in the words of an unknown laborer: "As sheepe or lambs are a prey to the wolfe or lion, so are the poor men to the rich men." It is only from that time on that men both in England and in Germany raised the question: "When Adam delved and Eve span, who was then the gentleman?" The idea gained ground that the land naturally belongs to the man who cultivates it. An irresistible tide, probably the strongest in modern social history, began to sweep the world in favor of the peasant's claim to his land. The artisans' guilds in the towns had likewise been losing, from the fifteenth century on, their tradition of regulated liberty and equality and had been developing a class rule of hereditary masters. Consequently, currents of unrest began to flow through the masses of their journeymen, as through the workers for the capitalistic monopoly companies.

The demand for independence centers on the property question. The significance of property lies in its human implications. Without property a man has no freedom. If the peasant were made personally free, but deprived of his land, what should he do? Abstract freedom is not even conceivable; freedom as a peasant within his own domain is the only freedom he desires. Property, as a necessary condition for personal liberty, is then a natural right of man: not in the sense of a money fortune that might serve to bridge a period of financial embarrassment, but in the sense of man's ownership and mastery in a given field of work.

Revolt against exploitation and domination is only the negative phase of liberty. The positive phase consists in the chance given to each individual for self-expression and self-realization. Each man's work, as soon as it is his own, enables him to experience the varied phases and qualities of human life and emotion: success and failure, effort and pride, trouble and tension, rebellion and resignation. If the work is in any way congenial, it gives him a social standing and a sense of self-respect and dignity as a human being that pervades his whole life. The relation between the peasant and his land, for example, is so profound that it is difficult to say whether the land belongs to the peasant or the peasant to the land; each shapes the other and determines the other's existence. It is no contradiction that the same property that binds man to his work makes him free in his work.

This conception of property as an instrument of economic democracy contrasts sharply with the legalistic conception of private property. The latter stresses the owner's exclusive right to nearly any use, whether socially wholesome or not. The democratic view, on the other hand, does not emphasize the exclusive aspect of property and concentrates on property as a requisite to self-expression and creative achievement. It does not justify any accidental or arbitrary distribution of property that may happen to exist, as "sacred," beyond reform. It considers the term "sacred right" as applicable only to the desire of every man to attain freedom in his work through property.

If this is to be accomplished, property as a natural and inalienable right must be accessible to everybody. It must not extend beyond anyone's field of work so as to encroach upon one's neighbor's field of work and thereby deprive him of his right. Private property consists in one man owning objects needed by others in their work. It is class property and implies the distinction between owner and worker. The property rights of non-working owners rest on a class of propertyless workers to operate those properties and are the very negation of democracy and liberty so far as the organization of work is concerned. In democracy private property in that sense could not exist; democracy rests on individual property restricted in size to what the owner operates or cultivates himself. In a system of small-scale manufacture and agriculture this form of ownership is easily attainable.

One man's individual property, thus limited, leaves

room for another's, in fact, for everybody else's. It enables everyone to be free of domination by others economically. The democratic character of individual property lies in the universal applicability of its principles. In other words, social equality is achieved through everybody having individual property. Everyone, since he is economically independent, is the social equal of everybody else. The widespread view that one has to choose between liberty and equality ignores the basic principles of democracy. Social equality rests on universal independence, but is perfectly compatible with the differences of income that result from differences in personal skill, industriousness, and energy. No system can avoid these differences; every system has to take care of the naturally handicapped by special provisions. The important point for democracy is that no excess income can be used, under universal small-scale production, to encroach upon the liberty of others. If anyone with an excess income attempted to hire workers in order to increase his wealth, he would find none to hire; or, if he found any, he would soon lose out as their work would be less efficient than that of his independent competitors. Inequality of income, under such conditions, cannot become very great and cannot lead to the social inequality that exists when one group dominates another. The fact that two neighboring family farms differ in size does not impair the neighborly solidarity any more than differing wage rates for different kinds of skill destroy the social unity of the working class today. As long as no able man starves and none wields the power of private property over others, fundamental equality persists. Liberty and equality belong together in the classless democratic society based on universal individual property.

The equalitarian feature of universal liberty and property promotes the co-operative spirit. Farmers in a demo-

cratic society, regardless of minor differences of property
and income, can and will co-operate in all matters pertaining to their mutual benefit. Occasions for co-operation
range all the way from fighting against enemies, fire, flood,
and pestilence, to providing irrigation and drainage, en-
tertainment and education. Nothing is more erroneous than
to attribute a self-isolating tendency to the small producers
with their individual property holdings. The truth is that
nowhere is the moral and material power of the community so conspicuous as in a group of equals where each
man's independence is accepted as an indefeasible right.
This community spirit is therefore very remote from the
spirit of communism; it is founded upon individual work
and individual property.

It is strikingly exemplified in the agricultural co-operatives that have flourished in Europe with increased vigor
from the time that conditions forced the farmers to meet
the requirements of the modern market. Today one can
hardly think of a moderately advanced country where
there would be a village without a modern co-operative or
a farmer not connected with one. Denmark, Sweden, Fin-
land, Norway, and Holland are only the most notable of
the countries using this technique; but that may help to
explain why an agrarian democracy has been best preserved among them. Germany, although not one of the
foremost co-operative states, had in 1930 some thirty thousand rural credit co-operatives with two million members,
savings deposits of $1\frac{1}{2}$ billion marks, a strong central organization for dealing with the outside credit market and
adjusting local deficits and surpluses of capital. Thousands
of co-operatives bought fertilizer and machines and
handled as much as one-half of the country's dairy products. The quiet and steady growth of the rural co-operative movement has not attracted the attention of the aver-

age urban intellectual, who believes that farmers are too individualistic and backward to organize effectively and form a sad contrast to the "rational and collective-minded" labor movement. The facts, however, disprove this easy assumption. The rural co-operatives in northern Europe are practically all-inclusive, but the labor unions in none of the leading countries have succeeded in organizing more than one-third of the workers. (This refers even to republican Germany, and the only exception is the most recent development in France.) In the United States millions of growers of fruit, wheat, and other crops have created such efficient co-operative selling agencies as to acquire a temporary monopoly in their field.

The co-operative tendency among individual producers is not restricted to farmers. A similar movement prevails among Continental artisans; their credit co-operatives are older and relatively no less effective than the rural ones. Without this co-operative spirit and organization, the individual pattern of work could not have survived, but this does not indicate an inherent weakness in the system of individual producers. It only proves that the system has sufficient flexibility to rise above a false philosophy of self-sufficient individualism and to achieve through voluntary co-operation a community of free and equal individuals.

Proof of the genuine character of the community feeling, for example among farmers, is given not only by their spontaneous co-operative organizations, but by their custom of never demanding interest or premium for neighborly aid through money, tools, or labor. These are simply regarded as services to the community which everybody has to render in order to be entitled to them when in need. This community spirit distinguishes the "co-operative individualism" of the socially equal from the "rugged," extremist individualism of men competing in a life-or-death struggle. In a dynamic system of rapid progress and increasing concentration of power those who are at one moment equal may become unequal any moment; everyone hopes to ruin his rival, but fears he may be ruined instead. Competitors may sometimes unite for certain purposes, as in the cartels that control the prices of independent firms throughout Europe. But once a cartel contract expires, they renew their competition or engage in a contest for the most favorable terms in the next cartel arrangement. Dynamic competition, within or outside the cartels, breeds a feeling of fear and hostility entirely foreign to the co-operative individual producers who live under conditions that do not lead to the progressive elimination of independent units of production. The co-operative spirit of farmers (and of artisans) has survived the depression and is building on the new technical possibilities opened up by science.[1] The farmer is not benefited by the ruin of his neighbor; and even if he were, he could do nothing to bring it about. Two big firms may undersell each other in a desperate fight for the monopoly the survivor would acquire, but that situation cannot arise among farmers, each of whom produces a microscopic portion of the total national or world supply. Moreover, if one farmer dropped out, the others could not increase their production because, again, there would be no laborers to hire. With universal individual property, nobody profits at the ex-

[1] It should be kept in mind that this chapter centers its analysis on the possibilities inherent in a system of universal individual property that was never completely realized in the course of historic events, but might have been if certain unexpected factors, discussed in Chapter I, had not intervened. In agriculture, which has been least revolutionized by technology, our analysis may be widely applied and verified even today. This is not to deny that ignorance and misery prevail among small farmers in many countries, but this development was not inevitable. Theoretical analysis and the experiences of farmers in the advanced democratic countries prove this. See the discussion in the text above and on pages 133 and 151.

pense of another and everybody gains through co-operation.

This entire analysis presupposes the special technological conditions under which the idea of democracy arose in
the eighteenth century. These conditions have only partly
survived. At that time a system of small-scale industry and
agriculture would have enabled each unit of work to be a
separate realm of liberty for the individual. The problem
of organization and regulation was simple and the solution
evident: every worker was to be independent by owning
his sphere of work. The comparative simplicity of the
underlying conditions at that epoch should not, however,
obscure certain general principles whose validity and applicability extend beyond the conditions that first suggested them. Democracy can be attained under a system
of individual work and individual property; it can be attained under a different system of work if an equally logical system of ownership is made to correspond to the new
conditions of work. It is the coincidence of the types of
work and ownership that makes for democracy.

B. Organization and Integration

1. The Problem

Any discussion of the institutions of liberty appears
practically useless unless it is made evident that these can
function as a living system. Whatever one's set of values,
there is no doubt that the preservation of society as such
takes precedence over the question of personal and group
liberty. Irrespective of the particular system, we must first
of all provide for the cohesion of society and thereby for
the survival and continuance of life itself. Life is by no
means automatically secured nor its survival guaranteed.

The more critical the situation, the more preponderant the question of existence becomes. What shall we do if free people do not reach an agreement on what system to erect and how to operate it, as for instance, under a democratic constitution, when no majority can be formed on account of an irreconcilable clash of interests between various groups? Here liberty would simply be destructive, and the preponderance of social cohesion comes to the fore. Similarly, since the difficulties of the free market have led to a crisis that appeared to menace the mere existence of men, their sense of liberty has been overshadowed by the need for security from the economic angle as well. The cohesion and functioning of the system of production based on the division of labor must be established at any cost. It is futile protesting about human dignity and spiritual values when people feel their very existence at stake. In the division of functions each group and individual contributes a particular function to the life of the whole, but each, in turn, depends on the correctly apportioned contributions of all the others. To make the specialized functions into an integrated whole is the primary problem of social life. Some inner or external force must keep the people together in some fundamental order in spite of the diversity and possible conflicts of their natures and interests; and institutions must be so constructed as to make the undisturbed flow and co-operation of specialized activities technically possible. In this comprehensive sense we speak of the necessary social integration and its spiritual and institutional requirements.

Democracy, for this reason, starts with a handicap in the race against authoritarian systems. In this world of ours there is little security and much danger, within states and between them. It is not even very difficult for unscrupulous politicians and vested interests, when necessary, to create dangers in order to impress people with the desirability of a united stand behind the government. This course is so easily embarked upon because everyone is familiar with the experience of actual emergency and distress constantly lying in wait. Loyalty to authority becomes a necessary virtue for those who hope that government protection will be their reward.

In the economic sphere, cohesion and integration must be cultivated daily if starvation is to be avoided. The particular dangers to which any division of labor gives rise form the reverse side of its achievements. Specialization increases the total volume of output and consumption owing to the better training, adjustment, and utilization of natural talents it fosters; it involves, however, a precarious dependence of every participant on all the others. Specialization on the part of any individual producer is possible only through co-operation with all others, and requires therefore an exact interlocking of the specialized activities. Specialization cannot be left to mere chance any more than the interlocking; some authority seems necessary to co-ordinate the various specialized activities necessitated by the division of labor and to assure the efficient production and distribution of goods to the community. Hence regulation by a feudal ruler or guild authorities or a state bureaucracy appeared technically necessary to secure the correct proportions in the division of labor and to keep the delicately balanced system in equilibrium. Authority as such, whatever its origin and character, has had to organize the division of labor.

2. Economic Institutions

A democracy based on individual property was out of the question until it found its own technique of integration. This is theoretically formulated as the doctrine of the free market and was revolutionary in its claim to superiority in practice over the authoritarian technique. It argued that Divine Providence implants in all natural beings urges that drive them unawares to contribute to and become part of a system of universal harmony. Every individual in seeking his own gain is "led by an invisible hand to promote an end which was no part of his intention." By pursuing his own interest he promotes the common good as well as his own. In a free economy everybody makes his living by supplying the needs of others and depends on the price he gets in exchange. The prices that they are able and willing to pay for different services indicate the variety and intensity of their wants. As the demands for various goods change, the prices change and lead the producers to adjust their output. The impersonal and automatic price system operates with great elasticity and speed in co-ordinating the varied activities of free men, each motivated by self-interest; no artificial authority is needed.

To the present generation, torn by conflict and tormented by fear, this theory, stated in the sweeping form used above, seems completely false. But this verdict is due to the failure to realize, first, that a theory may have been valid for a set of conditions no longer existing, and second, that it may still be valid within certain limits if properly qualified and reformulated. The doctrine of harmony was applicable to the pre-capitalistic era. A technically elastic system without fixed capital and overhead costs would closely follow the fluctuations of the price signals, adapt itself to the variations in demand, and thereby integrate the independent enterprises of the numerous specialized producers. The success of the system in practice is proved by the impetus it gave to the rise of modern industry and trade for a hundred years. Even today, with the increase in rigidity of the technological structure of production and its financial superstructure that has been going on for a century, the limitations upon the functioning of the free market are not so great as most people believe. The shrinkage of the market by thirty or more per cent during the depression is of course a terrible calamity and affords ample reason for investigating the source of the evil and searching for the most effective remedy whereby it may be overcome and its recurrence avoided. But the major portion of productive activities is being carried on even in the depression—and this fact should facilitate a fair estimate of a system that assigns the fundamental task of integration to the free market. After all, we survive while the free market provides us with food, clothing, and shelter from day to day—which it could not do if it had broken down completely or were in chaos.[2]

Important qualifications are necessary for an accurate presentation of the case. The doctrine of market harmony must not be stated as though it were of a strictly economic character, self-evident in any pattern of life. It depends for its full validity on undeveloped technological and financial conditions. This qualification reveals the totally conditional character of the system. But there are addi-

---

[2] To secure the statement of the text an anti-critical remark on the principle of economic theory may be subservient. American institutionalism is inclined to dispute the co-ordinating effect of the pricing process by referring to the fact that prices and profits are not determined by the free interplay of supply and demand, but by all sorts of organized pressure to influence the market through monopolies, the public through advertising, and the governments and municipalities in the direction of subsidies, tax exemptions, public purchases, and protective tariffs. While there is much truth in this objection, the argument, nevertheless, is grossly overstated, to the extent of missing the essential point. If it were true that the pricing mechanism had lost its co-ordinating function altogether and had become nothing but a means of pressure, graft, and exploitation, it would not be intelligible that we could survive with it. The fact that we do gives evidence of the presence of some order in the apparently unco-ordinated

tional prerequisites. A definite though by no means self-evident type of psychological reaction to price changes is pre-supposed in the most elementary formulation of the law of demand and supply. What this law requires is the automatic adjustment of production to the ups and downs of demand for the various products as they are expressed in the ups and downs of their respective prices and in the gains or losses of producers. But producers will follow these price signals—that is, withdraw from shrinking markets and turn to increasingly profitable ones—only if they do not prefer to stick to the tradition of their occupation or have no other ground for waiving a promised gain or accepting an imminent loss. The contrary attitude is neither rare nor unimportant today, what with political preferences, ethical judgments, boycotts, sanctions, etc. No matter what our opinion on these subjects may be, they all result in men buying dearer and selling cheaper than they would otherwise. The result is that the old market harmony is thrown out of gear and the automatic adjustment of production to demand is interfered with, as far as those tendencies go. The free market and the impersonal price system act as an integrating force only in an economic and social order where men are not overwhelmed by non-

division of labor, defective as this order may be today. The critics are interested in the disease of the economic body, and justly so; but they forget that, if the disease were the whole body and no normal functioning were left, this would be the physical death of society—yet they live. Biology cannot be given in terms of disease; the disease is accidental, not fundamental, because it presupposes a living organism, whose functioning is only hampered, not terminated, by the disease. It is remarkable how much Marx, being a faithful disciple of classical economics, is superior in method to the modern critics; he understands that the pricing process constitutes a definite order, which does not imply that he defends that order; he is in search of some other order. In the absence of a price mechanism that works somewhat adequately as described by economic theory, institutionalist criticism with all its merits would become senseless.

economic passions and where the technological and financial structure is relatively elastic and undeveloped.

The early advocates of laissez-faire had faith in liberty and progress along the lines of rational business and did not pay special attention to their psychological assumptions concerning men's behavior on economic matters because those assumptions underlay the age in which they lived. Hence a fair judgment on the market system from the vantage point of our much more divided world demands a thorough awareness of all the psychological factors. Within these limits and qualifications, the theory of the impersonal price mechanism as the integrating force behind a free economy retains its validity.

These qualifications contain a profound lesson of general applicability. Even the mere economic integration, the co-ordination of independent specialized activities to make them interlock, requires infinitely more than economic institutions—it requires a host of conditions both technological and historico-psychological. Granted the necessary technical stage, a certain conformity in economic behavior is also indispensable for securing the working of the institution called the market. This particular behavior is expressive of certain valuations with regard to progress and tradition, self-interest and political or ethical counter-interests, etc. Not any arbitrary sum of decisions, but a definite set of conditions intelligible in itself and characteristic of a definite type of man and society, is concentrated in the law of demand and supply. It is because men are molded by history to conform to the rules of the market game that they can be made free in the market. That conformity in economic behavior, which is a conformity in sociological type and personal ideals, is required to integrate the society of free individuals even in its economic functioning. A common belief must animate the members of this society in all their diversified activities: the belief in individual liberty and progress.[3]

3. Political Institutions

Social harmony depends not only on a smoothly functioning economic system, but also on a well-established state. A few writers have drawn from the doctrine of the free market the conclusion that the state is not needed in a world supplied by a laissez-faire economy. They assume that the only crucial problem underlying social unity is effective economic organization and that the need for a state exists only when there is no other mechanism for securing that end. None of the great champions of the new age, naturally not the state-devoted Rousseau and Fichte nor even Adam Smith and Jefferson with their belief that that government is best which governs least, took this position. Their sense of reality was too strong to allow such oversimplifications; it made them aware of the need for an ultimate authority with power to enforce order and preserve a unified organization when conflicts arose that might disrupt society.

In fact, even market harmony was found to prevail only under certain historical conditions. Not an eternal, unchangeable human nature, but a well-defined historical type of behavior that happened to dominate the eighteenth century enables the free market to function. This is sufficient to prove that the impersonal law of the market cannot replace the discernible power of the state. The reasonable self-interest which is supposed to operate the mechanism of the market may at any time be overwhelmed by

[3] The argument of this and the preceding two paragraphs has been recently given by Adolf Löwe, *Economics and Sociology*, London, 1935, and used as the starting point of his restatement of the relationship between the two fields of research.

passion. Rightly or wrongly, some party to the market may refuse to submit to an unfavorable verdict of the market and may seize what is withheld from it, which may lead to the social crisis of the market. The growth of fixed capital and overhead cost makes the structure of production inelastic and incapable of adjusting, which may lead to the economic crisis of the market. The conclusion that anarchists have drawn from the doctrine of the harmonious market belongs to its strictly mechanistic interpretation and crumbles as soon as man and society are viewed as historically changing, for whatever reasons and in whatever direction. The state as the ultimate safeguard of social cohesion remains indispensable even with the new economic organization.

As a result it becomes imperative for democracy to find new forms of the state that will reconcile Power with Liberty. Two different ways to this end present themselves. One is the etymologically democratic way, resting the power of the state on the will of the people so as to prevent a rift between the two; the people's liberty would then be safeguarded by the state. In practice, however, that state will be controlled by a larger or smaller majority, and the quest for the liberty of the minority therefore becomes crucial. Now the potential participation of the minority in the formation of the political will may be actualized by a shift in public inclinations and tendencies so that the minority becomes majority. But this presupposes that the minority will be permitted to move, act, criticize, and propagandize freely and that no majority decision will be allowed to infringe upon these constitutional rights. This leads to the second principle announced above, the liberal principle of reducing the legal competency of the political power and of creating state-free zones of life with liberty for the individual from state control. Since the minority is a part of the people, the merger of the two principles is logically necessary and has always suggested itself much more readily in history than the reconciliation of the two underlying philosophies developed by Rousseau on the one hand and by Locke and Montesquieu on the other. Both ways must be combined in any modern image of democracy; we have come to regard majority governments working under elaborate constitutional limitations as the only adequate form of political democracy.

This synthesis may be easily derived from the fundamental idea of liberty and equality we have developed above. Self-government unites liberty for the individual with co-operative action in matters transcending individual powers and of concern to all in the community. And political self-government, as economic integration through the market, depends on the citizens sharing certain fundamental principles. That is the only basis on which Parliament, Congress, and other national legislatures can operate. No debate can be carried on without a language intelligible to all the participants and certain standards of truth and social values to which all can refer ultimately. If there is no agreement possible on the primary principles owing to extreme disparity in social ideals and ways of life between different groups, then no minority will voluntarily submit to the will of the majority. The American Civil War arose from the rebellion of the South on the question of which type of civilization was going to dominate, and so does every civil war. Division of opinion in democracy may occur only over questions of secondary importance. The democratic code forbids any fanatical majority from exterminating the members of the minority or violating their vital, constitutionally defined rights. It also requires the minority to comply with the decisions of the majority as long as its political rights are respected and it is given the opportunity to compete in elections and possibly supersede the former majority party. The best example of this spirit of fair play is to be seen in the political life of England, with the high standards of political conduct it has built up. The British Parliament, "the mother of parliaments," continues to command the unqualified respect of its own people and those of other lands, whether or not democratic. But impressive as it is as an institution and symbol, it does not by itself hold together the British people any more than the free market does the members of a laissez-faire economy. Each springs from the common ways of living the people follow, the common beliefs they act on, and the ideals they hold in common. On this basis, each is able to use liberty as the means of integration in the political and economic fields, respectively, and requires therefore no force in laying the foundations of society.

This concurrence on fundamentals underlies the individual's freedom from state control. Nobody can fly in the face of convention by walking naked in the street, nor use his personal freedom for instigating the overthrow of the social order. Education, art, worship, and other phases of social life, politically important as they are, remain free from direct political control because the feeling of unity in the community is sufficiently strong to secure social cohesion without recourse to coercion. This sense of unity does not prohibit wide divergences in secondary matters. Freedom of thought, expression, criticism, and investigation benefit social unity in the long run far more than suppression. The freer any political organization is, the less fundamental opposition it will arouse: everybody has a chance to call the attention of the public to existing evils and invite co-operation in abolishing them. The result is that the organization can be altered to meet the changes in social life without any need for revolution. That in moments of emergency a stricter limitation and co-ordination is always applied is obvious, and it need not be repeated how easily this technical necessity is abused. The simple truth is that we need less coercion the more we hang together by virtue of our instincts and education.[4]

Still, an alarming problem exists in this attempt to reconcile liberty for the individual with the need for social organization. An unrestrained liberty for all logically leads to social chaos. On the other hand, complete uni-

[4] At this point and, in fact, for the entire discussion of conformity in fundamentals as the precondition of liberty, we must refer once more to Adolf Löwe, *The Price of Liberty*. The thesis of this important little pamphlet, however, requires a qualification. It is certainly true that the peculiarities of the English geographical-historical situation are responsible for the undisturbed growth of a very distinct type of man and thereby for a degree of homogeneity that permits giving the people civil and political liberties without fear of disruption. From this it seems to follow that such fortunate insularity, unique as it is, constitutes the sole and only possible basis of that spiritual integration which makes liberty workable. But the gloomy implication of this thesis is easily refuted by the example of France, wherein we find the core of libertarian occidental civilization. Only in one sense may the English case be said to be more striking than that of the French, and that is with respect to the tension between the democratic ideas and the highly aristocratic social structure that is accepted and approved by the free people. Most remarkable in England's case is that extraordinarily favorable conditions enabled her to solve an almost hopeless problem, namely, to shape a homogeneous type of man and produce a sense of belonging together that is strong enough to outweigh even the social strain and the conflicts of interest inherent to that structure. In France, contrariwise, the historical conditions may have been much less favorable, but the problem itself is incomparably easier. With more than half the French people being independent peasants and the rest mostly akin to them, the social structure is approximating democracy, and the sense of community and solidarity is much more directly attainable than in aristocratic England. To the extent that a voluntary agreement to preserve and develop independence and equality is more natural and rational than a voluntary agreement to preserve an aristocratic structure, the French example is more apt than the English to serve as the model for an investigation into the conditions of democratic cohesion. Much material in this direction may be found in the loving and beautiful book of Paul Distelbarth, *Lebendiges Frankreich*, Berlin, 1936.

formity in thought and action deprives the individual of any liberty worthy of the name. The solution for those who desire a free society that functions is a balance between the two opposed poles of liberty and organization, diversity and uniformity, that would achieve integration through unity on fundamental principles and yet permit the greatest degree of difference on all others. English democracy used to exhibit this desired equilibrium, but recently it has swung away from the pole of liberty towards that of conformity owing to the imminent danger of war. Fascist Italy and Germany may rightly maintain that they have helped to kill genuine political life even in democratic countries by making the question of national survival overshadow all other problems. This, however, is only half the story. The other half is that the eclipse of fundamental political debate by the armament question offers a convenient subterfuge to an opposition that has no coherent and constructive program to present as an alternative to the existing system, be it in domestic or foreign policy, after the breakdown of several long-cherished illusions. The political weakness of the opposition, in spite of its numerical strength, threatens to deprive British democracy of the vitality upon which the success of democracy depends in the longer run. This illustrates the positive relationship between liberty and integration in democracy. Liberty becomes possible through spontaneous integration, but it becomes real and efficacious only through exercise.

One should not conclude, however, that conformity on fundamental principles is the only prerequisite of liberty. The pre-liberal era in Europe and America had also known a regime of established order and agreement on primary questions, but it had not achieved liberty. The reason is that individual liberty requires not only a moral harmony among men, but also a specific organization of society. The anarchists who used the free market theory to bolster up their philosophy were sadly ignorant of the nature and dangers of human life, but were not completely absurd. They erred through a gross overstatement of a distinct truth. The state is necessary even with a functioning market, but we need less control by the state once we have a functioning market. Power, by Rousseau's principle, is reconciled with liberty when it is made the power of the self-determining free; but at the same time it is driven back by the principle of Montesquieu and Adam Smith and liberty put in its place. That within certain limits there is a spontaneous harmony attainable in certain provinces of life is a most novel and far-reaching insight, although it must not be discredited by an unconditional and sweeping formulation.[5] This partial harmony means that we may, within definite limits, let men act freely according to their own impulses and decisions and to that extent withdraw the compulsory agency formerly in charge of this field. Abolition of the state is absurd; democracy comes

---

[5] An important methodological observation may serve to supplement the statement in the text. Some indulge in denouncing the harmony theory today. But it is imperative to realize that a sweeping theory of wholesale disharmony and chaos would be equally faulty and even more faulty. Certainly the world of man and the free market in it are very far from acting harmoniously at large; but after all, we live, which we could not do if the world were nothing but chaos, and no coercion would be capable, in that case, of turning chaos into order and death into life. The truth is that the world consists of structures more or less loosely arranged and the process of our life takes advantage of this harmony as far as it arises spontaneously, and has to make up for the gaps and smooth out the conflicts between them, by deliberate and more or less artificial organization. The discovery of some partial structure and harmony therefore may be a great deed of liberation from a heretofore indispensable but unwelcome control by the state. And this is the true significance of the market doctrine when reasonably interpreted: the individual activities need not necessarily but do often interlock, in definite limits, without authoritarian guidance.

into being when the state's scope and power are reduced and liberty supplants state supervision wherever feasible.

It would be fallacious to infer that democracy could exist only as a liberal democracy, that it is bound to the functioning of the free market and becomes impracticable when the market fails. If the liberal technique for achieving democracy is only partly practicable because it corresponds to a pre-industrial and now widely antiquated structure of society, other techniques for reaching the same goal of democracy may exist in other social structures. Whether there are such democratic techniques corresponding to other social structures is, of course, a question of fact that has to be tested, just as the democratic significance of the free market had to be. In any case, our analysis of the simple model of democracy that is possible under simple conditions permits us to generalize the principle beyond the limits of the simple conditions. Democracy seeks the integration of society in the direction of what the people tend to do of their own accord.

C. International Unity

The democratizing and organizing power which the free market and price system wield under conditions of individual work is not confined to any one geographical area or state. Economic organizations concerned with the manufacture and exchange of goods can be extended more easily than political organizations that revolve about human beings bound together by tradition, language, and history, and tied down to specific places of residence and labor. So far as the exchange and bringing together of raw materials and goods for industrial production is concerned, no reason exists why the range of organization should not be expanded as far as it is technically possible. Since it cannot be denied that division of labor increases production and consumption, the logical procedure is to extend and deepen the division of labor wherever that is feasible. If selling in the market with greatest demand and buying in the market with largest supply is socially desirable, the practice should not be limited to each country separately. Two countries will supplement each other better than two sections of one country; two continents better than two countries. The wider the area, the greater the opportunity for the division of labor; and that means a larger output of commodities and a higher standard of consumption for all. The principle of the free market is progressive in its geographical application: it aims beyond a narrowly national system towards a unified world market.

This world unity has seemed to liberals not only desirable on account of its economic benefits to mankind, but capable of achievement owing to the trend of modern man's development, as they viewed it. The driving force behind the market is the rational and progressive self-interest of every normal individual. The national, linguistic, cultural, and religious differences that divide men in most spheres do not count in the economic sphere when the exchange of goods is involved. No inner restraints can, and no outer compulsion should, prevent business transactions from passing over non-economic borderlines. The market principle will regulate independent specialized activities, whatever their geographical range. It will integrate the free division of labor even on an international scale.

Great as the economic advantages are, they are far more than equaled by the achievement of world peace. Economic integration makes nations dependent on one another and thereby acts as a barrier to war, no matter what the inducement to war may be. Moreover, as people in different countries become acquainted with each other through trade and travel, the forces of national conceit and intolerance tend to lose their strength. Peace promotes the exchange of material goods and of ideas; in turn these strengthen the forces of peace. The natural law of free trade secures in this way the most profound integration of the economic and political order.

This whole development depends, of course, upon the prevalence of the conditions that had made possible the free market on a national scale, and had been considered natural by the early free-traders. These conditions are, first, an elastic and adaptable technique of production of a mainly pre-industrial character, and, second, a universal desire for individual liberty and progress. As the technique grows rigid through the huge modern investments the world market becomes exposed to the crisis as the domestic market does. At the same time, the wider the range one seeks for the free market, the less likelihood there is of finding the necessary psychological conditions for its extension, as the recent history of world trade shows. But until this change in trends occurred, liberals had support for their belief that free trade would bring world peace within the range of the occidental spirit. Under the mercantilist system protective tariffs and trade wars had been used jointly as means of one state profiting at the expense of others. Liberalism in the international field was a reaction to this practice; it argued persuasively that the people of one state can prosper most through peaceful co-operation with their neighbors. Free trade and peace would join in integrating the Western world and would be the crown to the structure of liberty planned by the architects of original democracy.

D. The Criteria of Democracy

The integrating principle in the system of original democracy is individual liberty itself. The assumptions of this philosophy were postulated, however, as belonging to human beings by nature, whereas in reality they are valid only for the distinct set of conditions that obtained during that one period of time. The claims once made for the universal validity of that formula are accordingly not maintainable. But the claims are not entirely void: when confined to certain conditions, they are indeed maintained. Here the doctrine of integration through liberty remains in force.

The fundamental significance of this fact cannot be exaggerated. Integration and liberty are by definition contrary to each other. Liberty, in any sense of the word, may or may not be desirable; integration, on the other hand, is indispensable because it is identical with the existence of society. There can be no compromise between the two. One may choose between a greater or less degree of liberty, or none at all; but between integration and chaos or death there is little choice. The best thing one may hope for is the insertion of some minor liberties in a system controlled by the integrating authority. The formidable confrontation of these two opposed principles now becomes suddenly crumbling as they prove to partly coincide. As the earlier champions of liberalism put it in their sweeping way, integration is taken care of by natural law if we take care of establishing liberty. Liberty, certainly an end in itself for any dignified human life, yet inferior in worldly power to the overwhelming claims of integration, is revealed as a means to integration, if properly arranged. This astounding coincidence of liberty and integration finds its institutional expression in original democracy.

From the start, the institutions of original democracy were deflected from their intended direction. The conditions under which they were conceived and to which they owed their significance soon presented a totally altered prospect. But the motive that had created those institutions remained alive and survived in changing forms and institutions under the pressure of changing experiences and influences. Original democracy is the repository from which all the genuine motives and basic ideas of the present political struggle have been drawn. In the disguise and transformation, degeneration and falsification of these ideas, we can discern the original motive which inspires the struggling groups and is responsible for what hope or danger we see in them. Man's desire for independence in his work is the innermost motive of democracy; to realize this motive by reconciling it with the need for integration is the constructive contribution of democracy. Under conditions of individual work, the technique for achieving democracy requires universal individual property and regulation of individual activities by the impersonal rule of the market. As conditions change in the direction of big industry, the institutional technique of democracy needs to be changed accordingly. The study of the simple democratic model suggests, however, a rule that can be more generally applied: namely, that liberty and equality are tied up with the coincidence between the types of work and types of property and that integration is to be sought in the direction of spontaneous activities. We shall discuss the implications of this principle in the following chapters.[6]

[6] The knowledge of the essence and true democratic significance of original co-operative individualism has almost completely vanished. It is forcefully and fruitfully presented and developed in our day by the lonely life work of Franz Oppenheimer in economics and sociology. He refers to Adam Smith as his one predecessor.

III

FIRST TRANSFORMATION:
CLASSICAL SOCIALISM

A. The Logic of the Socialist System

1. The Parallelism of Material and Human Developments in Capitalism

ONE OF THE pillars upon which original Utopian democracy rested was the belief in the superiority of small over large-scale production. Hence the supplanting in important industries of small shops by large plants, owing to the latter's superiority in efficiency and competition, proved a death-blow to democracy in its simple form, and resulted in the development of classical socialism. The one new factor, progressive large-scale production, when added to the set of conditions making for democracy, caused the logical outcome to be classical socialism. The vital elements of democracy were translated into a new language, but remained the same: liberty, integration on the largest possible scale, and the reconciliation of these two poles through pre-established harmony. This fact does not minimize the ingenuity and creative power displayed by Marx and Engels in the formulation of the new system. Grasping the inner logic of a new phase of history is always an original and ingenious act because no rule-of-thumb method can rightly interpret and correlate the qualities of heterogeneous factors as they arise in history. Social and political theory, however, is not interested in the individual deeds of the political prophets and leaders; it pursues the historical trend as such. That is why we deduce the political system of classical socialism from the conditions of original democracy and the one new assumption, the productive superiority and irresistible power of the large enterprise.

This new assumption originated in the daily experience of Marx's contemporaries and is plausible in view of the multiplication of human productive power through use of the machine. The taming of the natural elements increases the total output of man's work and reduces the work required for producing a given quantity of goods. The machine that lowers the cost of production per unit of the final product requires, however, a large original investment for its construction or purchase and is therefore only available to the capitalist enterprise. This is the starting point of large-scale production, with its relatively high minimum of output and sales displacing from the outset a correspondingly high number of independent producers. There is no end to this movement; it apparently aims at the infinite. The efficiency of the machine increases more rapidly than its size and direct cost, and new inventions accelerate this tendency toward a still larger unit of production. Hence the dynamic nature of capitalism, once the movement is started.

It is impossible either to defy or to check this development. Its power is overwhelming, and so are its achievements. Before organizational and technical progress was a generally known and approved principle, not a tenth part of what has actually been achieved would have been attainable if it had been dependent upon the consent of bureaucrats, workers, or political bodies instead of on the free initiative of pioneering businessmen. Their ingenuity cannot be denied by pointing to the logical and necessary path of technical progress from one step to the next. Not one of these steps could have been calculated in advance; inevitable as it may afterwards appear, each one required a creative imagination. Many have been driven by the profit motive, but not everyone has had the vision of an electrified world before there was electricity, or of a motorized world when there were only few expensive automobiles. A vision is never a matter of moral or immoral motives, because it cannot be intended or intentionally forced. It is not the morality of these men but their achievements that count in history. This point cannot be a matter for dispute between adherents and adversaries of capitalism. It was Marx himself who first discovered that it is the historical mission of capitalism to unfold the latent potentialities of modern production.

The more the technological principle has won the uncontestable rule over production, the more, however, its drawbacks and unsolved problems have come to the fore. They have sprung from the separation of property and labor. The capitalist enterprise underbids and ruins the propertied producer, prevents the rise of workers to ownership of property and independence, and enlists them instead in its own service and growth. This movement has been progressive and dynamic, has led to the centralization of production in fewer and fewer units, and has thereby increased manifold the number of propertyless workers who have to operate the growing plants of capital. This has brought about the familiar accumulation of wealth at one pole of society and of poverty and dependence at the other. As production grows the breach between them widens. This is the starting point of the socialist doctrine.

Numerous questions of detail in Marxian theory, interesting in themselves, but controversial and not strictly
necessary for the pursuit of the ideas of liberty and integration, may be set aside.[1] The fundamental development of
the economic and social order, as envisaged by Socialists,
proceeds on the two separate tracks of property and labor
and reaches its historical culmination in the social revolution, when these two tracks become united. A fundamental
economic development involving the transformation of the
structure of production, and a consequent but separate social development involving the transformation of men, go
side by side until they arrive at the eventual goal of history. The transformation of production gives rise, on the
negative side, to the crisis of the market, and on the positive side to the reorganization of production with the aim
of preventing crises through a planned economy. The
transformation of men consists, negatively, of their proletarianization; positively, of training them in a new communal pattern of work and thereby socializing them. We

[1] Among them we may mention the varying interpretations of the theory
of increasing misery, the doctrine of the centralization of property, which
is not identical with concentration of production, the explanation of the
crisis, and the supposedly fundamental theory of labor value. None of
them need concern us here because none is indispensable for maintaining
the main argument, even though each, if tenable, would impart color
and vivacity to it. The logic and the political future of Marxism do not
depend on those details. This implies, on one hand, that no refutation
of any of them really hurts the vigor of Marxism, and on the other hand
that our presentation of the main structure cannot be refuted by objec-
tions of a philological nature based on interpretations and quotations
from writings of unquestioned authenticity. The heir of an age-old controversy should take advantage of its outcome by discriminating between
the strictly vital and the accidental elements of the system. The presentation in the text does not aim at completeness, since it examines Marxism
from the particular point of view adopted throughout this book. As a
supplement, especially with regard to the economic theory of Marx, *cf.*
the author's article, "What Marx Means Today," *Social Research,* 1937,
number 1.

shall discuss the two pairs of conditions that, according to Marx, make for socialism.

Where a number of small independent shops once existed, the capitalist enterprises, favored by competition, tend to concentrate the growing output in fewer and larger units of production. This transformation, though justified by its driving force and accelerated productivity, gives rise at the same time to an increasingly bitter problem, the problem of economic crises. Whatever the theoretic explanation of the crises may be, one thing is clear: a society of peasants and craftsmen would not know these periodically recurring internal disturbances of their exchange system. The work of the big enterprise, when undisturbed, is far superior to that of the small shop, but its mechanism is far more complicated technologically and financially and difficult to handle. Sudden and fitful changes in market conditions can hardly be imagined in the pre-machine age, and such slight changes as might have occurred could have been easily disposed of by the flexibility of economic-minded men and their technical equipment. With modern technique and large capital investments, one innovation in one firm may shatter the whole market. The credit machinery is so elastic as to permit violent expansions and contractions in the total volume of credit and undermine rational calculations in advance of prices. The more rigid and specialized the given technical structure is, on the other hand, the greater the difficulty of making adjustments to changed conditions. The fixedness of the debt burden placed upon a firm may induce it to seek an escape from adverse conditions by increasing its output, if a withdrawal is technically and financially impossible; thereby the glut and the crisis would be intensified. In short, financial and technical possibilities lead to revolutionary innovations, but the rigidity of the existing structure often prevents any adaptation. Thus the development of the technical structure and its financial superstructure makes for increasing productivity and at the same time for more severe crises.

It is, however, one of the triumphs of Marxian dialectics that with the growth of this evil the remedy becomes visible. This develops from the diagnosis of the evil. If the automatic play of the market cannot perform the task of co-ordinating the private decisions of individuals, then that co-ordination must be provided for deliberately, owing to the revolutionary effects of these decisions and the conservatism of the existing structure. The decisions cannot remain private any longer; they must all visibly interlock and fit in with a comprehensive plan that pushes one group ahead and holds others back in order to safeguard them all. Now planned economy under these conditions is not only desirable, it is prepared for by the trend of history itself. With millions of independent separate shops such a plan could not be made, much less carried out; the fewer and larger the units of production, the easier the survey and the plan. The reorganization of capitalism by the capitalists appears to aim at the ultimate co-ordination of the whole process in one plan. In fact this reorganization creates a limited number of planning centers, huge corporations and combinations, equipped with every information and all necessary power within their respective domains. The percentage of specialized activities which are not co-ordinated by the market, but directly by the central will of a big firm or trust, increases. But at the same time the existence of several such partial and necessarily conflicting plans side by side aggravates the evil and strengthens the conscious want for one all-inclusive plan. The reorganization of capitalism from within in a few large units of production prepares for the planned economy it now only points toward.

What appears as the reorganization of capitalism from within under the point of view of production, appears as its socialization from the standpoint of the men concerned. This in a dual sense of the word. First, since the dynamic and progressive spirit, once restricted to a few, has spread among the masses, everybody is technique-conscious and convinced of the desirability of the greatest attainable progress. If at the beginning of capitalism individual initiative had to be lured by special incentives and protected from incompetent intervention, now such a system is no longer required. Capitalism may be said to have achieved its transitional task of education for the workers in the same manner that absolutism had done for the bourgeoisie. The universal absorption of the spirit of progress has made it possible to dispense with the profit system.

Secondly, and more fundamentally, the socialization of capitalism consists in substituting the collective type of work for the individual one and making it the predominant type for the first time in history. The significance of this fact cannot be exaggerated. Large-scale production is in itself collective work, and this in a much more refined and spiritualized sense than the group work which has always existed in certain fields of production, such as the building of highways or pyramids. Whereas in these fields it is the magnitude of the task that requires co-operation as a mere sum of individual forces, modern technique differentiates the functions and makes them interlock in a most subtle way. Hence a new type of worker is modeled by the new type of work—men trained in communal work and conceiving of themselves as forming a true community. In the beginning they may respond negatively to being uprooted from the traditional pattern of their life and work; they may turn conservative and reactionary as their tormentors, the machines, are progressive and revolutionary.

This stage cannot last long, however, when no vivid image of their old world remains. With the passing of traditions, memories also fade, as people are swept away from their shops or farms, from towns and villages, into factory halls and the slums of the big cities. Moreover, the productivity of the new technique makes a return to the old one manifestly impossible. Gradually the workers accept the new conditions and turn as progressive, revolutionary, and collectivist as the machines whose creatures they now rightly consider themselves. That is, they accept the new situation not as a permanent state, but as the starting point from which to work for new goals and as the foundation upon which to build up a new structure of life. Under the conditions of their new work, where tasks and experiences are shared in common, this new structure cannot be other than collective. As they toil under the control of and for the profit of private owners and suffer from unemployment due to private instead of central management, they set out openly to socialize a system that has become collective in nature but continues to be administered in antiquated private form. It is capitalism itself that teaches the workers the value of socialism.

2. *The Coincidence of Material and Human Conditions in the Revolution*

By combining in one process these two parallel lines of evolution, capitalism prepares the organization of production under a planned economy and trains the workers in the collective sentiment and action required for operating a planned economy successfully. With the organization of production and the corresponding proletarianization and unification of the working masses, the social revolution is attained. "The knell of capitalist private property sounds. The expropriators are expropriated." The separation of labor and property is done away with; communal property for the entire classless society is established in all plants and is used as the basis of a unitary planned management. Since private property through its control of industry had been the source not only of crisis and unemployment but also of domination over individuals, the revolution restores security and liberty to the people.

For the understanding of present problems, it is important that the doctrine of revolution be correctly interpreted and that one understand why the "social" revolution has a place in a theoretic system that considers social phenomena as derived exclusively from the basic economic phenomena. The social organization has, of course, to fit the underlying economic organization. Accordingly, the social revolution cannot be a truly original and fundamental event, but only the spectacular conclusion of and adaptation to the more fundamental economic revolution which has gone before. This economic revolution encompasses the whole era of capitalism; it is, however, a perpetual revolution, where the difference between the words revolution and evolution disappears owing to the duration and the automatic logic of the process. Although we described the development of capitalism to the stage of large-scale production and reorganization as a gradual and irresistible metamorphosis, the same process is known in history as the industrial revolution and is rightly so designated. The replacing of the time-honored and naturally static individual system of production by a progressively collective pattern leads to the final unification and planned management of industry and the most far-reaching changes for the workers who operate this changing system. The conscious social organization, however, particularly the legal system of property rights, cannot easily follow these daily changes of the economic structure. It lags behind, and private property as a result is in an increasingly tense conflict with a system that in other respects is being socialized. When social organization finally catches up with the economic development, it attains its goal through conscious will, the social revolution. Socialism finds everything at hand for its new social order in the structure of production and the type of men prepared by capitalistic developments; it only needs to take them over and follow the inherent logic of the economic process. By so doing, it proves itself the heir of capitalism.[2]

The dependence of the revolution on the ripeness of the conditions prepared by capitalism does not, however, reduce its claims on the moral and intellectual forces of the revolutionists. History models and remodels men and conditions, but it can never reach its goal without the fullest devotion of the men whom it has shaped and trained for their task. The revolutionary struggle for power is, in the classical doctrine of socialism, a struggle of practically the whole unified but armless nation against the remaining small number of all-powerful capitalistic rulers. This means that the number of the parties to the fight is in inverse proportion to their organized power. The rulers have the government, the army, and the courts at their disposal; the educators, and everyone else, depend on them for their existence in the given framework. The revolutionists have to overcome not only this strongly entrenched power but also the serious anxiety of people lest the struggle paralyze production and lead to physical catastrophe if a smashing victory is not scored at once. The re-

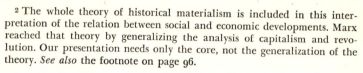

---

[2] The whole theory of historical materialism is included in this interpretation of the relation between social and economic developments. Marx reached that theory by generalizing the analysis of capitalism and revolution. Our presentation needs only the core, not the generalization of the theory. *See also* the footnote on page 96.

construction of society after the victory likewise requires the greatest devotion and ingenuity. Communal property and planned economy are the lodestars, but the realization of these general principles under specific conditions, and the allocation to everyone of his function in the huge work, involve problems of the utmost weight. The fate of socialism depends on the strength and faith of the Socialists.

Hence the ripeness of material conditions, although indispensable, is not in itself sufficient for the social revolution. The objective conditions give rise to the problem and make its solution possible, but men have to solve it. Man is both the product of history and its producer. He is free and responsible and may or may not achieve his ideals. But he cannot achieve them in the void; he is bound to the task of his day. Historical necessity and human freedom are not opposed; each postulates the other. This is inconceivable in terms of static logic; it is, however, the true structure of life as conceived by Marxism and any other religious dialectic, in Judaism, Mohammedanism, and Puritanism. An equilibrium between the preparedness of the objective structure and the responsible initiative of man is what the revolution requires.

3. Dictatorship and Withering Away of the State

The capitalistic obstacles to the reconstruction of society lead to the dictatorship of the proletariat as the most rigorous measure to break the resistance of the privileged, to secure the long-term plan, and to shorten the period of struggle and danger. As all past history proves that the holders of organized power will not surrender it voluntarily, the revolutionists must not wait for a counter-attack but must stamp out any such possibility from the beginning. Again, however, a correct interpretation is necessary to realize the logic of the entire Marxian system. From the basic assumption, universal spread of large-scale production and proletarian work, it follows that the dictatorship of the proletariat is the dictatorship of the huge unified majority over the small minority and their lackeys. In a somewhat unusual, yet consistent terminology the Communist Manifesto identifies the rise of labor to the ruling position with the establishing of democracy. For, as Marx and Engels put it, the labor movement is "the independent movement of the huge majority in the interest of the huge majority." Democracy here signifies the all-inclusive absolute power of a state based on the will of the majority, in line with Rousseau's theory and Robespierre's practice. In other words, the proletarian dictatorship is the militant rule of the majority for the enforcement of its will, the destruction of privilege and discrimination. It may, in this respect, be called a democratic dictatorship.

A second characteristic of the dictatorship is that it is to be transitory, not only in the sense that every human institution is doomed to extinction sooner or later, but in the strict and well-defined sense of an intended limitation upon its task and duration. As soon as the roots of possible resistance have been weeded out and the economic plan has got under way with the support of the whole working community, the dictatorship will begin to wane. According to the famous chapter on the historic tendency of capitalist accumulation in Marx's *Kapital*, socialization, in spite of its technical difficulties, will take "incomparably less time and effort" than the preceding transformation of pre-capitalistic scattered property into capitalistic property. For, when its form is revolutionized, capitalistic property is already being operated on a socialized scale. "Capitalism means the expropriation of the bulk of the people by the few usurpers, socialism the expropriation of the few usurpers by the bulk of the people." All this follows directly from the assumed effects of large-scale production. The political transition to socialism, having long since been prepared for by the social and economic transformation within capitalism itself, requires a majority dictatorship of only limited duration.

It is, moreover, not only the dictatorship which fades. Marx and his disciples use the word dictatorship as more or less synonymous with the word state. This is very unfortunate indeed because it now enables the Marxists to belittle the differences between existing democratic states and fascism, and by labeling both dictatorships of the bourgeoisie, to minimize the distance between the Marxist dictatorship and a true democracy. It blinds them to vital political issues and furnishes them glib but invalid arguments. Yet in itself that doctrine of the state is not only coherent but significant. It consists of fitting the accepted criterion of the state, coercive power to secure social cohesion, to the conditions of class society and its constant danger of insurrection. Political power is defined as the organized force used by one class to suppress other classes. It then follows logically that with the definite abrogation of classes, the state will "wither away." As long as mankind is engaged in its agelong migration through the desert of class domination, the state is indispensable. When society and production are jeopardized by conflicting interests, their cohesion must be taken care of by force. The free association and co-ordination of all interests is only the ultimate goal of history and requires elaborate and painful preparations. The goal cannot be anticipated, class society cannot be skipped, large-scale production can be developed only by capitalism. Until the conditions are ripe for socialism, one cannot complain of the existence of the state, as it is only a necessary concomitant of class society.

Class society being the form in which mankind has to exist, the state is needed to suppress the inevitable revolt of the exploited in order to safeguard the survival of mankind. Without the state mankind would not live to see its final salvation. (This result of dialectics again is analogous to the paradoxical fact that the persecuted Christians had to pray in the catacombs for the existence of the Roman Empire.) The abrogation of class division and exploitation, finally, liberates mankind from the state, the use of organized force. The free association and planned co-operation of free people requires many technical and administrative functions, but no state.

This theory is untenable, whether or not one adheres to the rest of the Marxian doctrine. It reveals extreme presumption to believe in the faultless goodness of mankind and to think that this will establish and maintain an eternal kingdom of undisturbed solidarity. Knowledge of the ambivalence of life, where creative forces change all too easily into destructive ones, precludes any such optimism. No pattern of solidarity can rule out the possibility of conflicts between different interests which may remain latent as long as the struggle against the common class foe overshadows everything else, but which will come out into the open once victory is firmly established and the spoils are to be distributed. When coal miners protest about the unique strain of their work and the superintendents of the power station about the responsibility of their physically much easier jobs, there is no yardstick by which to decide whether an exactly equal remuneration or a certain gradation is just. Some workers may complain about the power of the government planners to transfer them from one working place or one industry or one section of the country to another one and may seek to shift the burden to others. None of these or of the many other potential conflicts need be realized, but all of them might be. The danger lies in the fact that all these competing claims are equally legitimate. Such possible conflicts, and similar ones in the other spheres of life, education, sectional administration, foreign affairs, etc., force one to give up the doctrine of eternal harmony and to repudiate the argument that we do not know what unbelievable things man may achieve once the corruption of all human relations by the class order is cured. The doctrine of the withering away of the state positively asserts the unqualified goodness of man and denies the possibility of his being corrupted by permanent factors, of which the class order might be just one expression. Lenin occasionally suggested disposing of recalcitrant individuals by direct mass action, but this would mean the legitimization of any mob whim or violence. There is good reason for believing that, men being what they are, law and the law-enforcing machinery of jurisdiction and police will always be necessary.

This objection holds, however, only if one views the doctrine of the withering away of the state as a political theory. This doctrine, like the one concerning "the jump from the realm of necessity to the realm of freedom," betrays a way of thinking that is not susceptible to scientific analysis. With men as they are, a withering away of the state is inconceivable. In speculating on a radical and innermost change of human nature, we pass beyond the borders of empirical research and enter the realm of prophetic vision where the true significance and providential destination of man are circumscribed in stammering metaphors. If the lion and the lamb were actually to lie down together, all familiar political notions would be invalidated. Such an image is a symbolic expression of the prophetic urge for love and peace and may be taken as a guiding principle in the confusion and entanglements of this world. Similarly, we should interpret the theory of the withering away of organized force not as a practical program capable of being realized, but as a polestar to steer by. In this sense it constitutes the true criterion of socialist and generally democratic feeling.

Translated into the everyday language of realistic analysis, it implies a social organization that would reduce the need for organized coercion to the conceivable minimum. Thus the harmonious free market was designed in original democracy to make an entire set of authoritative decisions superfluous, and in classical socialism the urge for organized communal work leads to the same goal; moreover, in both cases the abolition of monopolies and class prerogatives removes a fundamental source of social conflict. Any society needs organized force for its protection within and without its geographical limits, but a society is free in so far as it is based on and integrated by the spontaneous actions of its members and needs no force, therefore, to establish and maintain its current procedure. A class society uses force, or the menace of force, on principle; a classless society uses either only incidentally. The extent to which force is absent in the foundations of a society enables one to judge the degree to which liberty prevails.

4. International Planning

This criterion of liberty applies to international as well as to national organization. Since socialism is the heir of capitalism, its geographical basis is the capitalistic unified world. Here, however, as in the narrower field of national economies, the integration achieved by capitalism has been partial and contradictory. The national differences tend to be wiped out, but the class differences are emphasized the world over. The side-by-side position of separate hostile camps is replaced by the hostile opposition of classes superimposed one upon another. Moreover, the effects of capitalistic large-scale production plunge all countries together into the crisis. And it is the crisis that revives those national antagonisms which were considered extinct and outmoded in prosperity. When no country wishes to buy and every country wants to sell, the idea of resorting to political power to make up for the disturbed economic equilibrium readily suggests itself. Political power backed by arms or military threats opens up new markets to the sale of domestic products, conquers and monopolizes the sources of colonial materials, and shifts the burden of the crisis to competing or backward countries. Thus the operating defects of capitalism lead to imperialistic conflicts, while production as such entangles all participants in mutual dependence. Cleavage and war instead of harmony and peace are the outstanding results of capitalism in its international aspect. This is the diagnosis given by the socialist doctrine.

Here, again, the organizational principle of socialism has its roots in definite historical conditions and solves the difficulties by deliberately removing the source of conflict. With the growth of international capitalism, the reorganization of production from within leads to the development of international cartels and trusts and prepares for that international survey and control which the world-wide extent of the crisis and the resulting political struggles make indispensable. But co-operation on an international scale that would be responsive to growing disturbances requires deliberate organization. This is rendered impossible by a system based on the pursuit of separate and conflicting interests through the inadequate national divisions of an international order. In opposition to this strife and disorder there is the universal interest of workingmen in overcoming the evils of the separate national systems through the

international solidarity of the working classes; this solidarity is the product of international capitalism in its disintegration. Socialism in a nationally restricted form cannot be realized under a system of international division of
labor that makes national economic units arbitrary and
far from self-sufficient. International socialism is, in a
broad sense, the necessary outcome of the process in which
the concentration of production and the consequent
growth of business crises and proletarian unity and power
were stages, all this on an international scale. Since capitalism fails to live up to the promise of peaceful co-operation and integration and turns to imperialism, the only
hope left lies in an international planned economy resting
upon the political power of the victorious workers and
their international organization. Peace through planned
co-operation in a world-wide system of large-scale production is the prize of the world revolution.

B. The Democratic Significance of the Socialist System

1. Liberty and Equality

The logic of classical socialism presupposes a system of
scattered property and a free market on a world scale; it
introduces the dynamic element of superior large-scale
production and leads straight to the progressive concentration of production. This involves the increasingly burden-
some costs of capitalist rule and the economic crises, the
progressively monopolistic trend in the reorganization of
production, the proletarianization of practically all working people, and their unification in collective work. It
culminates finally in the social revolution with social property and planned economy established on a world scale.

To secure the final stage, a transitional period of dictator-ship is required. The purport and goal of the entire move-ment, however, is harmony and peace, within and without every national group, evidenced by the abrogation of or-ganized force—the withering away of the state.

The parallelism between the final structure of Marxian socialism and that of Utopian democracy is conspicuous. Some specific points require further illumination. The question may be raised, what becomes of individual liberty under socialism? And what relationship prevails between liberty and property? Are not both liberty and property abolished and something like a totalitarian class substi-tuted for them? Is not the democratic idea of seeking in-tegration through liberty abandoned under socialism?

The current answers to these questions are in the affirm-ative among both friends and foes of socialist thought. The two groups do not differ on the interpretation of the classi-cal socialist doctrine, but only on the analysis of present-day society and its possible transformation. Liberty and property are, capitalists feel, the indispensable foundations of society; they boast of having established these goods. In their opinion, liberty permits, and the striving after prop-erty spurs, people to exert their productive abilities to the utmost in the direction of unsatisfied demand, as indicated by free price fluctuations. A regimenting plan would dull their efforts and the confiscation of property would en-tirely destroy all stimulus. It is sadly true, they say, that not all people are on an equal footing of economic well-being; but, they maintain, it is also true, and amply evi-denced by the rising standard of living, that all people profit by economic progress, which is secured to a very great degree by free initiative alone. The concentration of all power and responsibility in the hands of a central board, whatever its social composition and political origin,

is too heavy a burden to lay upon the refined machinery of modern economy and is infinitely inferior in flexibility to a system that decentralizes responsibilities and integrates them by the impersonal apparatus of the market. As to equality, the only practicable sense of this word is that a free society cannot tolerate legal discrimination. Social and economic equality, however, are excluded by the very principle of liberty and property, as nature chose to create men unequal. Thus capitalism decides for liberty and property, and against equality—and is thereby taken for the rightful heir of original democracy.

It gives evidence of an appalling lack of vitality and originality on the part of post-Marxian socialists to have submitted to this biased interpretation of their own tenets. By so doing they accepted the thankless task of fighting liberty and property and concentrating upon equality. Equality, according to this view, is necessarily of a propertyless type, since it involves removing property from the direct grasp of the individual to a social order where all people own all things together and no direct relationship whatever obtains between a concrete person and a concrete thing. In less radical utterances, abstractly communal property is waived with respect to consumption goods which may be owned individually, and is confined to the means of production. (This is the usual definition of socialism as only the first phase of communism and is now incorporated in the new Russian constitution for this first phase.) The means of production, at any rate, must be organized in an abstractly communal way, because their direct concrete ownership diverts the attention of people from solidarity, excludes equality from the economic order, and thereby leads to capitalistic rule. The trump card is of course the economic crisis and its origin in private property. The crisis demands for its solution an all-inclusive plan, but that presupposes the denial of property. As for liberty, it is not considered maintainable, however much one may regret the fact. Some Socialists are fond of the precious goods contained in personal liberty, but realizing that history always appears to reserve liberty as a privilege and a means of domination to the few, they agree that it must be renounced in favor of equality. Others spurn liberty altogether as long as they possess it; they do not even know what it means; they may argue, as Strachey does in evident earnest, that socialist liberty consists of a higher wage for the workers. This brand of socialism, then, agrees with its critics that it needs men without freedom, property, or a sense of independence and direct relationship to their tools—men watching over their equality with all the other members of an amorphous, homogeneous social aggregate.

Whatever one's taste may be, this picture certainly is in manifest contradiction to classical socialism. A rigorous logic derived the socialist doctrine from original democracy by the addition of the one dynamic factor of large-scale production. That procedure made it apparent how the original democratic motives were modified by the new environment and experiences and were compelled to change their direction—without, however, losing their identity. On the contrary, the reversing of direction is the very evidence of this identity. A single goal is aspired after in opposite directions if we start from opposite points. The same motive working under different conditions has to use correspondingly different means, since identical means under different conditions, or at the hands of different forces, lead to different ends. Public discussion is heatedly interested in the means, the institutions, as if they told anything in themselves. What counts is the living forces that create and animate these social forms and instruments. We do not understand the essence and functioning of institutions unless we understand the historical movement that uses or abuses them and the spirit that expresses itself through them. The inner motive with its ultimate goal is one thing, the conditions from which it emerges are another, the means it applies are a third. These are the phases of the problem we have to distinguish, although all are interrelated, and no motive or end can be recognized except by studying both conditions and institutions. It is in this sense that we affirm the spiritual identity of original democracy and classical socialism. The fact that they express their aims through contrasting institutions, in order to meet the contrast in conditions between small- and large-scale production, only confirms their identity.

Orthodox socialism is not the only movement to resort to collective institutions as a safeguard of individual liberty in collective work. Long before the rise of European socialism the first attempts at trade unionism in the United States received the warmest support from the Jeffersonians. These classical defenders of individual freedom wished to preserve the individual pattern of work wherever possible. But they did not impose individualistic forms where they did not belong; they realized that individual freedom in the collective work of industry had to be gained through collective organization, and they said so. Another impressive example of this approach is that given by Lujo Brentano, the foremost liberal scholar in Germany from 1870 on for more than half a century. He won fame both by his passionate attacks on socialism and his discovery that the labor unions were the means of restoring freedom in industry. As he put it, "the employer is a coalition in himself," and there is no equilibrium in the labor market unless there is in opposition to him a coalition formed by the individually weaker side, that of the workers. Brentano came to this conclusion through a study of British trade unionism, at that time in its infant stage. No discussion is now needed of how powerfully the British movement has developed and has been emulated in most leading countries. The sketch of British democracy we have given above (pages 29 ff. and 56 ff.) is incomplete without reference to the fact that the unions' collective organization has preserved certain elements of liberty and democracy in the system of capitalistic domination over collective work. Unionism certainly is not socialism, but it is not orthodox capitalism either. It is a partially collective organization, designed to secure individual liberty in collective work, an attempt to preserve the individualistic character of society by inserting a collective organization in that field where the pure individualistic form is directly destructive of liberty. It shares with socialism certain key ideas, only on a minor scale and without touching on the property question. Its clearest formulation is attained in the American program of the union's property rights in the jobs.

Under small-scale production, individual property is expressive of and creative of liberty; man is free because he is rooted in his work. The types of property and work coincide; everyone is granted his liberty, his property, and, consequently, his equality with all others. The small shop, however, has been gradually superseded by the big plant and the individual type of work by the superior collective one. Yet the old form of ownership has survived and proved to be a most useful instrument in that reorganization of production. Now it is obvious that individual property in the sphere of collective work is the contrary of individual property in the sphere of individual work. Individual property has become private property not because its legal form changes but because the objects of property change in character and size. The coincidence between the types of work and property and the universality of ownership have waned. The preponderance of the capitalist's sphere of ownership over his sphere of work has been balanced by the propertylessness of the men working on his property. They are not free in their work because it is no longer theirs, nor can they be the equals of those whom they have to obey, not for reasons of personal ability but of property. This organization with its inner cleavage, after fulfilling its historical mission, is supposed to give way to a new co-ordination of property and work, based, of course, on the new type of work.

Collective property, when viewed abstractly, appears to be the negation of individual property. But collective property in collective work is opposed only to individual property in collective work (and in a different way, to collective property in the natural sphere of individual work, as the next chapter will show). It is precisely parallel to individual property in individual work and is expressive of the same fundamental urge of man for independence in his work. The driving force of democracy, man's right to be free and rooted in a work that is his own, is thus not abrogated by socialism but transplanted to a new soil. Socialism attacks not individual liberty, but the liberty to dominate others; not individual property, but private property in excess of what the owner operates himself. It thereby restores the true meaning of liberty and property, and their connection with equality, under modern industrial conditions.

The logic proving the spiritual identity of democracy and socialism through the institutional changes is simple and rigorous and needs no historical documentation. Ignorance of the facts and indoctrination of both followers and critics of socialism are so widespread, however, that it is fortunate to find at least one witness to support the case. Karl Marx discusses throughout his earlier philosophical writings what he terms the "self-estrangement" and the succeeding "self-realization of man" as the true content of man's plight under capitalism and his eventual liberation from "the objective power above him." He also uses the term "real humanism" to indicate the point of view he has held in opposition to the idealistic humanism he has rejected, and therefore stresses the self-realization of man in the daily pursuit of a harmonious physical and spiritual existence, not merely in the world of ideas. The fact that the work of the laborer is not his own, but an item in the business calculation of somebody else, gives evidence of the "complete loss of man"; it "dehumanizes" man. The human objective of Marx's thinking is brought out particularly clearly in his bitter denunciation of the "Vulgar Communism," represented in his opinion by the French communist movement of his day. Vulgar Communism, instead of restoring to the worker the means of self-realization and abolishing the proletarian way of life, "is nothing but the generalization and completion of such an existence," it "detracts forcibly from talent," "denies the personality, and thereby proclaims kinship with that private property which is the denial of the personality." True communism must not accept the standards of capitalism, but must set up its own on a superior and more humane basis. The self-realization, humanization, and personalization of the workingman require that "private property be abrogated in a positive way; that man appropriate his own nature and his own work in a broader sense than that of material possession alone." Man is a "many-sided being" and realizes himself "in a many-sided way," he "appropriates his human reality" by living "as a comprehensive being" with "all the facets of his individuality." These views Marx elaborated over a period of several years into a comprehensive and detailed program of historical materialism. The dominant theme of his thought is that man's urge is towards liberty and property as the means of realizing himself in a world from which he feels himself estranged.[3]

These ideas cannot be ignored or disposed of by saying that they belong to the period antedating Marx's economic and political writings and are therefore repudiated by these more mature writings. The economic analysis of *Das Kapital* not only fits in with, but minutely outlines, the program that has to be followed on the road from self-estrangement to self-realization. The crystallized power of capital overwhelms man and strips him of his human dignity, but at the same time hastens the completion of its inner contradictions and its destruction at the hands of its victims. Whatever the merits or problems of this view, its complete accord with the earlier philosophical presentation is obvious. It is, moreover, explicitly emphasized by several passages of the *Kapital* itself; these have naturally escaped the attention of the professional Marx philologists because they did not understand this language. The most conspicuous passage comes from the celebrated but poorly understood chapter on the historical tendency of capitalistic accumulation. Immediately after introducing the "expropriation of the expropriators" Marx declares the positive significance of socialization to be that of "restoring not private property, but individual property on the basis of co-operation and of the communal possession of the earth and the means of production." Obviously the legal

---

[3] The quotations are arbitrarily chosen from hundreds of similar passages in the philosophical writings of Marx. These have been published, some for the first time, in Karl Marx, *Der Historische Materialismus*, herausgegeben von S. Landshut und J. P. Mayer, 2 volumes, Leipzig, 1932.

organization of society is expressed in this formula by the phrase "communal possession of the earth and the means of production." "Individual property" is not meant in the legal, but in the human sense. Socialization therefore gives to the individual an opportunity for individual activity and responsibility; it grants him the possibility of exerting his energies in work which he experiences as his own within the framework of the community and under its protection. As the community of workmen is master in the fields of its communal work, each individual can be free again in his respective sphere. Individual liberty on the basis of the communal organization of socialism corresponds exactly to the co-operative spirit arising from the individualistic organization of original democracy.

Insistence upon the reality of liberty precludes a merely moral or psychological interpretation. Liberty must be tangible, it must be experienced and practiced. A man's liberty is lost to him as soon as he abandons it to others to administer in his behalf. But in work that is basically communal an identification of liberty with arbitrariness is even more impossible than it would be in a system of individual work. In collective work two organizational limitations are imposed from the outset upon any individual decision: the essential discipline and co-operation that must exist in any collective management, and the technical nature of the work as represented by the rhythm of the machine itself. Hence many are prejudiced and believe that there is no room for liberty in a modern factory, that this work is mechanical once for all. There are, however, plenty of possibilities for human differentiation in the different types of technical work. Some of the problems that arise in any organized co-operation are: How to allocate the technically different portions of work to the members of the group according to their physical qualities and psychological requirements and preferences? Whether to plan a permanent allocation of men to jobs or a rhythmic shifting? How to judge the advantage of possible innovations from the standpoint of the working men? How the men may substitute for one another in case of illness or other personal handicaps without impairing the technical task and endangering the job? The general and abstract formulation of such questions must not give the impression that there can be any answer of a general legal or institutional character valid once for all. In fact the questions can never be decided definitely and universally; they have to be taken up anew in each shop as the productive task varies, or the technical or organizational structure shifts, or the psychological requirements of living men change. Despite the best communal system, labor will always entail trouble and hardship enough. On the other hand, the experiences of prolonged unemployment teach us that labor, even apart from the wage it brings, is among the vital requirements of human existence. If work can never be sheer joy, it surely can and should be part of a dignified human pattern, embodying human aspirations, experiences, tensions, and fulfillments. Only the workers themselves, granted proper guidance, are in a technical position to organize it as human labor. The self-government of the workers with respect to the individual allocation of their communal work is a necessary condition for the existence of a free community.[4]

2. Organization and Integration

The problem of reconciling liberty with the indispensable existence of co-ordination and integration appears, at

[4] Some more details are given in my article, "Democratic Freedom and the Organization of Labor," in *Political and Economic Democracy*, edited by Max Ascoli and Fritz Lehmann, New York, 1937.

first glance, to be peculiarly difficult under socialism. Under original democracy, the direct emphasis was laid upon individual liberty, and it required a theoretic discussion to show how liberty itself led to spontaneous integration in the market. The belief in this pre-established harmony of the market cannot survive in the presence of the deepening cleavages and disturbances of our day. It gives way to the idea of deliberate conscious co-ordination through an all-inclusive plan; capitalism itself starts on the way to such a reorganization of production. Disappointment with what liberty was able to achieve has led Socialists to place all their emphasis on integration. In fact it required a lengthy discussion to show how liberty can be preserved under a system aiming primarily at integration. We therefore appear to be a long way from establishing the kind of parallel between the two systems that would entitle socialism to proclaim itself the heir of original democracy in this new age. The connection between the pole of liberty and that of integration appears to be essential in the case of democracy and merely incidental in the case of socialism. As we discussed above, liberty is the very means to integration under original democracy, but it seems to be only tolerated by the independently achieved integration of socialism. In contrast to the coincidence of liberty and integration under democracy socialism seems forced to insert the element of liberty in a system that does not need it for purposes of integration, and might therefore dispense with it altogether.

This presentation falls down as soon as one takes into account the logic of the socialistic system and the forces upon which it depends. It is true that the technique of setting up and enforcing a plan requires nothing but an authority equipped with dictatorial power. The social origin and nature of the authority is irrelevant: it may be

traditional as in ancient Egypt, or revolutionary as in present-day fascism. The plan may or may not be equalitarian
and may or may not allow of some liberties, according to
the various possibilities arising from its origin. This conception of the plan, however, is purely technical and abstract, and disregards the historical foundations and dominant forces of a socialistic planned economy. The political
idea cannot be realized either theoretically or practically
unless it is imbued with the real sense of the particular
movement. If, therefore, the planned economy springs
from the movement envisaged by classical socialism, the
primacy of dictatorial integration, with or without the in-
clusion of some liberties, no longer exists. The structure
of socialism as a whole becomes visible and reveals an inherent connection between liberty and integration, parallel to that in original democracy. The same collective organization serves as the foundation of both liberty and the
plan. A planned economy may use any type of comprehensive unitary organization as its basis, but the idea arose
originally in connection with the idea of collective liberty
and property. Moreover, for seven decades it has been
monopolized by socialism. Propertyless workers in the
midst of concentrated and yet unco-ordinated production
have striven for that collective organization that will establish both human liberty and the integrating plan. As democratic individual property secures both liberty and integration through the instrument of the market, so collective
property secures both communal liberty (which includes
individual liberty) and integration by means of the plan.
Communal work educates and trains the workers in this
direction, this becomes their nature. Liberty that is sought
in the direction of solidarity and collective self-realization
is not opposed to the idea of a co-ordinating plan, as purely
individual liberty would be; communal liberty finds its

adequate goal in the plan. The plan is the true self-expression of men trained by capitalistic industry for communal action.

If any difficulty in this doctrine remains, it can be overcome by reference to the fundamental democratic idea of education. The workers of capitalism unconsciously yearn for communal planning, but are not, of their own accord, capable of conceiving the idea of planning. They need the superior wisdom—not of the state (they do not need to be compelled to do what they long for), but of the socialist movement, to complete their communal training under capitalism. The way Marxism interprets its own mission for the proletariat is, in this respect, the very model of democratic pedagogy. Any education has to fit the pupils for the objective tasks of life. In democracy these tasks are given and solved in the direction of the individual's spontaneous impetus. The wise democratic educator recognizes the inner urge of his pupils and helps them to formulate it in, and to reconcile it with, the given requirements of practical life. Marx did not create a socialist movement out of nothing, nor did he merely discover a socialist movement that existed before him. What he did was to study the newly formed proletarian men, to comprehend their blind instincts, and to express them in a coherent objective program of society that the workers could recognize for themselves. From what they were he drew the logical conclusions. He revealed to them the goal to be attained at the end of the road along which they were being driven by the inner necessity of their communal work; he showed them the meaning of their existence. The socialist movement, by following the principles of democratic education, confirms the desire of the workers for a communal reorganization of industrial work and teaches them that the culmination of their desire lies in the objective idea of a unitary plan.

Seen in this light, the constructive idea of socialism is exactly parallel to that of original democracy. The latter presupposes men who conform in their sense of individual independence and progress because nature so molded them. The inner urge of these men demands their individual property and through it achieves integration by the market. Classical socialism finds men whose sense of independence is remolded by the industrial revolution in the direction of collectivity. The inner urge of these men demands communal property for attainment of their liberty, and through it they achieve integration by means of the plan. The difference between the two systems lies in the fact that democratic harmony is regarded as given directly by nature itself (in any case, under the particular historical conditions of the pre-industrial period), whereas socialist harmony is regarded as the eventual outcome of a long and painful historical process. Democracy might, according to its own tenets, be started at once; socialism looks ahead to a salvation to come. The one relies on a static nature, the other on the necessary course of the future.[5]

Aside from this difference, the two systems are identical

[5] This formulation is not intended to belittle the difference between the two schemes. It encompasses the entire philosophy of historical materialism. The writer is convinced of the great significance of that philosophy and has studied it in several writings in German. Although we did not include it in our presentation explicitly, we did so implicitly. Historical materialism is, according to the socialist doctrine, the method that is bound up with the inner structure of capitalism and is derived from its analysis. It is therefore possible to give an orthodox presentation of the dialectical way of capitalistic history by merely following the causal connection between the stages of this development and without formally introducing the terms of historical materialism. Not only does the doctrine of the revolution as indicated above involve that relationship between the social superstructure and the fundamental self-movement of production

in that both teach the pre-established harmony and the co-incidence of liberty and integration, both make use of liberty as the very means of integration. Both take the spontaneous action of the citizens as the dominant force behind the social process and substitute this device for authoritative coercion. In both an anarchistic presumption is present in the form of the expectation of forceless harmony; this must be eliminated if either is to be practicable. In both this can be easily done; a significant distance in the direction of that Utopian goal can be covered by a sober examination of the two new social techniques. In each case the new social technique is used by men desirous of independence and specially trained through their experiences and does not rest on coercion. The state is not done away with, but the scope of its activity is reduced and liberty is thereby created. Original democracy is liberty organized under universal small-scale production, classical socialism is democracy renewed under universal large-scale production.

3. The Symbols of Democracy in Socialism

Two of the tenets of socialism attain, in this connection, the dignity of religious symbols. One was discussed above

which is termed materialism, but our entire discussion has shown the dialectical progress from undeveloped propertied labor, through the widening cleavage between property and labor, to the final harmony in the higher unity of collectively propertied labor. The reason why we did not use the terms of historical dialectics, though we might have done so without difficulty, is twofold. On the one hand, we chose to give the most simple statement of the case, and to this end used only such elements as are indispensable to the understanding of its inner logic. That is, we used the concepts of reality and did not need their duplication and generalization in the concepts of method. Secondly and chiefly, we are for our present purpose far less interested in the much discussed form of that process than in its much ignored contents. The logic behind these contents is the primary force of history in the doctrine of socialism.

as the anticipated withering away of the state; it was found in realistic terms to mean the reduction of organized force to a minimum. It is of course impossible to replace organized force by liberty unless that liberty, by virtue of its direction and technique, takes over the integrating function of which organized force had been in charge. If a plan of disciplined co-operation in division of labor is imposed by one group upon the others, it certainly cannot do without the use or the threat of force. That, however, is not the socialist idea. For socialism, the plan is only the technical form of a co-operation in which the whole people, trained as it is by communal work under capitalism, realizes itself. The idea of the plan is not imposed from above, but urged from below—nothing but details and technicalities can be controversial. As nature had been supposed to provide for that universal conformity in independence and progress which underlay the functioning market, so history is now supposed to provide for that sense of communal liberty which aims at planned co-operation. If it is not the eternal nature of man, it is at any rate his historically given nature that expresses itself in the plan. As democracy could do away with artificial integrating authorities that employed force because it discovered spontaneous integration through the market, so socialism believes in the withering away of the state because the idea of the plan is expressive of the spontaneous will of the people. In neither case is force needed to establish the foundations of society. Peace at home and abroad is the stamp of universal liberty and equality.

All these social and institutional conceptions, finally, are condensed into the methodological concept of historical necessity—the second of the symbols of the socialist creed. This notion is parallel to the notion of nature in the system of original democracy. Nature and historical necessity not only mold man, but act through him as well. According to democracy, man has to be free not only from serfdom, but also for spontaneous action as it arises from his nature and integrates social life through the instrument of the market. The same kind of idea, though more complicated and therefore easily obscured, prevails in socialism. As democracy posits the active nature of man as an end in itself and as the means of integration, so socialism posits his historically necessary urge toward communal self-realization as an end in itself and as the means of integration.

Historical necessity is usually interpreted to mean the technical changes and their effects. It is true that the technical changes are also encompassed by the term historical necessity, and rightly so, because it is this automatic process, enforced by dynamic competition, that engenders the new type of man and ideals. The point, however, is that this material effect of historical necessity is not in itself sufficient to attain the ultimate goal of the process. It is an indispensable condition, but depends on being completed and utilized by man. That this new man will in fact complete and utilize it is assured by his nature, by the combination of his original sense of independence with the positive and negative impressions of his communal work under capitalism. His inner urge is the decisive instrument of historical necessity. If by some mistaken and inconceivable arrangement the movement of production failed to produce that type of man, no appeal to historical necessity would be adequate to correct the mistake. To insist upon the technically necessary form if it happened to be refused by men, would be tantamount to putting production above men; it would be an act of arbitrariness and historically impossible. This case is of course inconceivable in the socialist doctrine, because history produces not only the material pre-conditions of socialism, but through them the urge of man that strives to complete them. It is this inner urge of man with which the final and decisive step of historical necessity is entrusted, just as it was the second-to-last step of historical necessity which created that man out of the nature of modern industry. Socialism is historically necessary because the inner urge of the historically determined man aims at this form of free communal work.

Historical necessity is therefore the methodical concept that belongs to the legal concept of communal property and the political concept of the withering away of the state. They are all expressive of the same fundamental democratic idea that man demands the right to be himself and to live according to the pattern of his nature. Given universal large-scale production, the nature of man finds its adequate expression in a planned economy based on common property. The overwhelming power of necessity implicit in this development strips the state of its artificially integrating function and establishes at one stroke liberty and integration, and with them, peace. This is the classical doctrine of socialism.[6]

[6] Our reduction of classical socialism to classical democracy attempts to achieve by systematic analysis of the doctrines what Henry de Man (Hendrik de Man) achieved by a comprehensive and elaborate historical presentation in his too-little-known book, *L'Idée socialiste,* 1933.

IV

SECOND TRANSFORMATION: COMMUNISM

Introduction: Syndicalism as Socialistic Idealism

WITHIN socialism wide differentiations soon developed in line with the national and historical differentiations of capitalism. Each brand of socialism used the elements of the classical doctrine for its own particular interpretation. As a result, the balance and comprehensiveness that were responsible for the symmetry and grandeur of the classical system were lost. This was the beginning of the decay of socialism.

The classical system of socialism turns on the symmetry between the two converging lines of development—the ripening of material conditions and of the workers for the decisive change. The ripeness of material conditions, the reorganization of production by the capitalists, is more fundamental only in the genetic sense that the remolding and ripening of men follows from that "materialistic" development. The spreading and intensification of large-scale production is the basic condition; it is paralleled by the proletarianization of the workers; and both tendencies converge in their common end. The systematic and practical symmetry of the two conditions must not be confused with the merely genetic primacy of the material condition. Historical necessity must not be interpreted as focusing on this primacy of the material condition as if the ripening of men were an automatic consequence of this condition. The more the material development takes care of itself, the more man has to take care of being equal to it. Otherwise the genuine ethic of Marxian dialetics is lost and replaced by the easy fatalism and optimistic inertia of the belief in "the amiable tendency of development" (as it was ironically called by Robert Wilbrandt).

This latter course was followed by German socialism, for many decades the most successful branch of international socialism and therefore long regarded as the legitimate interpreter of the Marxian doctrine. The mass movement there represented by the steadily growing unions and by an impressive political organization revealed a steady increase in the numerical power of labor. It looked as if this movement could not fail to include eventually the whole German people and take over all property when "the knell of capitalist private property would sound." The prevalent feeling was that this automatic process of capitalistic concentration and proletarianization should be watched, guarded from interference when necessary, and aided whenever possible. Genuine impulses and decisions were not encouraged in this set-up. Not the animating spirit, but the number of men counted; not constructive statesmanship, but orderly administration was demanded. Instead of leaders, German labor explicitly and consciously asked for "functionaries." No arbitrary action was to be taken, no unnecessary risk run, no spontaneous strikes allowed, as these might inflame the passions and lead to a premature conflagration and thus involve the war chest of the whole labor organization. The thing to do was to watch closely the progress of history, wait patiently for the necessary outcome, and meanwhile strengthen the organization. In practice this meant the undisturbed rule of the party and union bureaucracy, men who neither claimed to be nor really were rulers and leaders. Their calculation was right as long as economic conditions were on the up-swing and permitted labor to share in the benefits of capi-talism through the pressure of their organizations. But the true power of these organizations had long since been un-dermined by the movement's barrenness in leaders, im-pulses, and ideas.

The counter-movement to this restraint on true revolu-tionary spirit was syndicalism, a brand of socialism that flourished in France, Italy, and Spain, and was diametri-cally opposite to the German species. The German type corresponded to the systematic and often pedantic charac-ter of the German people; the Latin type is easily traceable to the Latin temperament. The difference in development of the fundamental material conditions between Germany and the Latin countries, however, has also been respon-sible for the deviation. As these differences in industrial progress became more marked during the latter part of the nineteenth century, the prospects of socialism in the more backward countries appeared somewhat discouraging. This resulted in a drastic change in theory: the emphasis was no longer laid on the material conditions, but on the fight-ing spirit of the revolutionists. To the one-sided material-istic interpretation of dialectics in Germany, syndicalism opposed an equally one-sided idealistic interpretation; against the conscientious and pedantic administration by centralized organizations, it set up the enthusiastic and spontaneous action of the rank and file. The syndicalists believed that representatives of labor in the parliaments and offices cannot be truly representative of the rank and file because they are no longer workers and do not per-sonally share the proletarian destiny and experiences, suf-ferings and hopes. What is needed in their opinion is the unrestrained spontaneity of the rank and file, united by a sense of a common cause in the various units of production as each group fights its own battle in its own shop and plant. It is true that these resorts to "direct action," since they are unco-ordinated, end in defeat again and again; but the example of heroism and sacrifice will inflame the hearts of the suppressed; the struggle will flare up and take final form in the general strike and ultimate battle.

This doctrine is unsatisfactory because it is incomplete. In passing over the material conditions of the revolution, it evades the question of what the institutions of a reconstructed society will be. It rightly stresses the element of vitality and spontaneity, but fails to place it under any integrating principle or in any integrated system. Without such a system, the units of production would have to be co-ordinated by the free market, as under capitalism. Since the units of production are also the units of the revolutionary organization, and are supposed to serve as the cells of the free workers' society, the effects of an unregulated market would soon be felt by them. Different groups of workers, through selective competition, would rise and fall on the ladder of economic and social power, and would be subjected to the perplexity and insanity of the economic crisis. Syndicalism has no institutional solution to such problems; it contents itself with stressing the idealism, morale, and solidarity of the workers and relies on the original or eventual goodness of man. In this respect it proves itself to be the proletarian form of anarchism.

Representing as it does the one element of vitality, syndicalism may, however, be reconciled with one integrating principle or another, as these arise elsewhere. British Guild Socialism after the war was an interesting, if not definitive, attempt to build up a democracy of industrial self-rule on the basis of the several units of production and their workers' councils, and thus pass on the direct impetus of the

rank and file to the co-ordinating institution, the industrial quasi-parliament. Soviet Russia derives her very name
from the workers' councils that sprang up spontaneously
in the unorganized insurrection of 1905, proved irresistible as units of battle in 1917, and are responsible for
whatever ingredients of democratic spontaneity may be
detected in the urban section of this dictatorial country.
Their initiative is invited, their criticism, suggestions, and
amendments to that portion of the all-inclusive plan which
concerns them is solicited by and passed on to the highest
divisions of the planning authorities. On the other hand,
the mere element of vitality, since it has no direction or
integrating principle in itself, may be harmonized with a
very different type of integrating principle—as in Italian
fascism, which glorifies heroic action as an end in itself and
utilizes Mussolini's syndicalistic heritage of fierce impetus
for an entirely different cause. This feature of mass spontaneity and its possibilities for abuse make it the reverse of
that mechanistic necessity which was supposed to achieve
its ends through administrators. At the same time the degeneration of existing democracy can be seen wherever its
driving force, the spontaneity of the people, is suppressed
and abandoned to its foe.

One more element of the syndicalistic doctrine of vitality must be stressed, the emphasis on the elite. Not all
workers nor all groups are equally exposed to suffering;
not all react with equal stubbornness and courage. As soon
as the mechanizing and leveling use of the labor and political organization is given up, the original qualities and
the natural variations between men come to the fore and
become relevant for history. History forges all its human
instruments from the natural raw material by subjecting
them to the pressure of social experiences and humiliations, but one set of its instruments proves better fitted to

force the door of the future than others. Some must take the lead, bear the main burdens, and win the main honors. The existence of a natural aristocracy, far from impairing democratic equality and solidarity, is the only means by which it may be realized. Every worker will recognize himself and his true destiny in the deeds and achievements of such an aristocracy; it has the genuine inspiring power of a symbolic representation. Only as an idea is embodied in living men, will other living men be convinced and transported. The whole emphasis on vitality, symbolic representation, and leadership is of course not new in itself: what is new is its emergence from socialism—in behalf of democracy and on a democratic basis. Together with the idea of spontaneity of which the workers' councils were the organ, this idea of ascetic heroic leadership has been taken over by Russia in the form of a secret order with severe principles of selection that has developed into the one ruling party.

It is impossible to exaggerate or emphasize too strongly the significance of this development for democracy, especially since this point cannot be further pursued in this book owing to the limitations upon its scope. Democratic liberty and equality must not stifle true leadership because a vital society is never an amorphous mass but an articulated entity, and leadership and initiative will assert themselves in abusive ways if not properly provided for by the official constitution. In a capitalistic democracy of the English brand, leadership is provided by the conservative group arising from the merger of the upper business class with the old nobility. But in orthodox democratic-progressive doctrine, whether individualistic or socialistic, there is no place for the authority of leadership: hence the danger of bureaucratic authority and inertia, as we have shown a propos of German labor. Marx, it is true, conceived the idea of intellectual leadership in the socialist movement to interpret to the workers their situation and their instinctive reactions, to arouse them to political consciousness, and to draw these tendencies together into an active force (see p. 95). This was, however, viewed in terms of intellectual enlightenment, not of practical leadership in responsible decisions and constructive measures. It is only through the doctrine of syndicalism that the full significance of social articulation and leadership was brought to the attention of the democratic movements, and Russian communism first erected a responsible constructive leadership in practice.

The problem implied in leadership as distinguished from domination cannot be discussed here. It must suffice to state how similar leadership and domination are in certain respects, and how vital for democracy the line of demarcation between them is. Only a mechanistic and decaying democracy tries to do without true leadership; a healthy democracy must realize and maintain the tension between equality and leadership. To contend that they are irreconcilable would be tantamount to denying the possibility of democracy at all, and of course the precarious character of this form of government cannot be disputed. On the other hand, no form of government escapes analogous problems; any dictatorship or aristocracy may easily lose real leadership owing to its transformation into a hardened bureaucratic institution and vested rights. Therefore, while it is true that without leadership no society can survive a crisis, it does not follow that any one particular form of government is more apt to meet the test than any other. This study, however, is not concerned with the comparative merits and defects of different political techniques, but with the historical development and transformation of the original principles of democracy and socialism. In turning to an analysis of communism in the light of classical socialism, we must keep in mind the ancient wisdom concerning the structural laws of any society that syndicalism revived and communism inherited and applied; we must also remember that whatever real or hypothetical forms and transformations of democracy we discuss, they can never be conceived as functioning without solving their inner constitutional problems.

The idea of leadership alone, of course, contains in itself no more guidance from principle than the concept of vitality. These qualities can be transplanted to other soils than that of democracy, especially as the foundation stones of democracy crack and the forces of vitality lose sight of the spiritual direction of democratic thought. This leads to the emergence of fascism from present democracy, as we have indicated above. While a loss of vitality and leadership may wreck an existing democracy, it is not in terms of vitality that the different political systems can be defined. What they signify is determined by the spiritual direction of their institutions and actions. It is to this discussion of the political principles embodied in the various systems that we turn.

A. The Logic of the System of Communism

1. Differentiation Within Capitalism as Starting Point of Communism

Classical socialism, as we have shown, stems from the premises of original democracy and the one additional assumption that large-scale production is universally superior to small. The two systems therefore have a threefold bond: that of historical sequence, institutional inversion, and spiritual identity. Leninism, however, is connected with classical socialism in a different way. To the assumptions of classical socialism it adds one more: the differentiation in economic progress among the capitalistic countries. This assumption does not describe a later stage than that assumed in classical socialism, but gives a more detailed picture of the development predicted by Marx and leads to the formulation of a more detailed and applicable program. Leninism claims historical, institutional, and spiritual identity with classical socialism, which it strives to fulfill through the study and use of new and important practical details.

Accordingly, the logic of Leninism is best displayed by starting from its additional assumption—the differentiation in capitalistic development of the various European countries. Recognition of this differentiation does not mean that the fundamental validity of the law of large-scale production is in any way impaired or called in question. The causes for the coexistence of large and small shops are regarded as temporary and provisional. One glance at the advanced countries shows how much more general large-scale production there is than in the poorer, more backward countries. This is supposed to prove that large-scale production is universally superior and that its final victory in all branches of production is assured, in the backward as well as the advanced countries. The difference between these two groups of countries is only a difference in degree of development. Like syndicalism, communism has to compensate for the lack of material ripeness in the backward countries by stressing the idealistic side of dialectics, as evidenced by the workers' councils and the Order of the leaders. Unlike syndicalism, however, communism has succeeded in reinterpreting the material side of dialectics and has assigned a positive function to the backward countries in behalf of the whole world.

What Leninism teaches in this regard is a division of labor in promoting a world-wide proletarian revolution among the differently developed countries. The more advanced countries present the model of development on the basis of which the young backward countries can study their own future. Not all countries, in spite of their interdependence through foreign trade, go through all the phases of capitalism at the same time. Not all arrive at the gates of the promised land together. Only the leading industrialized Western countries have kept abreast in their development, but to be one of them is not a privilege. For when they arrive at the doors of socialism, they find themselves unable to enter. The obvious conclusion to be drawn from the paradox of a powerful economic organization existing, but not preventing overwhelming propertylessness and shrinking markets, is socialization—but this step cannot be taken. With the growth and completion of capitalism the technique of power and organization has also grown, and the more unbearable capitalism becomes, the more unassailably it is entrenched behind the terrible efficiency of modern government. While the economic and social structure is ripe for the revolution, the political form is already too rigid to permit revolution.

History might have run into a blind alley if it were not for the greater mobility of the younger countries. There capitalism has not yet fully developed. Pre-rational looseness obtains in both their economic and governmental organizations. Not that capitalism and government are less ruthless in these countries, but they lack the efficiency and all-inclusiveness that developed methods give. The biographies of Stalin, Trotsky, and other revolutionary leaders tell how they were jailed or sentenced to forced labor again and again and managed repeatedly to escape and resume their political work. This cannot be credited only to the unconquerable stalwartness of these men, it also gives evidence of the lack of rational efficiency of an unorganized country in matters of political persecution. The same men would not have succeeded in escaping from a Russian prison or a German concentration camp today. This indicates why Lenin held it easier to attack and overthrow Czarism than an organized Western government. Moreover, the Russians did not need to wait for the completion of capitalism in Russia to comprehend the necessity of revolution and the ways of economic and social reconstruction. They learned these two points by studying Western capitalism, with its unbearable evils and the organizations it had prepared for the reconstruction as models. Thus the Russians were able to anticipate the logical outcome of that developed Western capitalism which could not, for technical reasons, resolve the deadlock in the countries where it flourished. The privileged position of the Russians lay in their being able to combine, for immediate utilization, the knowledge drawn from the study of the older countries with a still flexible and plastic organization in their own country. Their immediate task consisted in seizing power and reorganizing the country along the lines of productive organization existing in the older countries, but translated into socialism. The communist revolution in the undeveloped country is the product of its own flexibility and the economic and social experiences of the old countries.

The deadlock in the old countries is, however, a dangerous handicap to the socialist reconstruction in the young country. Since the economic interdependence of the old and young countries continues despite the new political differentiation, the capitalists can and will use this economic weapon to interfere with social reconstruction. For this material reason alone it is necessary for the revolutionaries to co-ordinate the older countries, quite aside from the desire on the part of the victorious workers to bring into the fold those fellow workers still languishing under capitalism. A clash hence becomes inevitable. It is only another form of the class war that did not reach its goal in the highly industrialized country as long as it sought an isolated solution. Now the deadlock can be broken. The rise and success of one or more proletarian states will accomplish in the older countries what the mere theory of historical necessity could never have accomplished. It will inflame the revolutionists, convince the skeptics, and undermine the belief of both the government and the people in the unassailability of the existing state. As the country second to Russia in ripeness for a communist revolution, Lenin occasionally named Spain, characteristically enough because it represented an exact parallel to Russia in that the two were just emerging from feudal inertia and starting on the way of capitalistic progress. From the two corners of Europe, he believed, the revolution would spread to its very center. The pioneering communist states would lead the world revolution and earn the honors of victory in the ultimate battle of mankind.

2. *Anticipation of the Development as the Criterion of Communism*

The fascination of Leninism lies in the way it has developed the fundamental Marxian analysis by applying it to the entire political reality of our day. It is as picturesque as it is logical. But the implications of its logic require discussion.

The argument of Leninism rests on the prime assumption of Marxism, the universal validity of large-scale production, and on the second assumption, the variation in speed of capitalistic progress in the different countries. It leads to the anticipation of the revolution by the lagging country. The latter can anticipate the revolution because it has learnt from the developed country its own capitalistic future and the inherent potentialities and necessities of reconstruction. It must do this because the example of the old country has taught it that economic maturity involves a rationalization of government that chokes any political possibility of revolution from within. In anticipating the revolution, the young country skips from an early and undeveloped stage to and beyond the final stage of capitalism. It is this skipping and anticipation that is responsible for all the problems of communism as distinct from those of socialism.

Classical socialism had assumed that the revolution would find men and conditions equally prepared. The communist anticipation means that the revolutionists find neither men nor conditions ripe. This is the negative side of the undeveloped state; the positive side is the taking advantage of the lack of rational methods in government. Communism itself is numerically undeveloped in the undeveloped country; it embraces only a relatively small number of class-conscious workers and their instructors in theory. Whatever the conditions and the ways and means of proletarian accession to political power, communism has to establish its own economic and social requisites, as capitalism has not been given time to prepare any. The economic and social development that was supposed to lead to socialism must now be achieved under the rule of communism itself. Instead of coming about as an historical process driven by the impersonal law of competition and concentration, it is now instigated by the proletarian government deliberately. Being a painful process of transformation, it naturally arouses resistance and requires force to be achieved. Communism has to take over the un-

pleasant task that capitalism was forced to leave unfinished.

It is an unpleasant task in spite of the fact that it is
undertaken with a happy end in view. In the classical doctrine, the collective liberation of the working masses
through communal property and planned economy presupposes their education in solidarity through collective
work; it is the logical outcome of their experiences in this
work under capitalism and their positive and negative adjustments to it. Under the communist regime this new
pattern is realized before the people concerned can appreciate the reason; the house is built, as it were, from roof to
cellar; a mold alien to the backward masses is impressed
upon them and they are forced to adjust themselves to it.
The magnitude of this task can best be seen in the fact that
at least 80 per cent of the Russian people were engaged in
pre-capitalistic forms of individual work when they were
surprised by collectivization. This is the statistical expression of their lagging industrialization, and can be considered a measure both of the performance of those who managed to solve the problem, and of the sufferings of the
people concerned. Through Lenin's inversion of the historical scheme the overwhelming majority of the Russian
people were condemned to a merely passive role in history
—that of being material to be molded by the rulers.

It would not be fair to suspect the motives of the rulers
or to impute to them a conscious abuse of their theory. It
is true that every system of domination in history has justified itself by referring to the backwardness of the ruled,
maintaining that domination is necessary for the good of
the people themselves. In the case of the Soviets, however,
the rulers do not simply turn to this facile expedient: they
strongly and honestly emphasize two distinguishing features
of their system. First, they themselves appear as trustees of

the future, not as rulers; no social or economic discrimination divides them from their comrades. Second, the dictatorial period is transitory, and the government, in remolding the people, pursues the definite aim of making them capable of self-rule. That there is no other liberty but that communal liberty which grows from communal work, is supposed to be evidenced by the previous attempts at liberty which resulted in capitalism. There is no other way to attain liberty except to transform life and work in the communal direction, as capitalism would have done—but without the implications of capitalism. This has to be done from above, dictatorially, but eventually it will be accomplished. The aim of this regime is to make itself superfluous. The doctrine of the withering away of the dictatorial state is not abandoned; it continues to occupy the central position in a program whose realization proceeds with amazing vigor.

All this, however, though it justifies the rulers, is no immediate consolation to those who are ruled and do not understand the view of the rulers. If they did, they would necessarily approve it, the theory says, and this would at once relieve the rulers of their function. But as the masses are not yet enlightened enough, they continue for the time being to suffer from what is not only inevitable but salutary, since it is the prerequisite of their own eventual liberty. The destiny of the agricultural masses is decisive in this regard, for they form the bulk of the Russian people and have just emerged from feudal bondage. Their emancipation had been initiated by the laws of capitalistic liberation one generation before, but had been completed and made effective only by the first phase of the communist revolution itself. The communist revolution had started from the alliance between the workers and the peasants as equals in the struggle against their oppressors, the capitalists and the landlords, who had been guilty of exploitation, war, and defeat. In this alliance, each of the oppressed classes seized what it had operated and coveted— the workers the industrial plants, the peasants their lands. The workers, trained in communal work, established their property rights in their plants on a communal basis; the peasants established their property rights in their respective lands on an individual basis, according to the natural urge of all peasants the world over. Whether or not this individualistic urge appears historically antiquated to the learned and to the members of the industrial community, it is natural as life itself to the peasant because it offers him the chance to root himself in his work through property and to win the liberty he values as a peasant. Whether, as an independent peasant, he would soon be ruined by competition and crisis, is beside the point. The only thing he is aware of is that it is not capitalism which expropriates him now, but communism. According to that program he must be deprived of all he owns as an individual in order to gain it as a member of the community. In the moment of his expropriation, his one feeling is that he is being deprived of all he has.[1]

3. *The Political Possibility of the Anticipation in Russia*

It may well be asked why the peasant submitted to his expropriation. The answer is implied in Lenin's reference

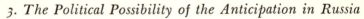

[1] The new principle of anticipation necessitated, and found expression in, a significant change in the accepted set of Marxian theories. The doctrine of the ripening of conditions has been dismissed and replaced by the doctrine of the "revolutionary situation." This situation is defined as a collapse of the existing order, which makes it possible to seize power. Of course, the old theory of ripening conditions had included the new one; once conditions demand a new order the old order cannot function any longer. But the reverse is not true; the old order may collapse without any preceding growth of the elements of a

to the undeveloped stage of Russia's history. Not only the government, but the whole people were lacking in organizational efficiency—with the one exception of the industrial workers. Capitalism arises when the ferment of progress, intelligence, and critical attitude operates on the obsolete forms of feudal society, and it imparts this spirit to all who are engaged in the growing industries. Moreover, in an undeveloped country like Russia, capitalism itself, where it exists at all, is not in an undeveloped form; it springs up late, but starts with the most recent equipment designed in the advanced countries. It benefits by the latest improvements in technical and organizational methods in the leading countries and transplants them to the new soil. No wonder that the proletariat of this recent and modern industry is as developed in critical intelligence and adaptability as it is limited in numbers. The rest of the country, however, the masses of the peasants just emerging from the dark ages, are as superior in numbers as they are inferior in enlightenment and organization. What they comprehend is their direct relationship to their land; they are far from being politically and economically educated and are still farther from any class-conscious organization and action. This may be explained by the fact of their illiteracy. They are not only unenlightened and unorganized, but actually unorganizable, because widely scattered people in remote villages and farms can be organ-

socialist society, and a non-socialist direction of reconstruction or the renewal of the old order after the elimination of the disturbance may be demanded by conditions. The old theory, therefore, is essential to the dialectical realism of classical socialism; if isolated, it leads to the hardened bureaucratic materialism of German labor, as discussed above, page 102. The new theory, contrariwise, by confining itself to a strictly negative definition, leaves room for anticipation and revolution at any stage and is, therefore, in line with the undialectical, voluntaristic approach of communism.

ized and instructed only by the written word. It is this wide gap between the class-conscious strength of the workers and the absence of any political organization in the peasantry that the workers took advantage of in establishing their rule and compelling the whole people to accept their pattern of life. The uninstructed and unorganized majority had to surrender to the enlightened and organized minority.

Another even more important point can be inferred from the reference to the opportunity of the undeveloped country. It is astounding to find no mention in all Marxian literature of the economic conditions that make a communist revolution possible. Marxism considers production in general, but without any further specification, as the fundamental and determining force in shaping life and society. Now the primary daily necessity is the production of food, and the interruption of the food supply may stop any social process and any revolution. In classical socialism the question of food supply did not arise because the universal validity of large-scale production applied to farming as well as to the industries and included the producers of food with all the other producers as participants in the proletarian destiny and as possessed with the will towards communal liberation. The communist anticipation of the revolution, however, has to deal with a social and economic situation in which the producers of food are to be found in the opposing camp. The reason is that farming still lacks reorganization on large-scale lines and that the peasants continue, or rather begin to insist upon individual work and individual property. It is therefore the production of food which first of all demands reorganization on communist lines if an all-inclusive communism is to be built up. This dependence of communism on the daily delivery of food creates a paradoxical situation that may prove to be dangerous once the peasants become aware of the power they wield. Their active political resistance may be smashed by political force, but no political force can positively secure production and delivery of surpluses in the long run. Raids to the country may take away the existing stocks but cannot enforce the current production of such surpluses as the cities need. The problem of food supply is crucial for any all-inclusive communism because it has to violate the feelings of the producers upon whom it depends for deliveries.

This problem could be solved in Russia because of its undeveloped condition again. If the people engaged in industrial work depend for their food on the agrarian surpluses, all evidently hinges on the relative sizes of the industrial and agrarian sections of the country. The smaller the percentage of urban people and the larger the rural percentage, the smaller the average surpluses of agricultural products that are needed. With 20 per cent of the people depending on deliveries of the remaining 80 per cent, the problem is solved with relative ease from the outset, compared with that raised by any industrialized country where the average surpluses per head of agrarian producer must be many times higher. Reckoning for the sake of argument in very crude figures, a Russian food producer would have to produce one-fourth in excess of what he wishes to retain for his own consumption. Even if he refused to deliver anything and reduced his production to the amount of his consumption, the government could still seize one-fifth of his stock without starving him to death. In an industrialized country like Germany, 70 per cent of the people depend on the deliveries of the remaining 30 per cent—which means that they are dependent, not only on the high productivity of agrarian work but also on the daily co-operation of the producers. It means that the average producer has to raise and deliver 233 per cent in excess of his own consumption, or, if we allow for a very large amount of imports, still 150 to 200 per cent, as contrasted with the 25 per cent necessary in Russia. In the United States 21 per cent of the gainfully occupied people are engaged in farming. In crudest approximation again the average producer of grain or dairy products has to produce for the city, and daily to deliver, four times as much as he produces for his own consumption. In the light of such considerations the economic foundation upon which the proletarian success in Russia rests becomes clear. The undeveloped stage of the country upon which Lenin centered the attention was responsible not only for the technical weakness of Czarism but also for the absence of anticommunist organizations among the peasants and for a comparatively easy solution of the problem of feeding the cities.[1a]

B. Verification of the Communist Doctrine

1. Verification of Communism in Russia

So far our analysis has moved within the bounds of Leninism and has been confined to a detailed examination and illustration of its underlying concepts: the uneven rate of capitalistic growth in various countries and the specific imperfections hindering the economic, social, and political ripeness in the revolutionary country. These problems were first attacked for merely political or, as it

[1a] The shifting of emphasis from industry to agriculture is not new. In economics, Franz Oppenheimer one generation ago has taken up an old motive by formulating his "geocentric" law to the effect that the growth of industry is limited by the available surpluses of agriculture. Now modern agrarian techniques are so productive as to suspend the economic validity of the law: the economic limit is not reached. But the political implications of the law are of overwhelming significance.

were, technical reasons, owing to the circumstances that the revolutionists had to take into consideration and were able to deal with so successfully. These originally technical details have given rise, however, to questions of principle which are increasingly significant. In an inquiry from the Marxian point of view the mere concept of technicalities is likely to be distrusted. In the classical doctrine everything converges upon the realization of the goal, all social reality and history are governed by one tendency, and all obstacles such as an individualistic pattern of life or the impossibility of the survey needed to establish a planned society are gradually removed by the developments of history. The new doctrine, however, is dependent for its realization more on cunning, on seizing the available opportunity, than on the majestic and awe-inspiring march of events impelled by historical necessity. Circumstances do not, as in the classical doctrine, precipitate the revolution: at best they must be taken advantage of, and at worst be fought. This passive view of the historic process, of existing conditions and living men, is nothing but the reverse side of the emphasis laid upon the knowledge and energy of the revolutionists, in contrast to the equilibrium between the material and human contributions set forth in the classical doctrine. However, as Leninism is derived from Marxism, the question must be put as to what this depreciation of objective conditions signifies for the goal and its historically necessary pursuit. Will a misinterpretation of the forces of reality cause the goal sooner or later to be missed? A future failure would demonstrate that the revolution was not allied with the logic of the historical process, and the reluctant historical process would assert itself. Speculation on the possibilities of a political failure of communism in Russia, long current among anti-communist Marxians, raised the question not only of political expediency, but of spiritual justification, of correct interpretation, of right belief. The philosophical principle of historical necessity cannot be confirmed except by the political success of a system of thought that claims to realize the striving of history toward its fulfillment in the final liberation of mankind.

It is therefore decidedly in favor of the communist interpretation of history that the prospects for its further political success in Russia are bright. Its anticipation of the revolution occurred when men and conditions were in a premature stage and were not only too undeveloped for resistance, but plastic enough to assume the form impressed upon them. The backwardness of the social and economic structure, moreover, has afforded the enlightened government a unique chance of combining coercion with persuasion by demonstrating to the skeptics the advantages of the new pattern. What the peasants are forced to accept is often the most modern, most efficient, most attractive of the devices of rational technique and organization. These bear witness to the superior wisdom and benevolence of the government, and the confidence thus created can be carried over to those matters which in themselves are not so convincing. To comply with the will of this government not only is advisable for political reasons, but can be advocated because of the unheard of prospects that the government is capable of opening up.

In this respect the function of Russian totalitarianism is very similar to that of Western absolutism in the early industrial period and to fascist totalitarianism in undeveloped Italy. Industrial life appears too strange and remote from the natural inclinations of the people to be taken over voluntarily by them simply for reasons of profit. The absolutistic tyranny over the bourgeois, capitalistic tyranny over the workers, and Soviet dictatorship over the Russian peasants seem to have been required if the knowledge and practice of industrial possibilities were to be diffused and made prevalent. The Soviet dictatorship, since it is younger than the others, draws the full benefit from the long and painful process of trial and error through which the preceding generations in the Western world had gone. Consequently it can save its people all the intermediate imperfect steps and take over the most recent and best-confirmed results. The Five-Year Plan has an irresistible appeal because it compresses into five or ten years what the pioneer industrial nations had to test out over one or two centuries of most troublesome history. This principle of accelerated progress is of course not monopolized by communism; it is applied by different political systems in Japan, and in Turkey and Palestine on a modest scale. Wherever a progressive-minded group seizes power in an undeveloped country, it naturally takes advantage of this possibility. Nothing new along technical and organizational lines seems to have been contributed by Russia thus far. Inventions there may not be possible so long as the known potentialities are not exhausted, and all energies are concentrated upon utilizing them. Nor are inventions necessary as long as the gap between Russian and Western technical developments provides Russia with ample room for progress. It is futile to speculate upon what capitalism or some other system might have done in Russia if communism had not intervened. The fact remains that the Russian dictatorship has been very efficient and has performed remarkable achievements in the direction of industrial development. It really leads the people while remolding them.

Nevertheless, it is questionable whether the results of all its endeavors will be communism as the Communists themselves conceive it. They believe that there is a one-sided dependence of all spiritual issues on the material ones, that in Lenin's famous phrase, "Soviets plus electricity make communism." They supplemented their positive technical and organizational revolution by attacking the forces of reaction centered in the church; they taught the people atheism along with the use of the machine which was considered its symbol. In doing so they were favored by another fortunate coincidence. The Christian Church as in most other countries was weak in faith, and narrow and reactionary in its political leanings; in addition, however, it seems to have been widely corrupt in matters of personal morality and not to have commanded much human respect. No wonder that the people were fascinated not only by the deeds but by the sobriety and devotion of the new leaders who obviously practiced what they preached. Yet the question remains open whether ultimately communism will absorb and remodel Russia or be remodeled and absorbed by her. Religion is not to be identified with an ecclesiastical institution and its incumbents —not even necessarily with the consciousness of fundamental dogmas. The religious genius of the Russian people may be deprived of supposedly obsolete objects and methods of worshiping and may still survive although without direction and self-consciousness. The peasant cannot suddenly understand a rational doctrine rationally: he has to translate it into his own way of thinking. We are told by a most competent observer what stupendous moral effects in every direction communism is producing in the Russian village. It is true and only natural that the people should be morally poisoned by an alien and misunderstood pattern which more or less violently impresses upon them, for the supreme goal of its self-assertion, the basest methods of spying and place-seeking and denunciation. This, however, is only one of the alternative repercussions we are told of. A neighboring village may show the most unheard of sublimity of human spirit, human devotion, human brother-liness. The religious genius of the Russian village may mis-take communism for a revelation of Christianity (and thereby give it an interpretation more profound and more correct than the interpretation of communism in terms of atheistic materialism). The institutional plasticity of Rus-sia which Lenin perceived and took advantage of may be due not only to her undeveloped, unorganized stage, but to a permanent spiritual sublimity that finds no ultimate value in the institutional issue and is creative enough to seize any occasion for its inspiration. This spirituality, through its victory, would refute communism, or would perhaps lift it to a level where even its inflection of wrong is, through the agency of a superior power, transformed into a blessing.

As for the communist leaders, they would not be likely to admit this even if it came to pass. Nor would they need to do so, as they themselves are concerned only with the institutional problems. In this political sense of the word, communism would of course be justified and strengthened by such a turn of events and would proudly point to the results of its penetrating political judgment. Whatever the spiritual interpretation, the political success was striven for and was attained. Lenin, the state-builder, knew ex-actly what he could afford to demand of his people and achieved what perhaps amounts to the most profound po-litical transformation ever witnessed in history. Still, the ambiguity of the spiritual outcome would once more em-phasize the unsolved problem of what the structure of so-ciety signifies in and for communism, if it is only by mis-apprehension that success becomes possible. Along with the political advantages of rural backwardness discussed above, the religious reinterpretation occurred to make communism possible. Lenin may deserve credit for having shrewdly steered his course with the aid of all these currents, but that dependence of his on these special factors may impair the validity of communism as a political principle. The more unusual the conditions of the communist success in Russia prove to be, the worse for the communist doctrine and its application abroad.

2. *Farming as the Test Point*

In this connection the question of agricultural economy comes up again, but this time not in its special application to the technical development in Russia and the spiritual reinterpretation of communism. It is the crucial question of what the principle of collective farming signifies for socialism, positively and negatively. This question would not arise in the classical doctrine, which assumed that large-scale production and proletarianization would assert themselves in farming as in all other important branches of production and hence urged the socialization of agriculture. This doctrine left, however, to the spontaneous course of economic and social history the task of demonstrating the procedure. The socialist form of ownership belongs to a collective type of work, which is expected to emerge as a result of the economic development of society under capitalism. Under conditions of universal large-scale production, socialism is the only adequate form and the logical conclusion to the historical transformation of capitalism. This argument can best be explained by reversing the order of exposition: if history did not choose to realize the program of large-scale production, socialism would be invalidated. It has therefore a conditional program of political and social adjustment, even though it firmly believes that history will realize its expectations.

The fundamental divergence of communism from socialism now becomes immediately apparent. What had been a conditioned conclusion is anticipated and put as an absolute commandment. Though Socialists had not doubted the eventual validity of large-scale production, they felt the logical necessity of waiting for it in order to be justified. This implies that they gave to history the opportunity of changing its mind and its course of development. The Communists, however, feel that they know the will of history and are at liberty to anticipate it. Since they are the rightful executors of the will of history, it makes no philosophical difference whether they wait for history to do the job or choose to anticipate it. In other words, by anticipating the revolution, they dispose of history—they deprive it of the chance of asserting a changing will with respect to the technical structure of production and make the one possibility into a certainty. They know for certain that history would prefer large-scale production, and they therefore need no justification for bringing it into existence by force and political means. On the contrary, they take pride in hastening the course of history, and thereby shortening the pains of transition that backward people have to undergo in any case. For the conditional socialist formula in the event of large-scale production, the Communists substitute their absolute will to communism and large-scale production.

Hence, the existence and progress of large-scale farming in Russia does not prove what communism desires it would. The old and the new patterns of farming do not compete on the same footing because individual farming is being discriminated against by administrative and financial devices, and all the power of the government is used to promote collective farming. Credit of any kind is expressly withheld from individual farms and reserved for collectives, and so is the use of the machines, mainly the tractors, which the government has gathered in special stations scattered over the whole country and lends out to the surrounding farms. Discrimination in taxes, in the delivery of seed and other necessities, in admission of the children to school, etc., work in the same direction. According to the official statements the collectivization movement sprang from the spontaneous urge of farmers who realized the advantage of large-scale farming; this advantage, or rather the disadvantage of persisting in individual farming, had been brought home to them in an unmistakable way. The idea of collectivization without this coercion is absurd: thousands of peasants would not have voluntarily decided to unite their thousands of plots into one farming unit of 55 square miles or more. The formation of a unit of such a huge size is in itself evidence that the peasants have been expropriated by the co-operative instead of contributing to it, for no personal tie of experience and affection connects this new pattern of their lives with the previous one. The idea of spontaneous transformation by the peasants themselves has been patently invalid from the outset, and has never been applied to the gigantic government-owned grain farms, the largest of which used to comprise 470 square miles.

Under these circumstances the progress of collectivization proves only its political success but does not prove that collective farming is more productive than individual farming. We do not know whether individual farming, if supported and subsidized by the same means, might not produce the same or even better results. The question of productivity still remains open. In two respects the Russians even had to retrace their steps. The original enthusiasm for things on the largest scale had led to farm units being set up of a size which turned out to be so impracticable that they had, in extreme cases, to be divided into hundreds of collective farms each. In the second place, the collective character of the collective farm has been gradually reduced in favor of individual utilization of dwellings and gardens and cattle. While a complete dissolution of the collective is of course out of the question, both the size and the intensity of the collective are at present in a process of shrinking. As this trend flatly contradicts the tendencies favored by the government and its theory, urgent reasons of productivity must be responsible for it.

But this is not all. If one is to believe the official story, collectivization became necessary to stop the growth of the "kulaki," the larger farmers suspected of capitalistic ambitions and possibilities. The truly manorial properties of the Czarist regime had long since been seized by the peasants or farm laborers who used to till them. The government's fear of the kulaki would be in line with its theory that the larger scale is superior to the smaller scale in farming as in industry. This is, however, far from warranting the wholesale destruction of small farming. Every political system has to watch over its borderline and defend it by special measures against possible infractions. A system intent upon barring the rise of larger properties might lay prohibitive taxes on such properties or might bar the hiring of labor without which they could not be operated and would become valueless. Instead of following such a course, the Soviet government pursued its supposed goal of annihilating the larger farms by destroying not only them but also the smaller farms whose existence was supposed to be threatened by the larger. If there had been any sense in this policy, it would have been borne out by proof of an irresistible concentration of farm properties in the period previous to the collectivization. But even an actual superiority of the kulaki's large farms would not have proved their superiority in general. The illiteracy of many millions of peasants naturally had given the larger and more educated farmers an advantage, but only a competition between fully educated peasants owning technically developed small farms and the kulaki could decide the question of superiority.

This entire hypothetical reasoning, however, is brushed aside by what one of the highest official spokesmen reports: [2] "During the period when small production predominated, the growth of the kulaki as a class was accompanied by the much more intensive economic growth of the poor peasants. They passed into the ranks of the independent producers, thus strengthening the class of middle peasants. This feature of the class differentiation in the Soviet village is the reverse of what takes place under capitalistic conditions. Under the latter the growth of market production leads to the enrichment of the higher groups and the ruin of the lower groups." This latter remark on the agricultural trend under capitalism follows the official Soviet doctrine, and the immediately ensuing description of the collectivization leaves no doubt either that the report is true to it. What matters, however, is not the unscrutinized repetition of a theory on the development abroad, but the authoritative assertion that small farming in spite of the handicap of its undeveloped stage did thrive in communist Russia when it was interrupted by the political drive towards collectivization. This is the contrary of the communist doctrine.

Orthodox socialist theory from the publication of the Communist Manifesto to our day has always assumed that agriculture came under the same laws of development as

[2] A. Gayster, member of the Gosplan and vice-president of the Agricultural Academy, in Obolensky-Ossinsky, Ronin, Gayster, and Kraval, *Social Economic Planning in the U.S.S.R.*, p. 116; reprinted in *World Social Economic Planning*, published by the International Industrial Relations Institute, 1931, p. 389.

industry. Large-scale production, through its superiority in productivity and competition, cannot fail to assert its dominance, ruin the small owner-operator, and concentrate production in large properties operated by the dispossessed who finally take them over as their communal property. When the Communist Manifesto listed as first among the immediate measures of socialization the "expropriation of the land properties," it only applied the principle of the "expropriation of the expropriators" to those who had expropriated the independent producers from the land.[3] When it became apparent, however, that the small farm would not vanish at one stroke, an auxiliary explanation became imperative to reconcile that fact with the accepted theory. Karl Kautsky elaborated all the economic arguments which have since been used without alteration or addition by all Marxians including Lenin. Kautsky's theory was that the small farmer survived only by overwork and underconsumption,[4] that he had to earn a living as a wage-worker in the neighboring factory or in the neighboring large farm,[5] that in the absence of such opportunity for proletarian employment economic and intellectual decay are inevitable,[6] that no education could raise the children to a higher standard of knowledge and skill because the small farm cannot give the children free time and money for attending a higher school,[7] and that the mortgage debt transforms the farmer into a proletarian ex-

[3] The brief demand, under number 8 of the same list, for the "formation of industrial armies, especially for agriculture" seems to betray some doubt in the validity of the main thesis, if that demand is correctly interpreted as meaning something like shocktroops for operating agriculture against the will of its operators—a passage most puzzling in theoretical content and most alarming politically.

[4] *Die Agrarfrage,* 1899, pp. 106, 300.

[5] *Ibid.,* pp. 174, 294.

[6] *Ibid.,* p. 294.

[7] *Sozialisierung der Landwirtschaft,* 1919, p. 22.

ploited by a capitalist, his creditor.[8] Kautsky's conclusion
was that the small farm was "irretrievably doomed"[9] and
would "lead to such decay, such misery that one might ask
himself whether he had a right to prevent its ruin if it
were possible to prevent it."[10] All attempts to help the
small farmer by co-operatives, etc., can only do harm by
"arousing illusions that cannot be realized."[11] As late as
1919 Kautsky contrasted his vision of a large socialized
farm where the farmers work five hours a day and have
one month vacation each, with that of the neighboring
small farmer who seeks through every means in his power
to become a member of that large collective farm,[12] in
order to get rid of his way of life, made "repulsive" through
overwork and undernourishment.[13] Private property in
land would cease to exist, first through the revolutionary
socialization of the large private estates, and then through
the voluntary action of the surviving small farms which
join the large ones.[14]

To an unbiased observer it appears unlikely that the
same size of organization would be equally suited to different branches of production. Everything depends on the
specific claims each type of work makes on the qualities
of men. The more individualized or refined the care of the
individual plant or animal has to be, the more an individualistic pattern of work will be required. The more the
product serves as raw material for further production, as
in the case of grains, the better the prospects of large-scale
production will appear. This rule, especially when applied

[8] *Sozialisierung der Landwirtschaft,* 1919, p. 16.
[9] Commentary to the party program of Erfurt 1891, Chapter 4, no. 8.
[10] *Ibid.,* Chapter 1, no. 4.
[11] *Ibid.,* Chapter 5, no. 14.
[12] *Sozialisierung der Landwirtschaft,* p. 75.
[13] *Ibid.,* p. 38.
[14] *Ibid.,* p. 76.

to agriculture, evidently requires many qualifications and is impugned by many experiences in recent times. On the one hand, animals may be bred on a very large scale; on the other hand, the most profitable form of grain farming seems to be a family farm with much capital. The first instance may be accounted for by the historically transitory stage where the most recent knowledge is more promptly realized by one entrepreneur than by many small holdings. The counter-instance is, however, certainly attributable to recent developments in techniques, particularly in electricity. It is a strange and most remarkable fact that the first phase of technical progress through the accumulation and multiplication of both labor and machinery in one plant had no application to agriculture; the recent turn to really labor-saving devices has benefited the one-man unit also and has enabled him to lower his cost. This even applies to some branches of manufacture, but is mainly true of farming. The more, according to a fundamental Marxian principle, the use of capital can be substituted for that of living labor, instead of combining the two, the more efficient an enterprise can be without employees. To combine the psychological impulse of individual interest with the highest technical efficiency seemed impossible to Marx, but appears attainable today. Powerful instruments now cultivate wide areas without hired or communal labor.[15] That means that neither capitalism nor communism is needed to organize labor. The expansion of the farmers' co-operatives for the use of machines by each farmer in turn corroborates this tendency. The spiritual foundation for the co-operative movement is the peasants' conception of property, which we have discussed above (p. 42 ff.). While the

[15] Heimann, "What Marx Means Today," *Social Research,* Vol. IV, 1937, page 46.

original co-operative enterprises dating from the Middle
Ages persisted into the era of the allegedly individualistic
system, new co-operative devices emerged gradually and
spread over all the advanced countries as it became imperative for farmers to meet the claims or dangers of capitalism. Their general objective was to support the individual
farm by supplementing it in such matters of mutual benefit as were beyond the scope of individual activity and
purchasing power. Through them the farmers put together
their savings for common purposes, provided for the purchase and use in turn of machines, for standardizing and
selling their crops and eggs, and for building and operating dairies, all this in behalf of the individual farm.[16]

Kautsky and Lenin declared that a success of the co-
operatives' attempt to help the peasant was "out of the

[16] The reader should carefully distinguish between a co-operative farm
and a farmers' co-operative as the representatives in agriculture of two
opposite political principles. A co-operative farm is a large-scale farm
owned by a farm co-operative and operated by its members (in English literature the term is spuriously applied to a farm owned by a consumers'
co-operative and operated by hired labor after capitalistic fashion). A
farmers' co-operative serves limited purposes of independent propertied
farmers. The first is the form recommended by Kautsky (and applied by
the Russians) for collective farming and is supposed to spring from the
revolutionary socialization of private large estates and from the voluntary
grouping of small holdings by their owners when they want to share in
the advantages of large-scale farming. Contrariwise the credit, dairy, or
machine co-operatives of independent farmers in all advanced countries
supplement and thereby strengthen the individual farms. The first form
corresponds to communism and centers in the communal work on the
farm, although it may permit the members of the co-operative some individual utilization of cattle and dwellings and gardens, as is increasingly
the case in Russia today. The second form corresponds to the co-operative
individualism discussed in Chapter II and serves to assist the individual
pattern of work and property in such matters as transcend the power and
scope of the individual farm. Our terminology is adapted from Franz
Oppenheimer's distinction between a production co-operative and a producers' co-operative, the latter term presupposing the existence of separate propertied producers.

question." [17] Kautsky's arguments were to the effect that the co-operatives are accessible also to the naturally superior larger estates,[18] while the most important technical innovations remain inaccessible even to the co-operatives of the small farms,[19] and the small farmers are too slow, inflexible, and uneducated to operate modern establishments.[20] The dairy co-operative was singled out as "depriving the farmer and his family of the milk they used to consume; while rescuing them in financial respect this device is certain to ruin them physically." [21] In opposition to this Eduard David maintained that socialism was dangerously misled in applying the Marxian theory to farming, that the small farm would neither vanish nor decay, but would prove to be the permanent pattern of agricultural work strengthened in all directions by the co-operatives.[22] On the basis of electrical technique and co-operative organization, small farming is invigorated and stimulated into making headway in all the advanced countries. The most impressive agricultural systems of the world, those of Denmark and Holland, show big individual capital equipment, supplemented by co-operatives, and betray no sign of being overwhelmed by the higher productivity of any other type.[23] (See also p. 151 below.)

[17] Kautsky, *Agrarfrage*, p. 129; Lenin, "The Workers' Party and the Peasantry," in his Munich paper *Iskra* in 1901, reprinted in Lenin's *Selected Works*, Vol. 1, pp. 54-67. Lenin's hatred of Kautsky was such that he never mentioned him whenever he followed his line of reasoning.

[18] *Agrarfrage*, p. 404.

[19] *Ibid.*, p. 121.

[20] *Ibid.*, p. 259.

[21] *Ibid.*, p. 269.

[22] *Sozialismus und Landwirtschaft*, 1903.

[23] Lenin, in a very elaborate analysis of the American agricultural statistics, written evidently in 1914 (*Capitalism and Agriculture in the U.S.A.*, unpublished work, mimeographed, New York, International Publishers, 1934), states that a farm small in size and considered therefore uncapitalistic may be operated on so intensive a basis as to require much hired labor and be a capitalistic enterprise. This is perfectly correct and an im-

In the case of agriculture it is very doubtful whether the organization promoted by communism for political reasons is at the same time the most productive organization. If it is not, communism will have sacrificed possible economic welfare to a political value considered supreme and hence worthy of the economic sacrifice. In so doing it will have deserted historical materialism which asserts that the economic interest is and must be the determining force of work and life, and will have embraced a political idealism that arbitrarily selects a certain form of life as politically

portant point. But a large farm operated without hired labor is equally possible in theory and is increasingly important today in fact. Lenin proceeds to build up a combined yardstick in order to measure the exact extent of capitalism in American farming. Even this does not bring him to the goal desired for the sake of his theory, as he has to admit in his summary: "Agriculture lags behind in its development. This phenomenon is characteristic of all capitalistic countries. . . . The contradiction between industry and agriculture has not only not been solved by capitalism but has on the contrary been further extended and aggravated" (p. 63). In this quotation the "lagging behind" of agriculture—as if agriculture followed the course of industry—is an erroneous theoretical interpretation of what is correctly recognized as the "contradiction between industry and agriculture." He goes on to say (p. 67): "Manual labor [meaning at the same time individual labor—E. H.] still prevails in agriculture. But the data cited above do not prove the impossibility of socializing agriculture even at the present stage of its development. He who controls the banks directly controls one-third of the American farms and indirectly dominates all of them." Two remarks must be made on this passage. Firstly, Lenin, much less careful than Kautsky in using Kautsky's argument, plainly resorts to indebtedness as a substitute for communal work as the vehicle to socialism. Whether that is possible we shall see later, p. 155. Secondly, in so far as Lenin discusses the technical side of the question, he is no doubt right that even with the millions of small units a co-ordinating plan can be carried out. But this adds nothing to the proof. The AAA in the United States has succeeded in co-ordinating the small farmers technically without socializing them at all, simply because they are accustomed to voluntary organization out of the requirements of their work. When one grants that farmers may be organized, the political question still remains whether they would submit to socialism or how they could be induced to do so. Lenin would be the first to agree with this statement.

desirable and embarks upon remodeling life and production accordingly. It would not be an anticipation of a revolution that would sooner or later be impelled by economic conditions, but be a political revolution against the economic reality.

If productivity happened, however, to coincide with collectivization, that would not in itself suffice to justify collectivization—though the situation would of course be more favorable than in the first case. Capitalism follows the criterion of productivity regardless of what suffering it entails for the workingmen; it ignores the possible degradation and abuse of men whenever the machine seems to demand it for the sake of productivity. For a workers' society this is unbearable. It is not only the result of their work that matters, taking them as consumers; it is their lot as workers, in their work, that is of vital importance. Though it is certainly out of the question to let the workingmen decide for themselves upon the technique of their work, since that may affect the whole community, the human implications of the various possible techniques must be taken into account as a major item in any decision on the subject. Otherwise the Marxian verdict on primitive communism with its "denial of the personality" and its generalization of the capitalistic "loss of man" would again be valid (see p. 89). This is incidentally the only tenable interpretation of historical materialism; its fundamental concept, the economic interest, must always take due cognizance of both the satisfactions and the dissatisfactions involved. Therefore, if the productivity criterion happens to apply to collective farming, the rightfulness of collectivization would still be questionable in view of the predilection of farmers for their individualistic pattern. The Communists, by using force to anticipate the desired technical development, destroy the possibility of forms had to face the problem of how to secure integration in a system of liberty). The nature of man, as he is, must always determine what forms and institutions are required to secure his liberty and self-realization. Communism, while supposedly developing this simple truth, destroys it through sophistry. Liberty is now interpreted as not immanent in man himself, but as conceived by an elite and imposed from above. Any member of that elite is considered a normal man; his interpretation is held binding upon all because the study of foreign countries is supposed to reveal him as the type of man aimed at by history. The right of man to be what he is, the inner urge of the suppressed, the self-realization of the working people, no longer count. This is the first and therefore the decisive breach of the tradition of liberty whose rise was joined to that of the modern world. Proof that it is a breach in tradition and not a positive development of socialism can be gathered from the wavering of communism in the use and abuse of the word liberty. This word at one time stood for the motive and élan of the communist movement, but since the accession of communism to power it has been consistently derided as a bourgeois prejudice and bourgeois pretext that can easily be seen through by an enlightened proletarian mind. The stamping out of the peasants' liberty destroyed the principle of liberty.

As for the concept of historical necessity, it is so closely tied up with the concept of liberty that it shares in the sophistical distortion of ideas. Historical necessity meant in the classical doctrine the convergence of all material and human realities toward the final salvation of mankind: the reorganization of production from within under a unitary management, and the parallel education of all the working people for communal liberty through proletarianization. Now historical necessity like liberty is so narrowed as to encompass only the life of the existing proletarians and to ignore the rest of society and the inherent tendencies within people to assert themselves. The pivotal principle of historical necessity is destroyed when its comprehensiveness is denied, and it is reduced to political arbitrariness disguised as necessity.

It is true that the peasants do not fight against this destruction of their liberty. That is because they lack political and economic power and because they are inclined, while submitting to the new institutional pattern, to adapt it to their own spiritual pattern. Even so, the abrogation of liberty has inevitable consequences in the theoretical and political fields. All the fundamental concepts of the classical doctrine are retained in letter but perverted in meaning. This is true with respect to the basic ideas of the dictatorship, classless society, and waning of the state.

Dictatorship, in the classical doctrine, was an emergency measure, of transitory nature, necessary to break up the organized and strongly entrenched resistance of the class foes. It is no question of constructive principle, but of the technique of political warfare. Its significance, seriousness, and possible duration must not be belittled. Marx certainly took it very seriously since all historical experience suggests that the beneficiaries of an antiquated order do not resign without resistance. This consideration, however, must not mislead us into assuming that the classical democratic doctrine of socialism authorized any kind of dictatorship, no matter what its objectives or duration might be. Though no absolute figures can be given to indicate the limitations placed upon dictatorship, for instance in regard to its duration, the entire trend of Marx's thought makes it clear that limitations were assumed. The dictatorship conceived by him represents an overwhelming majority and has to suppress a minority; it finds the economic structure prepared for a plan and men anxious to co-operate in the plan. Its task is fundamentally limited. The communist dictatorship, on the other hand, represents a small minority; it has to rebuild the entire economic structure, and to remodel the large majority socially and morally. It has to suppress not only the exploiters, but the majority of the people with their genuine will to liberty and property. Its task, as a direct consequence of the principle of anticipation, is many times heavier than that of the classical dictatorship. This is one of the cases where a difference in quantity turns out to be a difference in principle and spirit. The difference in principle can be seen from the difference in duration as envisaged by Marx and Lenin respectively. Marx had pointed out (see p. 76) that the task to be performed by the dictatorship required "incomparably less time and effort" than the preceding transformation of pre-capitalistic scattered property into capitalistic property. For "capitalism means the expropriation of the masses of the people by a few usurpers; socialism means the expropriation of a few usurpers by the masses of the people." Communism, however, means the expropriation of the masses of the people by a relatively small minority; it takes "incomparably more time and effort" than Marxian socialization because it necessitates the "transformation of pre-capitalistic scattered property" into communal property. Accordingly, Bukharin, when official spokesman of the Soviets, estimated that the Russian dictatorship would be needed for another two or three generations. If one adds the past years of the dictatorship to this calculation, the total period is about a century, a period approximating the whole duration of Western capitalism until the World War and the Russian Revolution. The coincidence of this estimate with that implied in the foregoing quotation from Marx is striking. The Russian estimate is, moreover, likely to be conservative, as its authors probably took into consideration the psychological effects it would have in the masses. The communist anticipation of the revolution not only implies that its material foundations and its social and intellectual prerequisites are absent, but substitutes a practically permanent minority dictatorship for the transitory dictatorship of democratic socialism.

In view of this circumstance, a closer analysis of the social consequences of the communist dictatorship becomes imperative. The Communists will not admit that it presents any social problem at all. They point with just pride to the modest salaries of their rulers, which show no discrimination between them and the proletarian masses. The importance and significance of this arrangement are very great. But it is not true that it precludes any social differentiation between the rulers and the ruled, the planners and the planned for. This misapprehension arises from the naïve and oversimplified interpretation of historical materialism that tied up the economic interests only with money incomes and not with the entire pattern of existence. As soon as the will to power is recognized as one of the primary human motives, and the exercise of power as one of the elemental satisfactions, the picture changes without being destroyed. A primitive exploitation theory believes that the exploiter, the employer, eats and drinks at the cost of his workers. The fact that he reinvests his profits is then traced to his desire to multiply the quantity of his final enjoyments by postponing them until the future; profits are transformed into additional means of exploitation. However, by far the larger part of profits is always permanently invested and reinvested as these accrue and is never eaten up. This does not mean that the owners forego the enjoyment to be derived from these profits: by investing capital they buy power over men and things instead of consumption goods because they prefer the satisfaction of power to additional or refined consumption. Power in a capitalist system springs from wealth and is permanently linked to it; but it can in other systems be established directly by legal or political fiat. A well-known example is the power, pride, and extraordinary social standing of officers and civil servants in Germany, and the striking contrast which used to exist between these satisfactions they enjoyed and the modesty of their salaries and standard of living. In the same way, but in an infinitely higher degree, the problem of social and political power arises in Russia, where the dictators wield more power over men and things than any known rulers in history with the possible exception of the kings of Egypt.

If there is any danger in this tremendous accumulation of power in a few hands, it is bound to be intensified through being ignored. This is strikingly exemplified in the history of early puritanism. By banishing the pleasures of consumption and ignoring the irrational power motive, it concentrated all the selfish energies of people in striving after economic power; by limiting the consumption of the successful and favoring their investments it contributed to building up capitalism as a system of economic domination. Similarly, the Russians limit the consumption rations of their leaders at the same time that they confer on them the formidable power which their huge task necessitates. Just as the Puritans insisted that they had to transform the world for the glorification of God without earthly reward (and the extreme modesty and sobriety of their living bore witness to this), so the Russians claim the same unselfishness with the same hypocritical reasoning. And not only are the Russian rulers directly endowed with this power—they are consecrated in it by an elaborate theory which states that this power is no ordinary power, that it is the realization of highest intelligence and morality, the vanguard of enlightenment and solidarity. Religious honors are bestowed upon the tomb where the remains of Lenin rest, and Stalin's picture in colossal size is displayed everywhere to inspire the faithful and warn the skeptical.

Power in itself is not bad—it is just an element of life and capable of being used for good or evil. No society can exist without a power to represent and order it, whatever may be the origin and nature of that power, and whatever the particular dangers it entails. What is objectionable is not the existence of power, but the flat denial of its existence and the problems it raises. The dispute between Stalin and Trotsky has given ample evidence that the personal power motive operates behind the discussion of principles. And even if an occasional individual proved sufficiently unworldly to be above the temptations of power, certainly the hundred thousands of party officials, who are accustomed to supervise and direct the lives of others, would not be likely to be equally high-minded. Speaking not in terms of ethics but of social science, one cannot dispute the fact that such tremendous power creates a social position for its holders, regardless of their salaries, and gives rise to their having a group interest in defending and developing this position.

Now the theory of communism asserts that it is the clearly conceived task of the new ruling group to make itself superfluous by leading the people to self-rule. Some very strong individuals may act in this direction and may put their pride and ambition in furthering such a transformation. They will have nothing to fear because their personal authority, strengthened by that performance, will assert itself anew under the new representative regime and will keep them at the helm of the new state as of the old one. But, in general, the ruling group consists of thousands and hundred thousands of members and will be composed differently in different regimes according to the qualities and abilities required for organizing and supervising these different systems. The ruling group in a dictatorship cannot hope to be kept in power by a subsequent democracy. What the communist theory amounts to is therefore nothing less than the assertion that pure unselfishness on the part of this ruling group will conquer the most conspicuous group interest. Historical materialism, on this point, resorts to extreme idealism to inspire its adherents and does not even attempt to prove the possibility of such a sudden and drastic change in the accepted human pattern of behavior.

If one grants that the ruling group in Russia would not abdicate with any better grace than any of its predecessors in history, the situation becomes exactly parallel to that involved in the transition from the seventeenth- and eighteenth-century absolute state to the bourgeois state. In each case there is an enlightened and progressive government to take the lead in developing the potential forces of the people for self-government. A bourgeois society developed under the protection of the absolute state, a workers' democratic society is desired and striven for by the proletarian dictatorship. As the social forces in such situations grow in consciousness and ambition, a clash between them and the bureaucratic tutelage becomes inevitable and may lead to the more or less violent overthrow of the authoritarian regime. This would be completely in line with the (dialectical) doctrine of the development of society through cleavages and conflicts to higher forms and would comprehend the idea of education through the dictatorship as a necessary step in mankind's innate striving for final liberty. But it still would not save the communist claim that the state, after the last and most formidable concentration of its power, will automatically wane away. History shows that, when the time was ripe for a bourgeois regime, the ruling groups were stupid enough to refuse to surrender their power and brought upon themselves the English, American, and French Revolutions. This, however, is the logic of history, especially dialectically interpreted history. One or two centuries of education by the enlightened state resulted logically enough in government by the bourgeoisie, but it required for its realization the horrors of many years of civil and foreign wars. In the same way, the simple and logical transition from rule over and education of the workers by an enlightened dictatorship to final democracy may require a true (dialectical) revolution in Russia. This is the only realistic forecast if we can assume that the will to democracy cannot be choked by the spirit of totalitarianism and will assert itself eventually.

The very concept of the one-party state serves to corroborate this analysis. The new democratic constitution of Russia, far from abolishing the one-party state, legalizes it by reserving the right to nominate candidates for the elections to the party and its affiliations. Accepting for the sake of this analysis the dictatorship over the non-proletarian majority is very far from demanding a one-party state and interpreting it as a workers' democracy. A democracy limited to a ruling class and more or less legally excluding other groups is by no means unknown in history; rather it may be said to be the predominant form of democracy from Athens and republican Rome down to the southern states in the United States with their exclusion of the Negroes. In its relationship to the ruled group this form is certainly dictatorial, but it is democratic in so far as it offers the right of free choice to those on the inside.[24] Liberty, although resting on unanimity in the fundamentals (p. 55), does not have its essence in unanimity but in the diversity that arises on that foundation. To move and act freely within an established social and political pattern is democracy; to move and act under command is dictatorship. Not the slightest reason has ever been given why the supposed workers' democracy should not grant the workers the freedom of decision characteristic of self-rule. The same constitution that reserves the rights of free citizenship to the workers might easily exempt the fundamental economic set-up from the range of their majority decisions. This would be perfectly in line with the traditional practice of democracy always to establish direct or indirect constitutional protections for the fundamental pattern of society. Just as a liberal-democratic bourgeois state grants its citizens manifold rights, but directly or indirectly exempts private property from the contingencies of majority decisions, so a workers' democracy might exempt its collective property from majority decisions by placing it under the direct protection of the constitution, the courts, and the state's armed forces. If words are to preserve their meaning, a workers' democracy must mean a democracy limited to the workers as the ruling class, based upon a socialist economy, and protected by the constitution. These simple conclusions are not, however, even considered worth refuting by those responsible

24 The definition of democracy as accepted by all political theorists from Aristotle down to Bryce and Kelsen is compatible with the exclusion from the decisive rights of women or slaves or racial or religious or social groups. The idea of democracy, of course, at least in its modern version, tends to include all individuals regardless of such differences. But an incomplete democracy is still a democracy in its inner structure, although it is a system of domination in regard to those who are excluded.

for the theory and practice of communism—so little do they know of the democracy which they claim to create, so biased are they in favor of their own unlimited rule. There is no room in this set-up either for democratic self-rule by the workers or for the reduction of the coercive power that is sanctified in the doctrine of the withering away of the state.[25]

All this is not, however, simply an avoidable blunder. It is deeply rooted in Lenin's original conception of this state and his general theory, and clarifies the disparity between the communist dictatorship and Marx's idea concerning the transitory majority dictatorship. Owing to the principle of anticipation, the minority dictatorship must speed through means of a maximum use of force a transformation of society which was only partly achieved but partly missed in the advanced countries after one or two centuries of capitalistic history. The disparity between classical theory and communist practice is made clear through the logic of the anticipation; it is increased by the inevitable social consequences of dictatorship: the interest of the dictators in the dictatorship. The more prolonged and intense the dictatorship has to be on account of the

[25] So confused are all political concepts today that even the underground movement of the German Social Democratic party in the one utterance which has reached the outside public proclaims the one-party-state as the natural form of a workers' democracy (*Socialism's New Beginning*, by Miles, New York, 1935). Norman Thomas in his foreword takes exception to this as to other points in the pamphlet. Among the followers of Marxian political theory Sidney Hook is particularly outspoken in his criticism of the one-party state, as are the Webbs. Of course the controversy goes far back. In 1904 Lenin (*One Step Forward, Two Steps Backward*) had demanded the hierarchical principle, which he called the bureaucratic principle, as against the democratic principle for organizing a revolutionary Socialist party, and had been bitterly criticized for this by Rosa Luxembourg, the outstanding personality in Western communism and its first martyr. Her writings are prohibited as counter-revolutionary in Russia today.

magnitude of its task, the more it strengthens the anti-democratic tendency of social stratification. Since the task is "incomparably" greater than in the classical doctrine, it takes incomparably more time and requires a permanent staff of dictatorial rulers. The duration and intensity of the minority dictatorship is justified in theory and in propaganda according to the incomplete degree of realization of the social and economic reconstruction; in fact it betrays the deviation of social development from the set program.

What remains is a new method of economic integration in a society politically integrated by the use of most highly rationalized force. In other words, what remains is economic security at the cost of liberty. We take it that the system does provide security, after having tormented the people with the literally murderous famine of 1932. True, the Russian type of planning is in harmony with the spontaneously collectivistic tendencies of the ruling proletarian class: it is the adequate economic expression of their liberty and is emphasized as such by the co-operation of the workingmen in drafting the plan which we discussed above (p. 105). This, however, is no new political principle in history, as the forcible authoritative integration of society is always along the lines of the natural inclinations of the rulers. One of the factors responsible for their authority is their specific talent for the type of function required in their system. Whether we admire the technical side of the Russian plan or doubt its wisdom on significant points, the coincidence of the plan with the natural inclinations of its formulators cannot be regarded as a particularly remarkable political performance, as a ground of special pride. The partiality of this liberty makes it a privilege and a means of domination. Not the liberty of the workers, in so far as it exists at all, but the force to be used against the majority of the people is the criterion of the plan. In view of this, the Soviet plan ranks with the authoritarian type of integration as against the democratic type which uses the elements of spontaneous harmony as the principle of integration.

4. Consequences on a World Scale

A. THE PROBLEM OF FARMING IN THE WESTERN WORLD

The use of force against the inner urges of the people might be expected to bring about a political catastrophe which would reveal that this is not the true method for solving the problem. Historical necessity should assert itself when certain primary impulses are infringed upon and demonstrate the historical impossibility of an arbitrary solution. The more this logical result is circumvented in Russia by an unusual combination of political ingenuity on the part of the rulers and strategic weakness and spiritual misapprehension on the part of the masses, the more we must look at the world as a whole to apprehend the logical defects of communism and its political consequences.

Communism claims to be a world doctrine and to lead a world revolution. The anticipation of the revolution by force in Russia is only the first act, to be followed immediately by reverberations in the other countries. But this is too loose a presentation of a connection that is essential to the principle of communism. It should be presented more accurately as a device of surrounding the enemy's flank where it is least strongly fortified in order to launch an attack from both the front and the rear, when an attack from the front alone would be hopeless. The combined action is a whole and must be examined as such. It is on a world scale that the distortion of the democratic principles bears its fruit.

In this connection, the brief statement of the agrarian productivity problem we have derived from the trends in countries with autonomous economic development gains fundamental significance. If the backwardness of pre-communist Russian farming were due to the prevalence of individual holdings, the progressive countries that have reached economic maturity and have big surpluses in farming would be expected to show large-scale farming. But one may safely say that the contrary is true. The trend in the organization of farming has been opposite to the industrial trend—at least up to the present. This qualification allows for unpredictable changes of technique and size in the future, but does not warrant a policy based on the prediction and practical anticipation of what has hitherto been untrue. Realistic examination shows that individual farming not only survives, but gradually advances at the expense of the large estates in the countries where there is free competition between the two types. This was most strikingly evident in Germany, where tariff and financial policies were designed, even under the Republic, to serve the interests of the big estates, but that did not prevent their gradual decay and the reduction of their number in favor of small holdings. It is no new observation that the most steady and enduring social transformation in Europe before and since the World War has been the emancipation of the free peasantry (although the urban transformations are of course infinitely more spectacular). This agrarian tendency is obviously in accordance with the emphasis on the producers' self-interest that had given rise to the early belief in the superiority of small-scale production and is upheld in farming by the adaptability of technical progress to the nature of the small farm. The distribution of electrical power and the growth of various forms of co-operatives have already been mentioned. Whatever the future may have in store, it is the forces of the present as they happen to be which shape present political problems and decide them.

When capitalism had supposedly run its course and was ripe for supersession, the predicted unification of society on the basis of the industrial pattern was found to be wanting. The problems which Russia has been able to solve by virtue of her backwardness had not been done away with in the advanced countries, but still existed there in all their severity. The Western peasants had not been exterminated as peasants: they were not changed into agricultural proletarians as had been expected; nor had they remained politically unenlightened and unorganized as in Russia. Their productivity had increased to such a degree that their number could remain stable or could slightly diminish, even though the tremendous increase in the total population demanded increasing crops. That is to say, their surplus production in excess of their own improved consumption had multiplied and these surpluses in turn permitted increased industrialization and urbanization. Of course importation from abroad had to contribute to the supply in many countries, but even in Germany the imports never exceeded one-fifth of the total food consumption and then were made up mainly of Dutch peasants' eggs, Danish peasants' butter, and Swiss peasants' cheese. The indoctrination and blinding fanaticism of Marxism has succeeded in concealing all this. The facts are that industrialism, whether or not socialized, rests on agricultural surpluses that are produced mainly by individual propertied producers. This is the true economic foundation of our lives. Whoever doubts this need only contemplate the ultimate test of power, the case of civil war.

The general strike of industrial workers has been glorified for a long time as the proof of their potential strength. But an organized strike of dairy producers against the city would bring an abrupt end to any urban regime and thus lay bare the true bases of power.[26]

This conclusion cannot be avoided by referring to the fact that the recent crisis of the capitalistic market swept over agriculture as over all other branches of production

[26] Many Marxians consider the farmers the born enemies of labor. The ideological reasons or pretexts do not concern us here; they are discussed below (p. 266 ff.). What counts at this point is the true proportions of economic power. These leave no doubt that the Marxist ideology is bound to bring disaster upon labor and that any hope for democracy, in whatever form, must begin with a sincere reorientation of principles and institutions. It may be useful to discuss some of the minor Marxian arguments. The farmers are interested in high prices for food; this fact is supposed to prove an inevitable conflict of interests. The argument, however, proves too much. In a society based on the division of labor, every group is interested in raising its own selling prices and in keeping all other prices down, but that fact does not preclude the possibility of social cohesion. The interests of miners, railroad workers, or civil servants might just as well be singled out as irreconcilable for all time with the interests of all the others. Moreover, this argument applies not only to capitalism, but to communism; it is not derived from any particular social order, but from the principle of the division of labor. The farmers, whether or not collectivized, wield the ultimate economic power in any industrial society. The importation issue is raised to prove that the antagonism between the worker and the farmer is unbridgeable in those European countries that subsidize their farmers through high tariffs at the expense of consumers. If it were not for the artificial support of domestic farmers for political and possibly war reasons, consumers would be provided with much cheaper food from abroad. Hence the communist authorities, when in power, should import in order to exterminate the reluctant farmers. This apparently would make communism dependent on foreign farmers and even on foreign capitalism, if we can assume that the necessary quantity of food happens to be available abroad at the moment of the domestic conflict. But all this is absurd. Planning is possible only within a politically unified body and has of necessity to give up the benefits of an unregulated outside trade if it wants to escape the drawbacks. We shall discuss the problem of the political range of planning below (p. 165 ff.).

and shook it to its very foundations. True as this is, it did not lead to the expected reorganization of farming on large-scale lines. Such reorganization would have presupposed that large units of farming had come off better in the crisis than the smaller ones, and the contrary seems to have been true, whatever the cause may have been. Large-scale units were ruined and had to be abandoned or broken up; small ones were nearly starved out but managed to get through. The decisive percentage of propertied producers in the capitalistic nations has remained fairly stable in Europe for the last three decades and did not change during the years of the last crisis. This percentage includes, of course, other groups besides the farmers, but this only serves to corroborate the argument. The percentage of proletarians has not increased during the last years or during the last decades. The relative distribution of the people among the different social categories appears to have attained a certain stability. This, of course, must not be mistaken for a slackening down of industrialization. Industrial progress has never been more intense and rapid, but it has widely changed its character and, as a result, its social effects. It does not as in former periods require the concentration of the working masses in a few plants; it often consists of saving labor per unit of the product directly and thereby making production in both industry and agriculture grow without increasing the number of workers. It becomes in many cases applicable to the small shop and enhances its efficiency and competitive prospects. With this process and many cross-currents in full swing, it is impossible to predict an indubitable tendency. What matters is the present state of affairs, where industrialization parts from proletarianization and therefore gives the lie to the socialist forecast and its communist anticipation.

The special benefit farming draws from this turn of affairs we have already indicated (p. 133).

Capitalistic reorganization of farming and expropriation of the farmers cannot be proved by referring to the financial and credit problems. Capitalism is a many-sided phenomenon, and one of its most conspicuous traits is the spread of financial rule not only in industry and trade but in farming as well. This would seem to make finally for the desired unification and proletarianization of the rural masses, if not in form, at least in significance and effect. The farmers, crushed by the burden of their debts, and certainly interested in escaping them, are led to see the source of their sufferings in capitalism, just as the workers are. The former are exploited as debtors, the latter as workers—which constitutes a difference in minor respects, but none in principle. As a result of meditating on the impossibility of escaping their growing indebtedness, the farmers would finally join the workers in the struggle for the overthrow of the system of exploitation. All experience teaches, however, that opposition to financial exploitation does not lead the farmer to communism. Attempting to get at a human, rather than purely monetary, interpretation of the farmer's economic interest makes one realize that the farmer defends himself not only against financial claims in general, but against being uprooted and proletarianized by the financial claims. Proletarianization does not mean earning little—this would apply to most peasants; it means working collectively. That is what the peasant rejects for himself—not because it is a worse lot than his own, but because it is a different way of life. He does not want just to save a certain amount of money; he wants to preserve a certain quality and pattern of existence, because it is his, identical with his nature and tradition and with everything he feels to be of value in his life. If he were interested only financially, he might turn communist to crush all the financial powers in the most radical way. Since he is an individualist in his work, such a course would entail for him suicide for fear of death. Conversion to communism might happen in a few individual cases, but it is unlikely to happen as a group phenomenon as long as there is the much more easy and logical expedient of canceling the debts. This is no permanent solution, to be sure, as the debt may accrue again and oppress his children. That does not matter to him, however, since he does not have the belief in permanent solutions; a solution for one generation suffices him, and his successor is at liberty to repeat what he did. As long as he can operate his farm, no debts will convert him to communism: it is not the abstract income scale, but the concrete pattern of work which determines the personality of the group. The idea of farmers being collectivized through the burden of their debts, and in this way being prepared for communism, is absurd from a practical standpoint and goes counter to the Marxian idea of the totality of human life. In other words, what the socialist doctrine needs in order to prove the inevitability of socialism in agriculture is not financial pressure, which always has obtained in history without leading to socialism, but large-scale production, which gives rise to the new collectivist type of man and through him to socialism. The necessary socialist definition of capitalism is not simply financial control by capitalists, but large-scale production under such financial control. In the absence of large-scale farming there is no hope for communism.

This observation also settles the question of farm tenancy. The wide spread of tenancy both in England and among the Negroes in the South of the United States is often quoted as evidence that labor is separated from property and that a natural urge toward communism is thereby created. The contrary is true. The former owners and present tenants in the United States have not lost their properties in any free competition, but through all sorts of discrimination against them. This separation of labor from ownership has so little to do with large-scale production in communal work that present large owners often do not dare operate their properties as entire units with hired labor, but must lease them out in small plots to individual tenants. Accordingly, the tenant or sharecropper has a natural and direct interest in saving on the rent or the share due the owner and establishing himself as the owner of his land again. His case is very similar to that of the mortgage debtor: the tenant and the mortgagor want to get rid of financial obligations, but nothing in their experience urges them on to a collective reorganization of their work. The analogy to both cases is not that of the capitalistic factory, but the feudal estate operated in several plots by individual peasant-serfs who can conceive of their liberation only as coming about through the individual seizure of their lands (p. 40). Most farm laborers, bound to the land by a small plot and dwelling of their own, will cherish the same idea; those on large units where individual activities are interlocked in a communal work may be impressed in favor of the communal pattern. Of course, farm laborers and tenants in the southern part of the United States resemble the Russian peasants of the pre-revolutionary era in the backward stage of their political and technical education and in the fervor of their religious life, and could be easily brought to accept an unfamiliar pattern; but it would not occur to them of their own accord to support it.

This flexibility is not found, on the other hand, among the farm tenants outside this district. Here, however, tenant farming may be conducted on a large scale as the tenants' capitalistic enterprise with hired labor, both in America and in England. This is contrary to the current interpretation of tenancy as one form of proletarian work, but in line with the leading ideas of Marxism independent of the tenancy question. The small tenants, however, including the American Negroes, line up for the most part with the small peasants of Europe and the independent farmers in America, from the point of view of an investigation into the political potentialities of the various economic types.[27]

In the light of all these considerations the agricultural structure is full of dangers for a socialism conceived as the uniform application of industrial proletarian principles. Of course socialism need not be and has not always been conceived in this way. We have already mentioned that Eduard David in 1903 devoted a voluminous and sensational book to demonstrating the thesis that agriculture has developed differently from industry and that this fact

---

[27] A current misunderstanding on the so-called distressed areas in the capitalistic countries needs correction. In the United States, for instance, these areas comprise several millions of people, in sections whose natural resources, such as minerals or wood, have been exhausted, or whose industries or agrarian monocultures have become obsolete owing to recent turns of technical development. No socialization could revive the bygone economic foundation of these people's lives. Distressed areas have to do, not directly with capitalism, but with the technical age of the country; any technologically old country in a rapidly changing world is bound to have some. On the other hand, although they cannot be blamed on capitalism, unregulated capitalism is unable to offer any cure, except by chance or in minor cases. The existence of such areas makes a strong and obvious case for some sort of economic planning including possibly the removal of the population to other sections of the country. But this does not necessarily require wholesale socialization. The huge constructions of irrigation works and power stations on the Tennessee, Colorado, and Columbia Rivers in the United States are intended to bring a positive and enduring relief.

demands plain recognition, confirmation, and promotion by socialism. Half a century earlier the great Proudhon, coming from a peasant environment like David, in a country half-peasant to this day, had focused all his thinking and preaching on the doctrine that the independent farmer "adheres to the land with all his roots, his heart, his blood, and could not give it up without perishing." His socialism consisted of destroying, partly by queer means, big capitalistic property and supporting peasant-proprietorship. These and some other examples may have little political significance, as Proudhon's ideas were swept away by the Marxian influence in the First International in 1867 and David could never assert himself against Kautsky in the German Socialist party, previous to the Great War.

Therefore it is incomparably more important to find that the leading adherents and representatives of the Marxian doctrine have been fully aware of the political dangers arising from their position on agriculture. A few years after Marx's victory over the Proudhonites, Wilhelm Liebknecht, the German Socialist leader, who used to work in close contact with Marx and Engels, published in 1874 a pamphlet designed on the one hand to support the doctrine of concentration and final socialization in farming and on the other hand to avert the political dangers implied in its propaganda. "To force the program upon the peasants would be sheer madness"—"the misunderstanding would be laughable if it were not so utterly dangerous." Kautsky, while elaborating the Marxian theory of agriculture in two books and many articles from 1891 on, never tired of emphasizing "the great interest which a socialist regime must take in an undisturbed continuance of agricultural production" and reiterating that therefore "it is unthinkable that one choose the method of forcible expropriation in order to provide the peasantry with the advantages of a more perfect production." [28] The solution he presented (as we have already mentioned on p. 132 ff.) was the immediate socialization of the large capitalistic farm enterprises without touching the peasants' properties: the economic, social, and technical advantages of large socialized farming would then induce the small neighbors to "gladly renounce their fictitious independence." Even the communist party of Germany, in its program of 1919, which leaves nothing to desire in vehemence, adopted the same policy and demanded the "expropriation of all large and medium-sized farms; the formation of socialist farm co-operatives under unitary centralized leadership throughout the Reich; the small farms remain the properties of their owners until these voluntarily join the farm co-operatives." Of all the leading theorists of Marxism, Lenin alone seems to have been silent on this point of political procedure.

The innumerable utterances by socialist leaders to the effect that the use of force against the peasants is "unthinkable" did not, however, appease the suspicious peasants nor win them over to the cause of an integral proletarian socialism. It is easy to find the reason. The socialist protestation centered only on a matter of political expediency. It was far from containing approval and confirmation of the peasants' pattern of existence, frankly predicted their "irretrievable" ruin, and promised to give them only the decision as to when to give up their "fictitious independence." Such a program failed to attract the peasants since it did not leave them alone in the building up of their future according to their own needs and ideas; it anticipated the wreckage of their ambitions, and it consoled them with the hope of the powerful and unobtrusive

[28] *Die Agrarfrage,* p. 442.

help from the workers. The numerous contemptuous phrases uttered by Socialists, from Marx on, only added to the outrage (see below, p. 266). Nevertheless all this might have been tolerated if the socialist forecast itself had been borne out by the experiences of the peasants; in case of a real decline the prospect of a distant and strange salvation might have appealed to them. But when they contrasted this forecast of their decline with their own feeling of constant growth in consciousness, organizational strength, and economic versatility, and their gradual rise from misery against many odds, they easily came to the conclusion that Socialists were liars and poisoners. In this the peasants were entirely wrong, the Socialists were only ignorant. But such a degree of ignorance on the part of political scientists and statesmen is unpardonable and has not been pardoned by history.

The socialist movement found itself in a blind alley. It could not hope to attain universal large-scale production and the ensuing universal socialization against the active resistance of those engaged in the fundamental branch of production, agriculture, yet it did not see how it could win them over. In the event that farming really proved to favor small-scale, individual ownership, Kautsky's plan of not touching the small farm would never lead to the voluntary socialization he predicted. In that event the choice plainly lay between a hopeless attempt forcibly to socialize farming and the abandoning of socialization in farming for the sake of securing the socialization of industry with the support or at least the toleration of the peasants. Naturally the Communists leaned toward the first alternative, in line with their usual overemphasis on revolutionary idealism. The Social Democrats leaned toward the second alternative, but would not admit this either to others or to themselves. In this situation Otto Bauer, generally regarded as the strongest of the younger socialist leaders, the party chief in the small agricultural country of Austria with the socialist city of Vienna, tried to break the deadlock and proclaimed the doctrine of the "eternal peasant." [29] According to this doctrine the social character of the peasant stood more or less outside the historical process of transformation, he had existed under feudalism, he survived under capitalism, and he would also persist under socialism. On this basis the Austrian party adopted a new agrarian platform, and so did the German party. This, however, was done so half-heartedly that the party members never realized even the existence of this platform, not to mention its fateful background. Only a little later its possible effects were overwhelmed and swept away by the surprising success of the Russian collectivization. The powerful state of the Russian workers found the solution of the agrarian question in the direction of an integral socialism, while the decaying German labor party gave up its claim to control agriculture. Otto Bauer himself revoked his heresy owing to the impression that the Russian events made upon him. Also the German peasants were more impressed by these events than by a platform in which its makers had apparently little confidence. The paralysis of Middle European labor was complete.[30]

[29] *Der Weg zum Sozialismus,* 1919.

[30] It is worth mentioning that the successful socialization of Russian agriculture used the economic forms contrived and elaborated by Kautsky, first in his commentary on the party program of Erfurt, published in 1892, and later in his voluminous book on the *Agrarfrage,* 1899. What he suggested was not state-owned enterprises operated on a wage-work basis, with freely fluctuating labor, and the profit going to the owner, the state, as in socialized enterprises of industry, transportation, etc.; but a co-operative farm with increasing property rights for the peasants including the right of succession, but excluding, of course, the right of selling one's share in the co-operative. This form is very similar in its organization to the producers' co-operatives of early socialism. The recurring failures of

These observations on the farmers can be extended to such other groups of pre-capitalistic origin and tradition as civil servants, artisans, and storekeepers. All these groups have long regarded the farmer as the representative and normal type of human worker. The artisans especially are very similar to peasants in that they are propertied producers, jealously watching over their independence while taking advantage of technical innovations as they have become available to the one-man shop. What distinguishes their social history from that of the farmers is the rise of capitalistic business in and from their own realm. The artisan used to be the typical manufacturer as the peasant was and is the typical agriculturist; the artisan, however, has been superseded by the factory and even compelled to seek employment in the factory in many branches of manufacture. Yet there are other branches where he not only survives but takes up new tasks in exchange for waning ones, as in the often-quoted example of the tinsmith who becomes a mounter in a progressive tra-

these early attempts Kautsky had attributed to the corrupting influence of the capitalistic environment; the particular forms of socialist agriculture he planned would thrive in the environment of socialist industry. What separated Kautsky from the Communists was not the economic forms of socialization, but the political procedure necessary to attain them. Fearing the repercussions of violent action in the developed countries for which he wrote, Kautsky hoped for a spontaneous development toward large-scale co-operative farming. In the failure of such a tendency to manifest itself, the Russians resorted to forcible action; Kautsky meanwhile failed to find any outlet at all. But it would be very erroneous to say that his political apprehensions have been proved groundless by the political success of his economic ideas in Russia, since he was concerned chiefly with the Western countries. This is a really tragic concatenation. So completely has the memory of Kautsky's achievements been eclipsed in communism that John Strachey, *The Theory and Practice of Socialism*, 1936, after paying a very legitimate tribute to Kautsky's "monumental erudition" and criticizing his political cowardice (p. 444), glorifies the Russian co-operative farm as "Stalin's great discovery" for which there was "no guidance to be found in Marx or Engels" (p. 456).

dition. The point is that the tradition of individual work is by no means entirely destroyed by capitalistic large-scale production and naturally resists a political overthrow of its existence by labor where it has successfully resisted the invasion of capitalism. These groups, with the possible exception of the civil servants, are much less strong in economic power than the peasants because their function is less vital. Their importance is mainly numerical inasmuch as they add to the number of those who prevent the workers from attaining a majority.

B. WORLD REVOLUTION AND INTERNATIONAL PLANNING

It is no wonder, in view of all this, that communism has not received political verification in the advanced capitalistic countries. The groups that reject the identification of anti-capitalism with communism are too many and too powerful. Whether or not they suffer under capitalism, they are opposed to communism because history has not educated them in the direction of communism. That is why, after the communist victory in Russia, the expected spread of communism to other countries failed, and the revolutionary attempts in Poland, Italy, Hungary, and such parts of Germany as Berlin, Saxony, Bavaria, and the Ruhr, were choked in streams of blood. In some cases, notably in Bavaria, it was a specific peasant organization that was formed and armed to suppress the insurrection. This was not, however, technically necessary. Awareness of the strategic factors, the stratification of the social structure, and the number and power of the conservative forces were so widespread that the more sober or timid group of workers opposed a revolutionary strategy which could only lead to disaster. Defeat was inevitable since the conditions of victory, as set forth in the doctrine of ripening conditions, were repudiated. The regular armies were rein-

forced by the militia of the conservative groups and supported morally and politically by the large majority of the
people. There could be no doubt of the outcome. No sympathy with the belief of the martyrs in the millennium of
communism can mitigate one's judgment that there was
no chance of political success. Yet success, in the communist doctrine, is the yardstick of judgment, since Communists maintain they are not stating an ideal but expressing the forces of a growing reality. In this orthodox
sense, the political catastrophe of Western communism
was a refutation of its principle.

The political impossibility of communism in the more
important countries naturally wrecked the program of
communist internationalism. There had been a twofold
purpose in this program of world revolution. It had been
intended, first, as a domestic revolution in the old capitalistic countries to be achieved with the aid of the young
countries, and second as a means of integrating the world
through international planning on the basis of common
communist principles. The fact that the idea of planning
could not, for political reasons, be put to the test of
international verification and was therefore confined to
verification under the Russian conditions of extreme
plasticity and natural wealth, may be useful to future work
in planning. The fundamental fallacy of communism, the
belief in the uniformity of social tendencies and contempt
for existing diversity, has been counterbalanced, from a
practical standpoint, by the application of its energy to the
most plastic country. But this same fallacy would have
remained without any counteracting forces in an attempt
at world communism. Something like an organized unitary
proletarian interest underlies the display of energy in
Russia, not only ideologically and politically, but mate-
rially as well. Nothing of the sort can exist on an interna-

tional scale, whether communism prevails as a political principle or not. Communism's demand for economic equality may be workable within an organized class, but it is certainly impracticable between nations, whether communist or not. As communist international planning focuses on redistributing the resources of the world, the question necessarily arises who, in such an event, shall give up what he holds at present. The popular answer that the thing to do is to expropriate the capitalists and to allocate their wealth to the exploited does not even approach the crux of the matter. For though capitalists own the resources everywhere, it still remains true that the workers in the various countries are each on a very different economic footing. It is this national differentiation in wealth which no doctrine of solidarity and equality ever takes into account.

Even if one were to grant that all workers would benefit in an equal degree by dispossessing their respective capitalists, national differentiations would still prevail. If they were entirely traceable to the differences in age and development of the countries concerned, there might be a chance of establishing a reasonable measure of equality within the world community by first promoting the development of the backward countries and bringing them up to the level of the advanced. But the economic conditions of nations and their workers do not differ only in consequence of uneven rapidity of development; history and nature have both contributed to this unhappy state of affairs. It is a simple fact that the English worker enjoys, as a member of the British Empire, certain economic privileges which are denied his Italian class comrade. Even if the Empire should be destroyed in the world revolution and its exploitation renounced by the British workers—whether voluntarily or forcibly—the natural distribution of raw materials among the several countries would continue to be as uneven as ever. It is a fact that, for instance, Russia is an exceedingly rich country, and that Germany, Italy, and Japan are naturally poor. The Russian and American workers—assuming that these are the most liberally treated children of nature—would have to give up part of their wealth to the naturally poor Italians, and this, of course, without compensation.

Now this idea may be extremely desirable from a moral point of view, but no historical tendency or prevailing interest appears to lend political support to it. One cannot see how a central communist board could force the surrender of natural resources by their owners except by waging war against them, and it is equally difficult to see how the naturally poor could wage war against the naturally rich who by this very fact are better equipped for war. The whole idea is too absurd to be pursued and leads to the conclusion that the most modest attempt at its realization would kill international communist planning at once. There is no other way to plan than for each country to plan separately, with subsequent adaptations by means of exchanges between them. But this, whatever else it may be, is not international communism and not international equality because everybody, whether rich or poor, gets an equivalent for what he gives up. National planning, as forced upon Russia as a consequence of the failure in revolutionary internationalism, is the only conceivable form of planning.

This remains unverified, however, and the international developments predicted in Leninism have already fallen short of reaching the world revolution. If solidarity and economic integration on a world scale were supposed to bring peace, that dream has evaporated with the fading of the prospects for world revolution. A bitter disillusionment was the inescapable consequence of a movement that substituted a biased principle expressive of the interest of one group for the ideal of an all-inclusive liberty which would have enlisted everyone in the revolutionary struggle. The encounter indeed between Trotsky, the creator of the Red Army, and Stalin, the maker of the glorious Russian nationality laws, was a tragic struggle between the two personalities who represented opposing principles. Whatever the personal implications of the struggle, it was only logical that Stalin's sense of reality should overcome Trotsky's Utopianism. The true significance of the decision must not, however, be obscured. Trotsky's willingness to set fire to the entire world was representative of the revolutionary pacifism that wishes to burn down this rotten world and on the ruins build the Kingdom of Peace. Stalin's retreat from the idea of world revolution through world war was tantamount to an admission of the necessity of sooner or later coming to terms with the bourgeois world and becoming entangled in its conflicts of interest and imperialism and possibly in its wars. While participation of Russia in the Internationale of Geneva and its substitutes is intensified, the Internationale of Moscow is convoked only in increasing intervals, and its fiery proclamations are as embarrassing to the real Russian policy as they are welcomed by the enemies of Russia and of labor the world over. Trotsky's expulsion from the proletarian empire he had been so instrumental in building symbolized the end of the communist dream of peace through revolution.

It would be ridiculous to blame Russia for this turn of her foreign policy or to demand that she retrace her steps. It is not merely a question of her foreign policy; it is a matter of crucial importance to her own structure and fundamental principle. Since she stands for the dictatorship of a class that is too weak in the other big countries to seize power, she is on the defensive and must fortify her precarious position by cautious diplomacy. Her cardinal mistake lies in her domestic decision. Educated to believe in universal proletarianization and therefore in the coincidence of proletarian rule and liberty, she has found herself face to face with the discrepancy of the two and has decided in favor of proletarian rule and against the universality of liberty. Because of her use of force against liberty, she can appeal no longer to the will to liberty. As the champion of the suppressed she would have been irresistible, and a world based on suppression trembled at her. When she turned to suppression herself, the magic she wielded was broken. She became a recognized power among the powers, and the world ponders the question whether her combination of partial suppression with partial liberties may not, under her conditions, be as sound as the old-fashioned combination in the other countries. This is the tragedy of communism.

Since the rise of fascism in Germany, Russia's policy has been undergoing further changes in the same direction. Russia not only has been making advances to the capitalistic world and dropping her anti-militaristic propaganda in the countries whose military alliance she is seeking, but has also been democratizing her domestic structure in important respects—from loosening the administrative pressure upon the peasants to drafting a new constitution. It is too early to judge the scope and significance of this new turn of events and to discern how much of it is merely for show, both at home and abroad, and how much real. To doubt the sincerity of this policy, however, only because it originates in the menace of fascism and in the desire to gain the sympathy of democratic groups and peoples is certainly not justified. In political as in personal life, it is by their mistakes that men learn—if they learn at all. The analysis of communism we have given in this chapter can only be confirmed by that possibility occurring. What the world knows as communism, the abolition of individual liberty and property in the name of proletarian justice, was bound to evoke a most violent repercussion. With Soviet Russia now inaugurating a change in order to stem the tide of fascism, much will depend on whether the revision of communism goes far enough and whether it will be made visible and credible to the middle classes throughout the Western world. As long as the communist program insists on the dispossession and forcible communization of individual farming it cannot renounce the most oppressive methods, according to its own fundamental proposition on political power as the means of suppression.[31] Therefore, if the communist claims to democratization are true, that would mean no less than the giving up of the core of the accepted communist doctrine—not only in Russian practice, but in communist teaching and program throughout the world. A sincere democratic revision of communism may stop the progress of fascism. But it comes too late, of course, to undo fascism.

[31] In 1933 the best American interpreter of a non-orthodox communism, Sidney Hook, in *Towards the Understanding of Karl Marx*, page 307, formulates the program regarding the alliance with the "petty bourgeoisie and peasantry" in typical fashion: "Concessions to these groups must, of course, be made, but only with an eye to their ultimate withdrawal." Such a program of deceit against potential allies can only drive them to fascism.

APPENDIX: ON A RECENT PRESENTATION OF THE
COMMUNIST DOCTRINE

A vast number of events have occurred in the last year that may be cited to bear out partly the democratic claims and partly the skepticism expressed above. Life in Russia is much easier, and free elections are announced. The candidates, however, are nominated exclusively by the monopolistic party and its affiliations; moreover, a wholesale extermination of any opposition seems to precede the elections. The huge trials at Moscow in the summer of 1936 and in January 1937 have given the impression of sincerity, but it could be proved that at least the details of what the doomed men fiercely confessed to are entirely untrue. The communist parties in most of the Western countries pursue a policy which is correctly said to be to the right of the Socialists. They support coalitions of bourgeois and labor parties, which they had denounced as the worst form of treason a few years ago; they vote appropriations for armaments without the reservations thought necessary by the Socialists, etc. All this may indicate a fundamental change, or it may be a tactical maneuver.

In the absence of an official Soviet declaration, which might be too embarrassing to release at the present time, one may turn for light to the most recent and authoritative presentation of *The Theory and Practice of Socialism* given by John Strachey in his book published in the fall, 1936. This book has been widely heralded as the first application of the communist principles to the special conditions of the Anglo-Saxon countries. Its attitude is entirely loyal to the party line, as is evidenced by the fact that in its five hundred pages Trotsky is mentioned only once as the champion of a faulty doctrine. The objective and achievement of the book consists in its emphasis on the human rather than the militant and terrifying traits of the revolution. There is no ground for doubting the author's perfect honesty. All these reasons make it the best available source of information on the present trend of official communist policy. The results of the consultation bear out one's skepticism. The only liberal deviation from the most old-fashioned and orthodox Soviet policy may be found in the church question where complete freedom of worship is promised and the contrary policy in Russia is explained as due to the extraordinary power of the Russian Church, while any attempt to eradicate religious beliefs from men's minds in Western countries is stated to be "impossible today and unnecessary tomorrow" (p. 239).

But none of the crucial problems that a realistic communism has to face today are mentioned in the book. The question of the workers' share in the profits of imperialism comes up in this form (p. 335): ". . . the funds out of which the British social services are paid come, in the ultimate economic analysis, not from competitively derived profit . . . , but from monopolistic, semi-feudal tribute, derived from Britain's vast dependent Empire. The exploitation of a whole sub-continent such as India . . . modifies the workings of the laws of capitalism in favor of the British capitalists. . . . [Otherwise] the British capitalists would not have a penny to spare for concessions to the British workers." No conclusion is drawn with respect to the economic interest of these workers in the Empire.

The elaborate discussion of democracy and dictatorship culminates in the statement (p. 164): "In order to establish a socialist economic system it is necessary for the working class to assume exactly that political relationship to the capitalist class which the capitalist class now assumes to the working class. Within the working class there will be effective democracy, just as today there is effective democracy within the capitalist class. Over the capitalist class there will be dictatorship, just as today there is dictatorship over the working class." This remarkable passage purposely ignores the fact that in capitalist democracy the workers enjoy personal liberty and certain political rights which the author in other sections of the book finds worth defending with every means at the workers' disposal, and whose value has become visible even to the blind from the experiences under fascism. These rights include the franchise and the right of free propaganda, which the "workers" and their theorists take ample advantage of. The author ignores these rights in order to deny non-workers corresponding rights in a socialist state. Otherwise the conclusion would be unavoidable that what corresponds to a capitalist democracy is a socialist democracy, a system of personal and political rights for all, based on a socialist economy rooted in the constitution, defended by legal jurisdiction and police, and therefore not subject to the chance wishes of fluctuating majorities. Instead, fascism is tacitly substituted for capitalist democracy in the above syllogism and the corresponding treatment is provided for those not members of the workers' democracy. Incidentally, the fact that Strachey's deduction presupposes fascism as the model to be followed and reversed by communism (the opposite of the historical succession) becomes conspicuous in his discussion of the workers' "effective democracy." This is not conceived of as a democracy limited to the workers and barring non-workers, but as consisting only of developed trade unions and workers' councils in a one-party state, that is, without political rights for the workers.

From these fundamental propositions the rest necessarily follows. The chapter on "the two classes" contains a foot-note of just one line to the effect that "there are other social groups and numerous distinguishable subdivisions of the two main groups" (p. 98). In a later chapter on the working class the nature of this class is delimited in the narrowest possible way, and any appeal "to the tech-nicians, the civil servants, or this or that category of the intermediate sub-classes" is denounced on the ground that "the greater number of these trained minds . . . cannot even imagine any system of society other than capitalism" (p. 323). If this means anything it must mean that the revo-lution must be made against the will not only of the capitalists, who are supposed to be useless in production, but also of the middle-class engineers and employees whose numerical and functional power is absolutely and rela-tively increasing at a rapid pace owing to the technical transformations which have taken place in this age of labor-saving devices. This statement is the only mention of the middle-class employees in a book of five hundred pages on the theory and practice of socialism in 1936.

With the agricultural problem Strachey deals in a simi-lar way. In a footnote on page 287 Thomas More is praised for having anticipated, not the restoration of individual farming after the expulsion of the farmers by the enclo-sures, but collective farming; and on pages 456-57 Stalin is praised for having solved "the vitally important ques-tion of how the vast field of Russian agriculture was to be brought into the ambit of a planned socialist economic system . . . [and] how Russian agriculture could skip the capitalist stage of development altogether." . . . "Collec-tivization was the biggest and hardest task which the Soviets have faced. . . . Its accomplishment is by far the most important event which has occurred in the world since 1917." This doubtless is true, the question being only, in which sense? No further mention of an economic or political problem of agriculture in the Western countries occurs; it is all "solved."

This neglect of the vital problems, however, brings out how great an emphasis Strachey must necessarily lay on the dictatorship as the means of overwhelming all these foes in any revolution to come. And it also makes understandable why the author loses his usual composure when discussing the secret police, the very incorporation of lawless tyranny (p. 220): "It is true that some of the technical methods employed by one secret police resemble those of another. But to leap from this fact to the conclusion that the secret police used by the Russian Soviets from 1918 to 1935, namely the G.P.U., was nothing more nor less than the old Tsarist Okrana under a new name is to evince incorrigible political illiteracy. The class which the Okrana held down wielded the weapon of the G.P.U. while the class which used the Okrana was held down by the G.P.U. Thus even if the methods of the two organizations had been identical, which they were not, they would have served precisely opposite social purposes. . . . Confusion between the two bodies is only possible for those whose intention it is to be confused themselves and to confuse others." This illuminating passage leads up to the statement that in England and America, where people have been accustomed to liberty for a long time, this tradition of liberalism will cause a "considerable amount of confusion" among "quite sincere and disinterested people" on how to suppress the "dispossessed classes," the supposed capitalists including farmers, etc., "and this confusion will, paradoxically enough, necessitate a more considerable temporary curtailment of the liberty of some sections of the population than would otherwise be necessary." If this indeed is a somewhat authoritative statement of modernized, democratized communism by its most educated, humane, and attractive Western representative, the chances for a further progress of fascism are bright.

V

THIRD TRANSFORMATION: FASCISM

Introduction: The Relation of Fascism to Democracy

THE ECONOMIC crisis under which the capitalistic world has been laboring for the past few years has made the Russian experiment appear increasingly attractive by contrast. The complete concentration of all important decisions has enabled Russia to co-ordinate effectively her economic energies, and except for the interruption caused by the famine of 1932, to carry through a program of increasing industrial output and social welfare, although confined to a low absolute level up to the present time. This development gained sensational significance when contrasted with the shrinking outputs of the panic-stricken capitalistic world. As people watched the decomposition of a system based on civil liberties and the paralysis of vital functions under the impact of permanent conflict, they learned to fear for their bare existence and were accordingly prepared to surrender liberties which appeared to serve no good end. But recognizing that Russia had paid a heavy price for her economic security, they began to wonder whether there might not be another way out than that of proletarian unification. They felt that the abolition of liberties should be limited, if possible, to the political and legal fields and should not encompass interference with the customary middle-class way of life, which communism so relentlessly abrogates. If the integration of society by force requires the use of one social type as the norm to which to subject the others, the middle-class type should be chosen as that norm and center of integration. This was the alternative to communism that fascism offered.

It is true that the analogy between the two systems must not be carried too far. Proletarian unification means something very different in form from unification under the rule of the lower middle class. Proletarian unification means universal proletarianization. This transformation is first possible in respect to social position, since it applies a negative criterion, the absence of individual property. Secondly, the generalization of the positive criterion of the proletarian pattern, the collective type of work, is more difficult, but not impossible. Where genuine large-scale production in one technical unit is not feasible, a spurious collectivity of work may be established by summing up the individual units into large units without changing the previous functions. In Russia, of course, large-scale production can be universalized very easily because it has been identified with progress, regardless of whether this identification has been found to exist in the advanced countries and whether progress is available only to large-scale production. The individual type of work characteristic of small middle-class producers, on the other hand, cannot be generalized in the presence of modern industry and transportation. A spurious division of a big plant into several individual units, analogous to that spurious addition of individual units into one big one, is impossible owing to the nature of the technical structure. A genuine return to small-scale production would involve sacrificing most of the gains in productivity which are due to industrialization and would destroy the basis of life of the correspondingly increased population. Hence a return to small-scale production is out of the question. Unification under the control of the lower middle class cannot and does not claim to make everybody a middle-class man: it envisages a stratified society with the middle-class principle as its dictated rule.

Fascism is more anti-democratic than communism, for the reason that unlike communism it is not directly and consciously derived from democracy. Communism aims in its program at an eventual democracy where everybody has to be an industrial worker and all are free and equal through self-government in their communal work. It becomes anti-democratic by enforcing this industrial pattern where it does not belong. Through fear of differences in social rank, it becomes destructive of differences in social qualities and of liberty. It treats different groups equally and thereby discriminates in favor of those whose nature finds satisfaction in this pattern. Its avowed legal principle is that of equality even though its human content is not. The scheme of middle-class rule, on the other hand, is openly anti-equalitarian and anti-democratic, since it demands a stratified society.

Nevertheless, it would be a mistake to neglect the traces left on fascism by its rise from democracy. These ingredients constitute its real strength. The pattern it posits as standard is, in its economic and social aspects, that of original democracy—a man's independence in his work through the ownership of his field of work. By assailing this pattern of democracy where it continues to prevail, communism becomes anti-democratic. By defending this pattern fascism takes on a partly democratic character which contributes to its strength. In terms of liberty, communism sets up as its ideal a proletarian liberty for all, at the expense of the peasants' liberty, and thus misses the

meaning of liberty. Fascism reverses this scheme and re-
fuses the proletariat liberty by reserving liberty for the
lower middle class alone. Fascism, moreover, takes advantage of the historical achievements of democracy by rejecting in principle any of the old authorities—monarchy, nobility, and church power—even where it has to compromise with them for political reasons, as in Italy. It cannot
be classed as an authoritarian or reactionary movement in
the familiar political terminology, as it lifts to the dominant position a lower social layer of recent organization
and self-understanding. It is authoritarian in the same
purely formal sense as communism: without relying on
any of the old-established authorities, it supersedes them
by its own authority. It is in this sense, again like communism, the beneficiary of democracy without being
democratic.

A. The Logic of the System of Fascism

1. The Dictatorship of the Lower Middle Class

Given these historical elements, the scheme of the necessary social and economic program of fascism can easily
be deduced—although it has nowhere been formulated in
this way.[1] The fascist goal is to defend the pattern of the
lower middle class by preserving the particular status of
the small propertied producers, which happens at present
to be a halfway position between that of the big owners
and rulers of industry and that of the propertyless workers.

[1] In presenting the logic of fascism we are far from denying the importance of accidental factors which have contributed to the rise of
fascism as they have to all other phenomena in history. Still it is of the
greatest theoretical and political significance to realize how far a logical
analysis of the primary factors can explain events once the conditions are
given. See below, § 5.

A generalization of this lower middle-class pattern by dissolving big industry is out of the question. Therefore the fascist course of action is to preserve the independent producers' particular status as a particular one in the midst of a society with a diversified class structure. The appeal of this status for the middle class is not their inferiority to the lords of industry, but their superiority to the have-nots. It is this position above the workers that has to be upheld, as it is being openly attacked by the workers. The workers, however, cannot be kept in their inferior position by the small owners who have no direct dealings with them on the owner-worker basis. Capitalism in industry is needed—not to foster the dominant status of the industrialists, but to maintain the medial position of the propertied producers outside of industry by putting the workers on an inferior plane.

It is this focusing on the lower middle class which forbids the easy identification of fascism with capitalism. As a matter of fact, there are in the developed countries of capitalism three groups, two of which are allies against the third in fascism; none surrenders its individual aims. A dictatorship of organized and concentrated big business resting on the support of the lower middle class is a distinct possibility and would in many respects resemble fascism. The reason why the rise of fascism was financially supported by big business as a measure of defense against labor was that big business planned to resume power in fascist forms as soon as fascism would prove incapable of solving the problems of a complex industrial society. German fascism came to power not only with the financial backing of, but in an open political coalition with, big industry, organized as the German Nationalist party of Hugenberg, Kirdorf, and Thyssen. It was the general belief of big business and outside observers that fascism had no program of its own, lacked talent, would therefore be confined within a short time to merely decorative posts, and would abandon the real power to those trained in ruling. Instead, fascism disposed of its partners in the coalition to the extent of outlawing them and exiling some of their leaders. This does not mean that the struggle is finished and could not bring forth a capitalistic dictatorship in a roundabout way, but it shows the fascist trend as having a principle of its own. The popular interpretation of fascism as militant capitalism concealed behind middle-class phrases is theoretically too easy and politically misleading.[2]

Two considerations contradict the interpretation of fascism as capitalism enthroned. First, the social principle of fascism, though it demands capitalism as a means of keeping the workers in an inferior status, does not do so in order to lift the capitalists to the ruling position. It is not to the advantage of the small interests to permit an unlimited accumulation of capitalistic income, wealth, and power. The more they come to regard themselves as the true representatives of the nation, inferior to the business leaders in economic shrewdness, but superior in natural vitality and national value, the more they will tend to equalize or smooth off the peaks of income. Big business fulfills a necessary technical function, particularly for modern armament; its managers are indispensable functionaries. They should be granted the freedom necessary

---

[2] Robert A. Brady, *The Spirit and Structure of German Fascism*, New York, 1937, pursues this line of analysis in an impressive way. His main argument is to the effect that in 1928, previous to the financial backing by big business, the National Socialist party polled 800,000 votes and two years later, with the support of big business, 6.4 millions. But it is precisely between these two elections that the economic crisis became manifest and the machinery of parliamentarian government broke down, as discussed below in § 4.

for doing their tasks but should not be recognized as national representatives or standards of morality. Their splendor does not add to the splendor of the community, as in a free business society of the American type where everybody feels akin to them on a minor scale and admires in them the perfected image of his own self. Their glamour is suspected by fascism as a perversion of the real values, as a confusion of ends with mere technical means. Therefore their political-social splendor is to be curbed, and so is its source, their wealth—to the extent that this may be done without hazard to the necessary business function. It is interesting to note that, with the exception of a few armament factories, it is not the big corporations that benefit the most from German fascism, but the middle and small ones, and that the quotations of stocks show a distinct equalizing or approximating trend. This is partly due to the enormous drain on big corporate profits and big individual incomes, not by means of state taxes, but through the compulsory "voluntary contributions" to the various collections organized by the ruling party for winter relief and similar purposes. Such sums of money are explicitly withheld from the control of the official bureaucracy. This demonstrates to the people the power of the party over both the bureaucratic state and the plutocracy, which had (with the general exception of the wealthy Jews, and a very few exceptions among other people) always been niggardly to a degree that is incredible in itself and incomprehensible to any foreign mind. Thus a direct redistribution of income through the party results in a transfer of social prestige from business to the party. In a great many cases, businessmen are constantly being watched and spied upon by party members on the staff of their enterprises, who are, as party members, not subject to ordinary jurisdiction but only to a party disciplinary procedure. Often entrepreneurs suffer personal humiliation. The publicity given such cases and the awareness of the omnipresence of the party create an atmosphere of fear in business which is in striking contrast with the idea that business rules society through fascism. The workers themselves feel a grim satisfaction at the dethronement of their old adversaries and acquiesce more easily in the loss of their liberties as they see that their class foes do not profit thereby. Both business and labor realize that it is an independent third group that is in control.

In our discussion of basic principles, the second interesting point is the discrepancy between the economic and the social hierarchy. The fact that the social stratification need not conform to the hierarchy of business and income is by no means new in Europe, least of all in Germany. The business aristocracy of the country, since they have been educated in Luther's rigid concepts of feudal morality, have always considered themselves inferior in social dignity to the caste of feudal lords, who could not compare with them financially. It is well known that there never was a bourgeois revolution in Germany. The preeminence of the old feudal layer appears also in the fact that the civil and military service had been poorly salaried and had been indemnified by the real power of the office and by extraordinary social esteem; they mostly came from the nobility. The whole much-ramified system of decorations, titles, and ribbons was designed to stimulate ambition without offering money prizes, and found ample response as long as the monarchy survived. Only in a business community is wealth directly correlated with ability, and the hierarchy of income directly interpreted as a social hierarchy. Post-Marxian communism takes as its model a society in which all qualitative differences of social articulation are wiped out and the money yardstick is the only measure of social rank. Accordingly, Marxism regards all deviations from the monetary hierarchy as mere remnants of an already doomed irrational system, just as it regards the panic-stricken peasants as potential proletarians. That system is, however, a reality of long standing, and easily traceable to, if not fully explained by, German history. Moreover, a new order may more easily set up its own standards as superior to those of business, when the new rulers, by virtue of their political supremacy, wield the power to favor or menace the business world. Hundreds of thousands of party officials, and civil servants who got into the ranks of the old bureaucracy as substitutes for ousted officials, are animated by this consciousness of power and are trained to give it adequate expression. The tradition of Germany confirms the possibility of a political hierarchy side by side with, and in fact superior to, the economic one. Fascism renews this tradition in favor of a new group and new ideas.

The above analysis is incomplete, however, if it demonstrates only that the hierarchy of power can be changed and made independent of the question of property. There must also be some concrete and overwhelmingly important function by virtue of which the political power can force submission upon a reluctant business power. In the fascism of today there are two such functions closely intertwined, but each alone sufficient for the end. One is the obvious dependence of business on the political power for protection against labor, once the two have embarked upon the mutual enterprise of suppressing democracy. Business then is defenseless and realizes that fact as does the ruling party. The dissolution of the German Nationalist party gives evidence of this mutual awareness. If business is not loyal, it is always possible for the state to vex it with all kinds of trumped-up troubles, including labor unrest, and to pose before labor as the adversary of capital rule and as the trustee of the ordinary man. That this is being done we have already mentioned; that it can be done is due to the political situation that business finds itself in. The official institution of the labor trustee, which has superseded the old machinery for settlement of labor disputes, is in this sense a weapon to secure the recognition and support of the German business people by reminding them of their precarious situation, individually and socially. What frightens them most, however, is not the bureaucratic institution alone, but the possibility of "direct action" by party cells in the plants, by the workers stirred up by them, or by the compulsory labor organization interested in presenting to its twenty-five million members some conspicuous achievements in order to keep them loyal. Having sided with business against labor, the fascist party is politically in the position of the "laughing third" and therefore at liberty to impose any humiliation it wishes upon business.

Yet there is another stronger ground for business submission to fascist rule. Our analysis thus far has considered only group interests, with their conflicts and alliances, as if the very existence of society had not been at stake. But fascism's true claim to power rests on its promise to reintegrate society after the disintegration of its entire existence in the crisis. The economic system found itself incapable of solving its own problems on the traditional lines of free transactions in the market. Credits were withheld from businessmen by foreign and domestic creditors owing to their fear of an economic breakdown, transactions and outputs had to be adjusted to the shrinking volume of working capital, purchasing power was lessened by this reduction of employment, sales suffered accordingly, and so on in the familiar vicious spiral downwards until the bitter end. To interrupt the spiral and start a new expansion, something positive had to be done to the course of business by an authority strong enough to stem the flood, impressive enough to be believed in, and powerful enough to co-ordinate the reluctant. But it was evidently not within the power of business itself to do so: it was in principle up to the state. Russia preached that there was no salvation except that of sacrificing the entire old system, and gave the fascinating example of a reconstruction and reintegration on the basis of a state power amazing for both its novelty and its scope. The Anglo-Saxon capitalistic democracies, after a period of hesitation, recovered their resolution and justified, by the success of their intervention, the authority on which they had acted. German democracy had already vanished by 1929. No majority could be formed, no political action was possible in the chaotic state of things. In this situation, fascism offered to achieve the necessary reorganization by creating a power capable of forcing authority on all and co-ordinating the decomposing elements. "Co-ordination" was the magic word which proved irresistible, just because it was so primitive and purposely failed to indicate the different possible directions of co-ordination. Fascism has succeeded in absorbing a considerable fraction of the unemployed in conscription, labor service, and militia. It has increased armaments by huge additional government expenditure and thereby caused industry to increase its output by billions and to absorb another considerable fraction of the unemployed. It has coped with the financial dangers of this bold policy by a most severe regimentation of business and finance. There are weak points in its program, of course, and its ultimate success is not certain.

Real wages are going down, which may cause trouble; they are not, however, falling in proportion to re-employment, with the result that family incomes and total purchasing power are slightly increasing. The financial strain on the government is very heavy and doubtless handicaps the progress of the program. All such doubts and dangers, however, important as they are in the practical situation, are aside from the main point we are aiming at in our discussion of principles. That point is that the business system was revived by an extremely active state policy and continues to be co-ordinated by an extremely rigid regimentation. The primacy of the state over business cannot be, and is not, doubted. The political idea of reintegrating society by a middle-class dictatorship over both capital and labor has been proved to be practicable, at least in the short-term view.

2. *Fascism as the Alternative to Communism*

The influence of communism on this fascist program cannot be exaggerated. Fascism is deliberately conceived as a counter-blow to communism—it claims to be the only alternative—and is in consequence largely determined by communism, partly positively and partly negatively. The communist interpretation of bourgeois democracy and capitalism has been taken over, with its emphasis on the economic crisis, its denunciation of the anarchy resulting from private decisions, and its contempt for liberty as a bourgeois ideology destined to palliate the greed for money. Through its diagnosis the general lines of the fascist cure were suggested. The fascist "co-ordination" is a synonym of the communist "plan": in fact, the term co-ordination had been in frequent use in socialist and communist discussions during the Republic. In a disintegrating society, co-ordination under a plan requires a dictatorial power, be it proletarian or some other type; not only the idea of dictatorship, but its technique—from radio monopoly to disposing of critics without trial or publicity—were invented and elaborated in Russia and from there passed on to Italy and Germany. The enthusiasts in both hostile camps, though not the political technicians, used to be aware of these affinities, and while killing each other spoke of each other with a certain chivalrous respect, until everybody ran wild in the bitterness of the final fight. More important, however, were the joint political enterprises, which culminated in the big traffic strike in Berlin less than three months before fascism came into power. It was a political action of the first order in size and success, organized by a strike committee which consisted of an equal number of official delegates from the communist and fascist parties, and designed to stir up the population against the Republic on the occasion of the approaching elections for Parliament—the last election under the Republic. Of course, each side hoped not only to destroy the Republic with the aid of the other, but to win over the adherents of the other side at the same time. The fact that such a tactic was possible proves how much they felt they had in common beyond their strife, for it is very often not the particular content but the general style and concepts of thinking which are decisive, both in intellectual and political history.[2a] Finally

---

[2a] Of course, this policy of the German Communists did not spring from inadvertence or whim; it is in line with the political doctrine laid down by Stalin himself. He had officially declared that the principal enemies of world communism were the Social Democrats and the Christian trade unions of Germany and that one had to take into the bargain a temporary rule of fascism in Germany because its historical mission would be to do away with those worst enemies of communism. In the latter respect the program has come true. Nevertheless its wisdom seems to be doubted even by the Communists today, as indicated by

and most important, the word socialism itself, as officially used by the German Fascist party, indicates the influence of communism—whether or not this is a welcome thought. It is true that the word socialism first appeared in modern history with a definite proletarian connotation as an analysis and critique of capitalism that heralded the proletarian solution; but the word had also been used for some time—most conspicuously by Spengler—without this social implication, and the right to such a usage cannot be denied. In this more formal sense it denotes the abrogation of, or restriction upon, private decisions in favor of a strict regimentation, and therefore the supremacy, in economic and social life, of the political will, whatever its origin and direction.

All this does not diminish the keenness of the conflict between the two alternative dictatorial solutions. It is of extreme importance to ask in what sense and direction a dictatorial power shall be made use of, if it is to come into existence at all. Nevertheless, it remains true that communism and fascism are alternative solutions, and this means particular solutions on an equal footing as opposed to the originally-aimed-at universal solution. As particular solutions, each must attempt to assert its claims as paramount—in fact, as the only valid ones. This is done in communism by stating that the communist worker is chosen by an inescapable process of history as the standard social type of the future and that therefore he only helps and hastens history by remolding all others in his own image. The same is done in German fascism (this decisive issue will be discussed later) by stating that the representative of fascism, by virtue of his extraction, is chosen

their recent coalitions with Socialists and "petty bourgeois" parties in several countries. Such minor blunders, of course, cannot affect the communist claim to infallibility.

by nature as the standard type, and helps nature by re-molding all others in his own image. Both claims are indicative of the common democratic origin of commu-nism and fascism, since both of them imply that the group will to power and even the necessary cohesion of produc-tion and society are not sufficient grounds for violence. Hence they do not justify the use of force, as a purely authoritarian regime would, by asserting that they are divinely ordained to rule all others and to decide all con-flicts in order to provide for security. Instead, they follow the democratic line of reasoning, inasmuch as they proph-esy that everyone will spontaneously agree to their re-spective program after a time. The democratic coincidence of self-expression with the specific requirements of inte-gration will finally come into being in the one case through the will of history, in the other through the in-exorable processes of nature. These are by no means the-oretical constructions for outside consumption; they are constantly referred to in order to prove that communism and fascism, respectively, represent real democracy—the only title to recognition in modern life, as conceded even by the enemies and slayers of democracy. Both commu-nism and fascism still remember the democratic conscience to which they owe their origin in part. But they are not democratic: they transform the fundamental democratic idea in such a way as to make it indiscernible. The com-munist statement regarding the future course of history has been refuted by history thus far; the fascist statement regarding racial superiority cannot, and does not want to, be proved theoretically. So both parties, in order to assert the universal validity of their particular rights, have to resort to force—not incidentally, but as a principle.

Another claim to uniqueness on the part of communism plays a very important role in all technical discussions of the economic crisis and the problems of planning. This is that any successful planned economy requires the unification of property in the hands of the planners and must not leave any remnant of individual control. The argument stresses chiefly the necessity of unitary management to preclude any such dualism of control or interest as might result from the coexistence of the planning power and the individual property owner. In general, however, the frictionless coexistence of a plan and individual property will become possible as soon as the central power is so impressive as to discourage any offense against its will. This is evidently the main aim of fascism, and it appears to be realized. Of course an offense, in order to be punished and suppressed, must be discernible; and some have challenged the technical possibility of detecting an offense. No public control of private means or profits can penetrate the thicket of modern business entanglements and bookkeeping. A financial transaction of any producing firm is bound, however, to precipitate a change of stocks on hand, and in case of a lasting investment, an increase of machines and buildings, and can be discerned the moment these material effects become apparent. If it is primarily the changes, increases or shifts of investments which affect the smooth working of the plan, these changes can be watched in their technical, if not in their financial, form. Only international transactions may remain without domestic precipitation and require a directly financial supervision—which, however, is not impossible, as proved by the German example.

Nevertheless, what can private property do, and what is its value, if it is really to give way to central supervision at any step or in any transaction? This objection is met by referring to the fact that central intervention is necessary only where it is to the interest of a private

owner to counteract the plan—and though this may frequently be the case, it is by no means always so. The plan
may be such as to permit of many everyday activities without modification. The baker, whether an independent producer or an official, will always have to distribute his
bread in the same way (except in case of rationing, which
every plan hopes to avoid). Whether or not to include
the working of private property in the plan will depend
on the social structure aimed at by the plan. An equalitarian program pointing towards equality of income has
no room for private property; an unequalitarian program
may have it. Accordingly, those pleading for complete
socialization not only demand equalization of income, but
are inclined to identify the concept of planning with such
an equalization. This, however, is a confusion. Whether
or not equality is necessary for other reasons, both an
equalitarian and an unequalitarian society can be planned.
Each plan may or may not succeed, depending upon
whether the suitable means for the respective ends are
chosen. It may be deemed desirable to maintain an aristocracy with, or even without, economic functions. The
question of how to make the various links of the plan
interlock and serve the common end must not be mistaken
for the other question of what ends should be pursued.
From these considerations it follows that the technique of
integrating the industrial system by a central plan does
not prescribe one distinct social organization and preclude
the rival one. In other words, the technicalities of a
planned or co-ordinated economy, important as they are,
do not anticipate the fundamental political decision.[3]

[3] The author is well aware how poor and inadequate these brief statements, as well as the later remarks on the economic technicalities, are.
Being a professional economic theorist, he has devoted many years and a
number of publications to studying these (and the more fundamental)
economic technicalities and implications of planning. The reader who is

The prevalent illusion to the contrary is intelligible only when one considers the historical development of the idea of planning. As long as the opposition to capitalism as a system was represented by labor alone, the idea of planning was a monopoly of labor. Not only did labor predict that everyone would before long join its ranks, but it claimed, in addition, to possess the remedy against the scourge of the economic crisis. The second claim was logically connected with the first, because planning is, by definition, the opposite of private management. When the first part of that prophecy did not become a fact, and people did not all agree to regard themselves as proletarians, labor insisted all the more stubbornly that the economic technique indispensable to fight the crisis was workable solely within the proletarian scheme of wholesale socialization. This argument was politically powerful as long as there was no rival scheme equally able to tackle the problem of the panic-stricken market. When this rival movement emerged, however, and took over from labor some of its fundamental ideas, labor found itself not only deprived of the monopoly in planning, but unprepared to carry on the fight on a different level. This applies not only to the Communists, but just as well to the Social Democrats, whose main objection to fascism, during the last years of the German Republic, was to the effect that fascism could not succeed in co-ordinating economic activities because it did not envisage the abrogation of indi-

specially interested and trained in these economic problems may turn to the author's recent articles on the subject, "Planning and the Market System," *Social Research*, Volume 1, November 1934, and "Types and Potentialities of Planning," *Social Research*, Volume 2, May 1935; both articles reprinted in *Planned Society*, edited by Findlay MacKenzie, New York, 1937. In the present treatise on political principles the economic problems may be passed by because they contribute nothing positive to the discussion of, and decision on, the fundamental principles.

vidual management. The fundamental issue was thus reduced to a merely technical one: the decision between the two political programs turned on the question of whether the necessary co-ordinating technique was attainable only under the proletarian scheme or was compatible with some form of private management as well. Even now, Communists seem to rely mainly on the hope that fascist co-ordination will break down because of its inherent deficiencies, just as the capitalistic world for many years anticipated the breakdown of Soviet Russia. Should a fascist breakdown occur—which is against all likelihood— that event would naturally be of enormous influence. Yet it may be questioned whether it would bring about the final decision on the principle involved and whether it would not be attributed to incidental mistakes in handling the principle—just as the communist principle might have survived even if Russia had succumbed in 1932. This fact leads us to the conclusion that the issue between different plans cannot be decided on the level of the technique of economic administration because it requires a consciousness of political principles and their spiritual significance. These, however, have long since been discarded by communism. Fascism and communism are two particular class solutions of the social crisis on an equal footing in deadly hostility.

A particular class solution gives liberty to some and denies it to others; it integrates society along lines expressive of that class's particular interests, and therefore must resort to the principle of violence. A universal solution seeks the integrating principle that will reconcile the different patterns of liberty and therefore does not require violence as a medium of basic integration. Whether such an integrating principle exists and is applicable is, of course, a matter for special investigation, but it certainly cannot be ascertained if nobody feels obliged to search for it. In fact, no one has searched for it; everyone has taken for granted that the only possible thing is a particular solution, and has promised to make this universal by using sufficient force to change the typical behavior of the suppressed. This is a very practical application of a very differently intended American philosophy, which considers only external behavior and suggests that anyone can be made to conform with anything provided enough pressure is brought to impress the corresponding behavior upon him. Such a thing may or may not be true. But there may also be in man genuine nature; however shaped and reshaped by history, it lives within him as his true self, may revolt against external pressure and be broken by it. This idea does not occur to the worshipers of violence any more than the thought that there may be an irrecoverable value in that particular nature and an inalienable right to its existence. Awareness of such values and rights constitutes the first step in liberty and justice.

3. Autarchy [4]

In the international field, the social-economic principle of fascism can be applied only negatively. There is no positive contribution of the lower middle class toward establishing a unified world and securing world peace— such as both partners of the industrial principle, the lais-

---

[4] The word autarchy has been widely used on the European Continent during the last decade to indicate the economic self-sufficiency of a politically organized country, and has been taken over into English political terminology. This has had unfortunate results because of different orthographic usages. In Greek, the word is spelt with the equivalent of k where the English spelling substitutes a ch. Etymologically "autarky" means self-sufficiency, while "autarchy" means autonomy. We shall use the word, however, in the sense of economic self-sufficiency, as a technical term, irrespective of etymology.

sez-faire capitalists and the Communists, claim. But this claim—even if realizable in principle—has not worked out thus far in the communist case, inasmuch as the despised autarchy of fascism is exactly the practical policy of Russia (though not its official program). The capitalist Internationale has indeed succeeded in forming a world market, but it is wholly questionable whether there is any integrating value in it, since its shrinkage in the crisis evokes and intensifies the conflicts of interests more than its rise ever lulled them. Hence, what appears at first glance as a defect of the principle of the lower middle class can be easily understood as a merit. The national economy, according to this doctrine, should be rooted in the soil of the fatherland, which the people should cultivate under the protection and guidance of the state. It should confine itself to its own national limits, as otherwise it might fall prey to foreign and hostile interests. This is the ideological and sentimental source of autarchy.

The workability of this device is disputed by the critics of fascism, and the early downfall of the National Socialist regime is expected to demonstrate the Utopian and antiquated character of its policy. Again, fascism shows a much stronger sense of reality and of real possibilities than its critics, whose international policy is so hopelessly involved. Not only has the liquidation of ruinous commitments had a strong psychological appeal: its practical effects, as well, demand serious consideration. Autarchy is, of course, more precarious and its limits more defined in a smaller and naturally not rich country like Germany than in the immense and abundantly equipped Russian continent, but this is for geographical, not political, reasons. The smaller a country is and the more entangled in the world market, because of its specialized production, like Belgium or Switzerland, the more devastating a policy of autarchy in the neighboring big countries would be for the small country. There would, in fact, be only one outlet for it: to conclude a trade alliance or tariff union with its big neighbor, whose own difficulties would thereby be diminished and whose economic rule would thus be expanded to include the nationally different small neighbors. This is certainly a very strong argument against autarchy from the point of view of the country too small for autarchy. But the attractiveness of the program to the big power may even be increased by such considerations. In more general and technical terms, autarchy does not necessarily need to be realized 100 per cent: as a prevailing tendency it may permit as many direct barter treaties as may be desirable or necessary to supplement the domestic equipment or to suit some political purpose. The only thing it precludes is free unregulated exchange by private sellers and buyers in the world market. Autarchy in this sense is one element of planning, in Germany as in Russia.

The main question is, of course, the impairment of economic welfare through autarchy. This will be serious in any case. A very considerable part of present international exchange cannot be translated into barter contracts: this occurs in all triangular or many-cornered transactions, where a man in A sells to a man in B and buys from a man in C, while leaving it to C to buy from B, either directly or through any number of intermediary hands or lands. As long as people buy abroad because it is cheaper to do so, and sell abroad because it is more profitable, all the participating countries are enriched—since such transactions make up for deficiencies in the national equipments. There is, however, no possibility of administering such transactions from the central board of any of the participating countries, because the government of A, though it can indeed find out and supervise the dealings of its citizens with B and C, cannot supervise the dealings of B with C, or with X or Z, who also deal with C. These many-cornered transactions, covering the whole world, constitute the bulk of international trade and the main benefit drawn from it. That one and the same country should be in need of our products, and at the same time the best supplier of what we need, is very likely to be an exceptional coincidence, yet this is required to warrant a reciprocal agreement of barter character. Hence many of the triangular transactions and their beneficial results would be canceled without substitutes being provided, and others would be replaced by reciprocal agreements of less satisfaction and value. In the first group of cases, the export industry would try to shift to domestic production of the previous import goods, which, if naturally and technically possible at all, would involve a serious diminution of the previously obtained quantity of goods. Furthermore the entire program may suffer from decisions against exchanging goods with countries not regarded as politically desirable. All these losses would not, of course, be adequately estimated in terms of the previous profits directly and indirectly derived from the transactions. The shrinkage in the quantity and the rise in price of many materials, and the complete absence of other goods, would necessitate a far-reaching adaptation and reconstruction of the economic system as a whole, particularly since existing plants closely connected with those goods would go out of use. In a country whose foreign trade represents 10 per cent of its total turnover, the destruction of foreign trade is likely to inflict losses of much more than 10 per cent.

Nevertheless, it might be possible for Germany or any other country desiring autarchy to stand the strain and to compensate for this in part. The positive possibilities of the situation must be taken into account. If there had never been foreign trade, a rise of industry in several countries separately would certainly not have been an impossibility. It would have constituted a serious handicap, to be sure, to have to manage with less abundant and less suitable materials on the one hand, and with less profitable markets on the other. But a rational technological development of domestic resources, supplemented perhaps by a few reciprocal transactions on vital raw materials, might still have led to great results, if on a narrower basis and therefore on a smaller scale. This fundamental consideration invalidates the position of those critics who aim at proving the impossibility of autarchy instead of weighing its inevitable difficulties. As an autarchic rise of industry is not impossible in itself, the inauguration of a policy of autarchy today may be conceived of in two phases. The first phase, the turn from the world market to autarchy, involves all the losses described above, and will mean, for the country as a whole, a terrific shrinkage of productive opportunities and economic welfare. But the country need not persist on this plane. Once the transformation and reduction are achieved, a new though more modest rise on different lines, with partly different techniques and industries, may be started.

Two auxiliary factors support this main thesis, both of them connected with the dynamic rise of population and of industrial techniques. First, the number of nationals and their average purchasing power is today several times what it was a century ago; the result is that an industry which could not have developed under former conditions may find the domestic market sufficiently large today. Second, many technical possibilities, though known, are not utilized by the bulk of the small producers today —as for example in farming; inventions and improvements may be forthcoming in the future. These could have arisen equally well under an international system, and would, in case of its functioning, have increased its benefits. Under autarchy, they would contribute to a positive rise from its lowest level and would help to compensate for the loss incurred by the transition to autarchy. Furthermore, it is unfair to weigh the merits and possibilities of autarchy in comparison with a perfectly working world market which has a purely fictitious existence. The true balance between the two systems depends not only on one's estimate of the possibilities and dangers of autarchy, but equally on one's estimate of the future possibilities and dangers of the world market. This brings us finally to the question of war, which may wreck all other estimates and justify even a high sacrifice of economic welfare in peacetime for an increase of economic security in war. Autarchy is certainly no ideal program, but neither is it impracticable—whether in communist Russia or in fascist Germany.

The political conclusion to be drawn from this economic survey is one of extreme skepticism concerning the international field. World trade, in the first phase of internationalism, had appeared as a means of integrating the life of mankind; world planning of world trade offered similar hopes in the second phase. Neither the practical autarchy of Russia nor the programmatic autarchy of Germany pursues any such ambitious aim. Their potential contributions to world peace, if they have any, lie in the negative direction of avoiding and getting disentangled from commitments that cause as much bitterness as interdependence. Against this advantage must be weighed the increasing bitterness of those who have to suffer from the disentanglement while it is in process. More important than this, however, is the fact that the absence of those economic entanglements which had been recommended as a guarantee of peace cannot, by itself, guarantee peace. It is true that if there are no economic contacts, there are no economic conflicts either, and those who believe that economic imperialism is alone responsible for wars ought to put their hopes in the most complete isolation of the nations through autarchy. Still, those causes of war that lie outside the purely economic field find no counteracting or restraining force in the system of autarchy.

The old pacifist argument that economic interdependence makes war more difficult does not prove that interdependence is sufficient to prevent war; it is confirmed, however, by the nationalistic striving after autarchy for overtly military reasons. To say that the technique of autarchy breeds war is absurd; but it is true that while autarchy removes possible economic conflicts which might arise from economic interdependence, it also removes a possible handicap on warfare. Moreover, that secondary implication of autarchy, the discrimination against the small countries which compels them to join the closed economic system of some big neighbor, will turn out to be the source of much economic and political imperialism and much competition between the rival imperialisms. It is worth noting that the political principle of national organization of big and small nations alike is not compatible with autarchy, which abandons the small nations to the mercy of the big ones. The principle of national organization demands that international trade be organized and relieved from its inherent ailments. Taken all in all, autarchy may remove certain dangers but adds other dangers. More than this cannot be concluded from an abstract and general economic analysis. All then depends on the spirit in which the one or the other program of economic policy is applied.

The idealistic hopes of internationalism are exposed to the double threat of political abuse for imperialistic purposes and of technical defects which are immanent in capitalism and cannot be removed today by international planning. The realistic skepticism of autarchy contains, however, no international organizing principle; it renounces any solution and repudiates any obligation. It believes that this planet is inescapably a chaos. This idea has been inculcated into the thinking of the German people, in an indelible manner for a long time to come by the policy of the World War victors, from the Versailles Treaty down to the threat of war against Germany in case of a tariff union with starving Austria in 1931. Never was a sincere and believing people eager with faith and hope for peace and good will more drastically disillusioned than that of Germany after President Wilson's promises. No wonder that all efforts at an international organization have since been ridiculed, and that fascism has appealed to the experiences and sentiments of the German people when it concluded that there can be no organizing principle for world peace. This belief is psychologically explainable and it is possibly correct. Yet it makes practically all the difference in the world whether one acquiesces in that statement and organizes political life accordingly, or whether one puts all one's strength in striving after peace, although fully aware of the danger of war. Peace is not the absence of conflicts and hostilities: if peace should ever be more than a matter of transitory chance, it must be the result of a positive organization of justice. Just as surely as any organization may prove ineffective and fail to offer a guarantee of peace, so peace will be missed unless we seek for it. Not in the economic technique of autarchy, but in the contemptuous indifference

to an organizing principle of peace, lies the true danger
of fascism.

4. The Emancipation of the Lower Middle Class in Germany

Hitler and the other leaders of the National Socialist
movement built up a genuine middle-class state in modern industrial society. Their plan had to maintain the particular status of the lower middle class and integrate German society by erecting a dictatorship over both business
and labor which they supplemented through autarchy.
It offered itself as an alternative program to communism
and contended that it was the only alternative—thus reap-
ing the benefits of any aversion to or fear of communism.
Systematic analysis and four years of historical experience
show that their program is workable, though it gives rise
to grave problems. This fact verifies our theory to a sufficient degree to make the logic of the fascist social and
economic program visible. Our entire deduction makes
use, however, of historical conditions not implied in our
discussion of the primary fascist principles. These conditions have to be added explicitly if we are to pass from
the National Socialist program to the facts and implications of its realization. We must ask why it is that in
Germany this program conquered the competing programs presented by Russia and the Anglo-Saxon countries
respectively. The failure of communism and democracy
in Germany that made fascism the only remaining possibility makes it necessary for us to turn to an historical
sketch of the German situation.

Any presentation of the rise of German fascism is misleading if it does not start from the fact that German
democracy, far from being overthrown by fascism, had
already died in 1929. Fascism stepped into the vacuum

thus created only in 1933. A defeat of democracy in a real struggle would have been bad enough; this fact renders the situation much worse. For it means that democracy had proved incapable of managing its affairs. It is certainly true, and cannot be stressed sufficiently, that the constant humiliations in foreign policy discussed above contributed greatly toward undermining the authority of the Republic. If the victorious democracies had been animated by any genuinely democratic spirit, they would have spared the self-respect of the young German Republic. If part of the responsibility is thus shifted from German democracy to the shoulders of the older democracies, this does not, however, strengthen the case for the principle of democracy. Moreover, the inner constitution of German democracy was weak and unlikely to stand a real strain, quite apart from the coincident events in foreign policy. Owing to its particular structure, the German Republic was exposed from the outset to the danger of paralysis and died of it.[5]

[5] This is not the place to describe the great achievements of the German Republic that an impartial historian will present one day in a balanced survey of its history. It was a highly spiritualized society, eagerly seeking progress, animated by a severe and critical sense of justice, and distinguished in learning, science, and art. This must be said although the experimental atmosphere and the lack of definite standards resulted in some aberrations and violations of good taste. The virtues by far outweighed the defects. Through social legislation and municipal socialism the standard of living was raised considerably; the average life expectancy was extended by ten years within ten years; an elaborate system of labor rights was designed to penetrate and transform the structure of capitalism. But all this cannot mitigate the judgment on the inherent political weakness and blindness of German democracy.

Both in Germany and abroad the impression has been prevalent that German democracy was corrupt and that the National Socialist revolution, whatever its right or wrong, had to clean the house. This impression is a triumph of what is termed today the technique of political propaganda. The facts are the following: The German Republic had inherited from the Monarchy a provision in the penal code which was designed to pro-

A parliamentarian democracy, in order to function, must be able to create a majority among the voters, and if no single group is able to form a majority, it requires a practicable coalition. If one examines the social structure which underlay the German political groupings, one finds the three characteristic groups of advanced capitalism. First, an upper layer—or perhaps rather two in close connection and alliance, though not without conflicts between them—the owners and managers of the big rural estates and the big industrial and financial enterprises. Second, the propertyless workers operating these properties through a collective technique. Third, the independent producers—farmers, artisans, storekeepers, and (for particular reasons mainly connected with them) the clerks of the big enterprises.[6] The crucial point for the failure

tect political writers but made the prosecution of slander virtually impossible. An editor who used an untrue statement in the political struggle had only to testify that he had honestly believed in the truth of the rumor, and thereupon was granted by the court the recognition that he had acted "in pursuit of warranted interests" and was acquitted or at best punished with a nominal fine, which did not dishonor him, much less prevent him from continuing in the same vein. This was the loophole used by the new technique. The mild sentences were interpreted to the effect that something in the incriminated statements must be true, and the country was flooded with rumors of embezzlement and bribery. These rumors became much too numerous to be prosecuted at all, and a great many prominent officeholders, in the administrations of the Reich, the states, and the municipalities as well as in the trade unions, were involved, often in the form that allegedly they had accepted bribes of foreign powers. When finally fascism came to power, some of these men fled abroad, others were arrested and detained for political reasons; but literally not one of them could be prosecuted for embezzlement or bribery.

[6] Recent political discussion has paid much attention to the growing differentiation of industrial occupations and population strata and much less attention to the relationship between the industrial population as a whole and the so-called old middle class of independent producers. Now the latter class belongs in the center of attention because the full diversification of social types in present-day society must be taken into account when examining all the political potentialities. This consideration applies

of the majority principle of German democracy is the statistical proportion of the economic classes: there were some 40 per cent of proletarians with the same percentage in the medial group—a situation which had existed for three decades without change, in the face of an increasing population. Furthermore, the extreme rigidity and class consciousness of the social hierarchy has to be taken into consideration. A man's economic status was regarded as fixed once for all and as determining his permanent social status. Decisive for the coalition problem, however, was the fact that the medial group was not conceived of, either by itself or by the others, as an independent and separately organizable group, but as a mere annex to the ruling group—feudal owners and big bourgeoisie. Since they were owners on a smaller scale, they were taken as bourgeois

especially to the tiller of the land who feeds us. But our emphasis on the old rural middle class is not, of course, meant to belittle the very great significance of recent differentiation within the urban sphere. Its source is the same labor-saving technology that was found to reform and modernize small farming. In its application to industry this technique leads to the growth of machinery and output without an increase of labor, if it does not even result in unemployment. At the same time, however, as the machine becomes more and more refined and complicated, it requires more engineers and technicians for supervision and more clerks for accounting. The distributive system of middlemen and salesmen grows too as production becomes concentrated in relatively fewer places and the consumers are spread over the entire country and beyond it. For all these reasons the new technical development, while modernizing and stabilizing the older type of work where it has survived, as in farming, favors a more rapid growth of the new salaried middle class in industry than that of the laborers. It is true that the white-collar workers share many features of proletarian life, but it is also a fact that they for the most part do not regard themselves as laborers. This cannot be discussed here, it has been best presented by Alfred Bingham, *Insurgent America,* 1935. One important conclusion has often been noted, too: pure proletarian labor parties can never win the majority as the numerical discrepancy between labor and the aggregate industrial population widens.

Another important point that needs to be made concerns the tactics of labor in the industrial struggle. The strike was originally conceived as a

by the representatives of labor, and since they felt themselves included in the latter's general assault on property,
they sought and found their natural representatives and
leaders in the big owners. The big owners, finally, could
have no objection against an interpretation from which
they drew the main benefit. Their political parties, the
more liberal German People's party and the more conservative and monarchistic German Nationalist party
thrived on the support of the many millions of small
owners. The whole situation, after the early elimination

means of demonstrating to capital that the true seat of all productivity is
labor alone. It found expression in the German labor slogan: All wheels
must stand still when your strong arms so will. This has become a very
dubious doctrine. In a literal sense it remains true, but even so it means
little as one need not be a worker to stop a machine; any rowdy can
throw a bolt into it. Apart from this, however, the positive idea that the
operation of the machinery depends only on the workers no longer holds
true. When fighting the employer, labor may find itself opposed not only
by the public in general but especially by the white-collar workers whose
work the strike stops directly. Other classes in the community may be
similarly affected. A strike in the largest American chocolate factory resulted in the striking laborers being thrashed, routed, and driven to work
by the enraged dairy farmers of the neighborhood whom the laborers
had not even thought of contacting when depriving them of the daily
sales of their milk to the chocolate factory. Such a result in one form or
other, if nothing worse, is inevitable as long as labor, a limited group of
the working nation, acts as if it were practically all-inclusive; it is not a
question of predilection for labor, the farmers, or some other class, but of
facing the facts. In short, although the strike was designed to manifest the
one-sided dependence of capital on labor and the latter's monopoly in
productivity, since labor forms only one productive group out of many,
the labor strike may hit these other groups also and arouse them against
labor. It is astounding to see the traditional strike ideology and tactics
persist in the presence of such far-reaching changes. In comparison with
European and American labor, Chinese labor shows imaginative force. It
organized, for example, a traffic strike in Shanghai by running all cars and
busses without, however, collecting the fares, and thereby won the laughing applause of all classes and left to the employers the odious decision
to shut down the traffic in order to avoid losses. This device is incapable
of generalization owing to technical reasons, but it proves how keenly
Chinese labor is alive to its dependence upon and responsibility to others.

of a progressive Democratic party, was complicated by the existence of two Catholic parties which included members of all social groups. This made them fit to join and strengthen any coalition. Under these circumstances, the only possible solution of the question of government was a coalition between labor and property; in practice this meant a union between right wing labor and the politically more moderate party of private property, the German People's party. If one reduced the complex social structure of the country to the Marxian scheme of two classes, owners and non-owners, no other possibility of a coalition existed than that between organized labor and big business.

Everybody, of course, realized that this was no true solution and could be accepted only provisionally until a more stable and homogeneous government became possible. As a matter of fact, the coalition had some temporary success as long as conditions improved. It became inoperative and paralyzed when the emergency of the economic crisis made decisive steps imperative, to the left or to the right; no decision at all could be obtained. As something had to be done, the government was declared temporarily independent of Parliament, with a view to restoring the rule of the majority on the return of normal conditions. This was the end of German democracy as a working institution, though the civil liberties of the people survived until fascism came into power.

A constructive policy could have broken the deadlock and built up a real block of democratic power by combining the groups of potentially democratic interests and including their requirements and experiences in a comprehensive program. To this end it would have been necessary to reveal the uncapitalistic character of the small propertied producers and to emancipate them from capitalistic leadership on the one hand, and exempt them from—and reconcile them to—the claims of labor on the other. This possibility was missed because those who were supposed to represent democracy did not understand how it operated. The crucial significance of the problem of the lower middle class was well known to labor and was even responsible for the rift within labor and the additional weakening of the Republic which resulted. But both wings of labor stuck to the Marxian scheme of two important classes, and relied on the familiar assumption that the middle-class element was doomed by history. The Communists insisted upon disposing of it according to the Russian model. They believed that this model was generally valid and applicable to German conditions. They were unaware of the unique conditions prevailing in Russia. The Social Democrats were aware of the inapplicability of this program. In fact German society, owing to its education by the capitalistic system and universal knowledge of Marxian class theory, was as strongly organized economically and politically as the Russian people had been ignorant. No proletarian minority, even if it had been united in itself and had not been opposed by the Catholic workers, had the slightest chance of surprising the majority by a coup d'état. Moreover, the professional army was in the hands of elements far to the right, since labor had always kept its members from joining it. Finally Germany, as an industrialized country, could not afford to violate the peasants on whose supplies it was entirely dependent. For these reasons, communism was out of the question, irrespective of how many millions of workers would have voted for communism. The inferiority of labor in political, economic, and military power was manifest. The Social Democrats had nothing practicable, however, to offer instead of the communist program. They did not perceive the possibility of combining politically with the independent producers against the rule of capital and the menace of the crisis. Nor did they recognize this possibility as a necessity —as the only outlet from otherwise certain ruin. Since it appeared impossible to do away by force with the embarrassing power of the lower middle class, they believed that the thing to do was to wait for history to take care of it through the further progress of capital and crisis. The interim period had to be bridged by orderly administration in a coalition with whoever was interested in it. This policy was tantamount to the abdication of democracy when put to the test of emergency.

One cannot say that the conflict within labor made it impossible for the Social Democrats to switch over to that new policy. Their negative policy of shunning any such move did not keep any communist sympathies which they might have jeopardized by a drastic action. With the communist papers preaching every day that Severing, the socialist Minister of the Interior, was "worse than Hitler," the relations between the two wings of labor were such that they could not get worse any more. On the other hand, there is no reason why a swift and decisive action should not have brought about the reconciliation within labor which was impossible in theory. For such action would have been by no means a mere demoralizing retreat but a reorganization of the fighting troops. If the Social Democrats had broken the existing state of paralysis, seized the initiative, formed an alliance with the peasants, and launched a vigorous attack on the economic crisis incorporated in the dominance of big business, the Communists might have denounced this new treason but they would have concurred in the attack. It would have been impossible for them to keep aloof without losing their followers. In the hour of emergency the scene is easily changed, and much may become real that appears fantastic in normal times. The switch was possible and imperative; and while the responsibility for having aroused the hatred of the peasants rests primarily on the advocates of Russian methods in agriculture, the responsibility for having omitted the positive solution rests entirely on the Social Democrats. It is they who sacrificed German democracy to the Marxian theory.

The development of fascism in Austria was very similar to that in Germany and teaches the same lesson. The social and political structure of this small state presents the purest type of that even division between urban and agrarian forces which directly leads to paralysis as the ties of common conviction between the two groups disappear. The conflict over social policy was intensified in Austria by the strong allegiance of the Alpine peasants to the Catholic Church and the hostility to it on the part of the Viennese laborers. Immediately after the war, in the wake of the wave of democracy and socialism that swept Europe, the democratic constitution of Austria worked smoothly, and the semi-autonomous city of Vienna demonstrated what admirable achievements municipal socialism was capable of. As social differences and the economic crisis became more acute, the Parliament in 1933 failed to elect a president, without whom it could not function constitutionally. It thereby invalidated the constitution and abdicated in favor of a government by decree. No outside interference was responsible for this absurd event. Subsequently the shifting weight of international relations contributed to the democratic catastrophe. When the Western powers let it be understood that they would not use armed force to defend Austria's independence against German National Socialism, fascist Italy stepped in and demanded as the price of its aid the crushing of the democratic forces in

Austria. In February 1934 the organization of labor was beaten and outlawed, and an authoritarian constitution was put into operation; but democratic government had been buried one year before.

It frequently occurs in history that an inescapable fate announces its approach by a symbolic event. The die has already been cast, but now the initiated understand that all hope is lost. The symbolic event in Germany was the uprising of entire villages, under the black banner and with scythes as arms, against the forced sales of foreclosed farms: an event unheard of in so disciplined, orderly, and law-abiding a country. The bailiffs were compelled to retire in spite of police escort. The Communists were jubilant, they invited the peasants to persevere and to join the revolutionists by forming farm collectives instead of clinging to their obviously untenable individual holdings. The Social Democratic press foamed with rage and insisted that the authority of the Republic must protect the historically necessary progress of capitalism and transformation of farming. The capitalist press warned the peasants that the mortgage credit of agriculture was at stake if creditors were cheated out of their legitimate claims. This confusion was the dance of death for German democracy. The Fascists understood that fact.

The true structure of the German Republic was brought out by this event. Paralyzed as it was by the division between capital and labor within the government, and between the two wings of labor outside the government, the Republic was, nevertheless, homogeneous in its general assumptions and standards. All organized forces within and without the government (with the exception of the Catholic parties) agreed that the progress of capitalism was necessary and welcome. As a whole they represented a highly stratified urban, intellectual, progressive society. Its various limbs were hostile to one another, but recognized their common reasons for existence and were connected through mutual experiences and intellectual discussion (even if from opposite angles). The middle-class people could and should have been used to carry the fighting parties of the capitalistic struggle to victory—either to defend property, since they were proprietors themselves, or to attack it when they became stripped of their own by that system of property. They were organized as allies to the capitalistic side of the struggle; by virtue of their pending social transformation they should have been reorganized as allies to labor. But they were not recognized as representative of, and animated by, a genuine independent principle of their own: they were considered unorganizable as a special group, negligible by themselves and doomed to be overridden by further progress on intellectual lines. In economic policy a great deal had been done in their behalf, as for any numerous group of voters; but this was not in the program of either capital or labor, it was forced through by their latent power, and the atmosphere of the Republic was alien to their tradition-minded, conservative mentality. Since they were excluded from sharing power in the progressive Republic their response was to support fascism as the revolutionary method of winning their emancipation.

The emergence and the direction of their reaction can be traced to the social-political conditions in Germany. The clock of their emancipation should strike at a time when the urban discussions were resulting in a complete and hopeless deadlock and the entire people were shaken by the crisis and longing for the government to act. It is only natural that the people should be disappointed, discouraged, and disgusted, and that they should turn away from democratic methods which exposed them to the immediate peril of chaos. The newly emerging group had not been represented in the endless discussions of the coalition, it had not been worn out nor compromised. It proclaimed decision instead of discussion, action instead of programs, leadership instead of progress. It substituted the immediate unbroken impetus of nature, as the true source of strength and power, for the disintegrating influence of critical analysis. Through close contact with nature in the daily work of their fields and the eternal recurrence of seed-time and harvest, birth and death, and remote from the intellectual approach to the principle of progress, they raised their belief in the "holiness of blood and soil" into the symbol of salvation from the curse of intellectual barrenness. This is perfectly logical in view of the situation, and it is as genuinely expressive of their real existence as the progressive revolutionary spirit of the machine is expressive of the proletarian reality.

One must not conclude that peasants are driven toward fascism by anything like a natural law. Given their existence as peasants, they will certainly put all their energy into the effort to preserve and strengthen it. But there are plenty of ways in which this might be done, and only one of them is fascism. Which way they choose will be determined by the entire set of conditions under which they act and interpret themselves and the external world. No natural law compels them to seek subjugation of others regardless of objective conditions, just as no natural law compels the workers to seek the extermination of individual peasantry, and none compels a nation to seek the subjugation of its neighbors. Antagonism and imperialism are only one of the possible forms of relationship between groups; the other is alliance for common action and mutual aid. Every man and every group can try to gain at the expense of

others or through co-operation with others, and the alternative will be decided by the nature and behavior of the
partners. To recognize and revere the sanctity of nature,
therefore, is far from using it as a fighting slogan and exclusive political creed. Such fascist tendencies as those in
Germany are more likely to arise as the tension between
city and country leads to an actual political deadlock and
is not lessened and outweighed by common political traditions and loyalties.

The outstanding example of a tendency to the contrary
is France, where the peasants received their lands through
the Revolution and where their indebtedness to political
liberty obviously is one with their attachment to their
lands. The heritage of the Revolution is the dominating
fact of French political life; it is common to city and country except in the Northwest, and it forms an integrating
power of mutual understanding and recognition. Of
course, this has not always been so. In 1848 and 1871
sectarian communist uprisings had been quelled with the
active support of the peasants, and all sorts of reactionary experiments had preceded and followed these catastro-
phes. Gradually, however, as the left learned to respect
the peasants' independence, anti-libertarian tendencies became isolated in some aristocratic and financial quarters
of Paris, and today the spirit of libertarian civilization is
penetrating and vitalizing the entire ancient country and
chooses the peasant and small town-dweller as its representative figures. It is a process of sublime logic.

This development, however, finds no analogy in Germany where no liberal revolution has ever taken place and
consequently no tradition of political liberty has been
woven into the average peasant's sense of property. It is
true that some sections of free peasantry have existed from

the Middle Ages, and their tradition of defense against feudal claims has accustomed them to democratic ideas. But free property for the bulk of the rural population was established by governmental decrees designed to prevent an outburst similar to the French one and were carried out half-heartedly with a view to maintaining the authoritarian structure of the country. Property was granted by the authorities, it was not won as the prize of a struggle for liberty, and had no conscious democratic implications. Political life in the country, consequently, was always weak; democratic ideas developed as the result of a distinctly urban movement and remained strange to the country. The effect was one of mutual alienation, suspicion, and isolation. The democratic potentialities of the country, with millions of independent properties and ten thousands of co-operatives, were ignored and ridiculed by those filled with proletarian hostility, and fascism was the outcome of the deadlock.

As a minority party, the Communists could not win control. Since the parliamentarian Republic had been overcome by its own ineffectuality, there was in fact no alternative to fascism and therefore no resistance. Some, when all their old beliefs were wrecked, were transported by the vision of a new system; others felt defeated and frustrated by the failure of their system of liberty and justice. Everything had been tried except fascism. It was impossible to refuse it a trial, as it had promised to secure the cohesion of society in the face of the threatening chaos. What fascism rescued Germany from was not, by any means, communism. Only such forms of government as the organized farmers will at least tolerate are possible in an industrialized country, and communism is not among them. What fascism rescued Germany from was the lack of strong government in a great emergency. In the clash between liberty and security, security triumphed once more.[7]

5. *Some Qualifications: Germany and Italy*

To claim that all this logically follows from the conditions under which fascism arose may expose us to a double misunderstanding and must be guarded against. Firstly human actions and reactions are never predetermined in the sense of a mechanical necessity; an element of free

[7] The thesis that fascism is a reaction to the communist substitution for democracy of a universal proletarianization which history does not spontaneously produce is not novel. Particularly impressive formulations to this effect may be found in the brief statements under the title, "Why I Am Not a Communist," by John Dewey and Morris R. Cohen, in the symposium, *The Meaning of Marx,* edited by Sidney Hook, 1934. Dewey says: "How communism can continue to advocate the kind of economic change it desires by means of civil war, armed insurrection and iron dictatorship in the face of what has happened in Germany and Italy I cannot at all understand. . . . I am firmly convinced that imminent civil war, or even the overt threat of such a war, in any Western nation will bring fascism with its terrible engines of repression to power. Communism, then, with its doctrine of the necessity of the forcible overthrow of the state by armed insurrection, with its doctrine of the dictatorship of the proletariat, with its threats to exclude all other classes from civil rights, to smash their political parties, and to deprive them of the rights of freedom of speech, press, and assembly—which communists now claim for themselves under capitalism—communism is itself an unwitting, but nonetheless powerful, factor in bringing about fascism."

By far the best presentation and interpretation of the entire range of problems is contained in Alfred Bingham's *Insurgent America,* 1935. While his economic Utopia suffers partly from a popular interpretation of supposedly marketless Marxian economics and partly from a related belief in an economy of abundance without economic laws, his socio-political analyses of European fascism and of diversified tendencies in America are of the greatest realism and originality. His study of the question, What is "the stake of the middle classes in capitalism?" and his answer that it is not a property stake but a job stake—thereby bringing individualistic property closer to labor—may become the basis for a realignment of political forces and for a reorganization of society. It is these chapters which make the book the outstanding performance of present-day political literature.

choice, whatever its philosophical interpretation, enters every decision, and we can therefore never strictly calculate the future course of history in advance or interpret past history as if we could have calculated it in advance. It was not inevitable that the industrial workers should preach the necessity of exterminating the independent producers; and even when they did, the counter-attack need not have adopted at all the forms of fascist wholesale repression as a permanent system of government. To point out the logic of the fascist program, therefore, is not to apologize for it as something inevitable; our approach simply tries to make the fascist program plausible as a human decision without defending it for one moment.

Secondly, one must consider not only the element of free choice but the element of historical contingency. In a critical situation much may depend on the sickness or death of outstanding individuals, or on their personal qualities which, however necessary in a biographical sense, are not calculable in a political decision. Napoleon certainly could not have achieved what he did, or failed as he did, without the wave of the French Revolution first carrying him to power; on the other hand, the French Revolution would certainly have taken another course without his unique military and political genius. In the history of the World War Lawrence of Arabia was a somewhat similar figure, less spectacular indeed, but more fascinating as a human being. A logic of historical events, therefore, would badly overshoot the mark unless it made allowance for the small and large effects of such incalculable elements as the personal qualities of great men and other contingencies. Marx not only formulated the principle of socialism as a form of society towards which reality tended, but gave the socialist movement consciousness and indelibly impressed it with certain features derived from his personality; any other discoverer, a Proudhon or Lassalle, would have stamped it in a different way. It is obvious that these considerations must have a bearing upon a system which professes the "principle of leadership," as does fascism. A grave objection to our attempted logic of fascism, therefore, may derive from the fact that it does not mention the names of the leaders whose part in history is so prominent.

It would certainly be very erroneous to dispute the contributions made by certain individuals to the making of fascism. If this account claimed to give the complete history of fascism instead of a systematic survey of political principles, they would figure in it in a very conspicuous way. In such an approach as ours, however, the fact that political principles are proclaimed and carried out by a few noted individuals is not in itself evidence of how far the influence of these individual achievements or contingencies reaches. The personalities concerned may be precisely expressive of objective tendencies which would be sure to find another personal symbol and mouthpiece if the existing leaders had been prematurely destroyed by some chance events. This is not to reduce all the spectacular events of fascist history to impersonal tendencies of lower-middle-class policy; it is only to warn against the contrary error of attributing them all to the personal greatness, political shrewdness, or moral wickedness of the protagonists. Far from having any methodical or philosophical bias, we have, in our survey of political principles, simply tried to see in each individual case how far the objective tendencies of history assert themselves through personal actions, and our attempt at a "logic" of politics carries us surprisingly far in the case of fascism as well as in that of communism.

Skeptics attribute to the contingencies of personal and historical life the fact that Stalin conquered the more colorful Trotsky. Dogmatists attribute it to the infallible instinct of the proletariat for its true interest. The latter opinion is not convincing because exactly the same justification would be given by the same observers if the proletariat had decided the other way. The skeptical interpretation, however, would be acceptable only if there were not the plausible explanation that the champion of a national policy conquered the advocate of an international policy and that the victor was a man of at least half-Russian stock while the loser was a Jew. There can be no doubt that such factors operate and that they may come to the fore and decide an issue when the balance is otherwise even.

It is noteworthy that in Germany the rise of fascism was not dependent upon one individual since there were, beside Hitler and independently of him, at least two other candidates for fascist leadership, Ludendorff and Erhardt. This fact accentuates the objective forces behind the German trend to fascism. It is true that the decision between these potential rivals must be attributed to contingency, and each might have impressed fascism with different features if he had come to power; but this concerns only secondary traits as compared with the primary principle of fascism. The familiar differences between German and Italian fascisms, although popularly ascribed to the personal qualities of Hitler and Mussolini, are actually traceable in the main to the differences of conditions in the two countries. Anti-Semitism and the theories of racial differences and superiority on which it is based in part are of course the very core of fascist ideology in Germany (and are analyzed as such in a special sub-chapter of this survey). But they would have formed too narrow an ideological basis for fascism in Italy, which has considerably less than one-tenth the Jewish population of Germany. On the

other hand, anti-Semitism is perfectly compatible with
Italian fascism, and such germs as occasionally make their
appearance may or may not develop; all depends on considerations of general policy. As the Italians attempt to
stir up the Arabic world against the English by pointing at
the Jewish colonization in Palestine under English protection, official anti-Semitism becomes more likely than not.

Fascist Italy is much less marked than Germany as a
lower-middle-class state, and Mussolini personally is not
at all in favor of the "petty bourgeoisie"; that is why he
uses the contemptuous Marxian term. Italy is far less advanced than Germany on the road to capitalism, industry,
and rationalization of life in general, and while in Germany little can be done further to develop the industrial
and technical character of the country, much still remains
to be done in Italy in this respect, whether this be an advantage or a defect. Mussolini may be compared to the
leaders of the absolute-mercantilist states of western and
northern Europe in the seventeenth and eighteenth centuries. Like them he places his hope and confidence in
capitalist efficiency and initiative; unlike them he confines
the capitalist class to business proper and founds the supremacy of his state upon the vitality of the lower classes.
Still the capitalist-industrial ingredient is stronger in Italy
than in the German brand of fascism because of the un-
exhausted urge for industrialization; in seeking economic
progress and political power, Italian fascism takes advantage of the potentialities inherent in capitalist energies.
The original fascist impulse, therefore, was the desire for
industrial growth rather than for bourgeois wealth, its concomitant. Nothing bears out this suggestion better than
the undisturbed good terms which Italy maintained with
Soviet Russia during the first fourteen years of fascist regime, as evidenced by the fact that fascist Italy was the

first great power to recognize the Soviet government and was also instrumental in bringing Russia into the League of Nations, while Russia on her part continued her deliveries of oil to Italy throughout the Ethiopian war and thereby positively contributed to the Italian triumph. Despite the conflict between the two regimes over sociopolitical ideas a certain sympathy with each other's efforts in industrialization and rationalization has united them for many years.

Of course this stage is over. The emphasis of Italian development has definitely shifted from industrial growth to capitalistic power and imperialistic expansion, and at the same time her friendly relations with Russia gave way to mutual antagonism. This development can be understood as quite logical in itself. The lower-middle-class basis of fascism is not apt to develop an undeveloped industry; thus one has to resort either to Capital or to Labor. In the beginning the industrial growth as such was in the forefront, while later its bourgeois character became increasingly conspicuous. Both stages, however, belong together although they are separate and distinct stages, both showing the deflection of Italian fascism from the pure principle of middle-class dictatorship, such as a developed industrial country like Germany had used as an outlet from the crisis.

The turning point between the two stages was Italy's triumph in the Ethiopian war which simultaneously was a triumph over England and the League of Nations. The war in Abyssinia had been initiated with very distinct anticapitalistic reasoning as the attempt to gain an outlet for the poor and their children in their overpopulated country. It had found the ardent support of these lower layers and had met with the almost unhidden disapproval and even some counter-maneuvers of the bourgeois and business people, who did not believe in the profitability of the enterprise and were afraid of arousing the anger of the English. Now it has all changed into its very contrary. The aggressive hostility of the Abyssinian tribes continues unabated, and while the towns and the lines of communication are effectively guarded against them, the hopes for Italians to settle as farmers are revealed as futile for a long time to come. The continued military engagements in Africa and the added and increasing sacrifices in Spain seem widely to create disillusionment among the lower layers, while the bourgeoisie and the intellectuals are in raptures at the huge investments in Abyssinia and the diplomatic victory over England. No conversation among Italians of the higher classes seems to miss the favorite topic, the imminent destruction of the British Empire. A distinct bourgeois imperialism appears more and more to become the political content of Italian fascism.

In post-war Germany there has been no more room for enthusiasm over industrial growth. German industrial capitalism is virtually complete, it has brought about the economic and political crisis and was both rescued and superseded by the middle-class dictatorship which uses capitalistic industry as an instrument of its policy. With no enthusiasm for industry German fascism, unlike the Italian, could never be on friendly terms with Russia either; there is nothing to mitigate their mutual political suspicions. It is true that the commercial and credit relations between them are of considerable and even increasing importance. But since each is aware of this arrangement strengthening not only itself but its potential adversary, this purely economic tie of common interests should not be given too much weight in an appraisal of their relationship. The negative fact that both are skeptical of capitalism does not reconcile them as everything else in their positive ideologies separates them. As we have seen, Lenin said that electricity plus Soviets make communism; it may be almost equally correct to say that electricity plus militia or corporations make fascism in Italy. But this principle is not applicable to a country like Germany where electricity can no longer figure in a revolutionary program because it is a familiar fact. German fascism encourages any invention which may contribute to making the country self-sufficient in peace and war; but it does not share by any means the Italian and Russian enthusiasm for progress and is highly skeptical not only of capitalism but of large-scale industry. German industrialization is virtually complete, and the German people's concern for the future of industry centers on its unsolved problems rather than on its further prospects.

In respect to both the ideological and socio-political programs, Germany presents a more characteristic brand of fascism than Italy.

B. Fascism as Anti-humanism [8]

1. The Problem and Its Political Significance

Two different considerations show that our attempt to derive German fascism exclusively from its socio-political conditions is neither comprehensive nor deep enough. One

[8] The following section bears witness to the deep influence that the teachings of Paul Tillich—both literary and personal—have had upon the author for many years. See Tillich, *The Interpretation of History*, 1936. We also refer with deep gratitude to Reinhold Niebuhr's recent book, *An Interpretation of Christian Ethics*, 1935. As the manuscript of this book goes to press, the message and decisions on *Church, Community, and State,* of the Ecumenical Conference at Oxford on Life and Work are published, and lend their great authority and impressive formulations to the point of view here discussed.

thing that cannot be derived from the socio-political conditions of Germany is the scope of the new revolutionary radicalism. Any narrow interpretation of historical materialism fails in the presence of the question why and how the political dictatorship was extended to include even a religious dictatorship. With the Protestant Church of Germany traditionally loyal to the state and careful not to mix in politics, the political ends of German fascism could have been much more easily reached by restricting the dictatorial rule to the worldly affairs and abandoning the other world to the Church, as Mussolini, after some wavering, had found it advisable to do. If his example was not imitated in Germany and the stubborn opposition of both the Protestant and Catholic Churches was arbitrarily invited, in defiance of all political expediency, strong forces must have been at work. An adequate analysis of these factors is far beyond the scope of the present treatise and the competence of the author, but a few broad strokes may give the main features of the National Socialist philosophy.

Some may object that this enlargement of our program is concerned with spiritual problems and can be dispensed with in a presentation centering on political problems. This is an error. The explanation we have given of fascism as a dictatorship of the lower middle class must not convey the impression that its rise had not been supported by millions of industrial proletarians, in particular from the ranks of the unemployed. This support, which may be credited with having greatly contributed to the final victory of fascism, certainly breaks through the Marxian view that political alignments are determined by people's social position. And yet this view is partly true, since the proletarian wing of fascism continues adhering to its socialist ideas while transplanting them into the new climate of fascism. Not only is there a strong and radical socialist wing in the fascist movement, but a socialist system of fascism is logically conceivable and politically not impossible. The two socialist possibilities are more or less identical in economic principles, but since they apply the principles in a different spirit and for different ends they are deadly enemies. It is obvious that this involved situation cannot be disentangled by a discussion of mere institutions and corresponding interests. Hence, the tangible problem of political alignment and the seemingly more remote problem of the Church struggle demand a consideration of the standards of belief and behavior that underlie German fascism.

It is true that this supplement badly impairs the architecture of our book. What is lost in symmetry, however, is gained in truth. The rise of the fascist spirit disrupts the unitary foundation upon which capitalism, democracy, socialism, and even communism rest and which has made it possible and necessary for the preceding chapters to start from the assumption (see pages 39, 88, and 97) of a definite type of man and a definite direction of human aspirations which are regarded as natural and are more or less unconsciously presupposed by the various competing programs. This assumption concerning mankind is vigorously disputed by fascism. While that "natural" type of man is shaped and reshaped by the experiences, possibilities, and pressures of changing conditions and events described in the preceding chapters, the belief in his natural or historical necessity is refuted by the rise of fascism and its new conception of man. That is why any study of the rational type of man proves inadequate to a full understanding of fascism and must give way to an explicit, if necessarily incomplete, discussion of the ultimate principles of social philosophy.

2. *Humanism as the Foundation of the Occidental World*

For several thousand years the evolution of Western mankind had been moved by humanism, by spiritual forces permeating human life and organizing the world. Logos and cosmos, reason as the all-pervading genuinely constructive force, and the harmonious universe, were the fundamental concepts of classical culture. The Hebrew prophets taught that the oneness of God was the primary principle underlying the world universe and resulted in the unity of all he had created and the oneness of his justice being all-inclusive and permitting of no exception. The Greek and Hebrew prophetic heritage became merged when, in the Gospel of St. John, Christ was proclaimed the logos of the world in whom all human souls partake.

This event, of course, did not bring about harmony in the world or in Western philosophy. The tension between the static natural concepts of the Greeks and the dynamic historical concepts of the Jews was a decisive issue within Christianity for many centuries, and the divinely ordained unity of the world continued to be violated by the destructive forces symbolized as sin. So strong is the power of sin in natural man that he generally must be protected against himself by the force and authority of the state, and in individual cases his body had to be burned to death in order to save the participation of his soul in Christ. The history of the Christian churches and peoples permits of no optimistic progressive interpretation. The fundamental principles of the Christian religion were warped in their application and remodeled into their very opposites; and the actual content of what was regarded as reasonable or sinful frequently testified to the narrow and reactionary mind of the interpreters rather than to their self-conquering sense of justice and love.

After all these qualifications, it is, nevertheless, correct to assert that the history of occidental mankind for two thousand years or more was ruled by the problems of humanism—of unity and reason, truth and justice, of how to interpret and how to apply them. Their absolute stringency and unconditional validity were universally recognized and presupposed in all human activities. Not in the sense of being realized in us, since we are sinful instead of being just and truthful. Still less, however, in the sense of an other-worldly separate existence, since the urge for truth and justice arises from our consciousness and drives us forward from within. The Commandments are inherent in our nature and aim beyond our nature at something which has no real existence as yet, but may and should acquire it. The paradoxical character of the fundamental monotheistic concepts is that they are not other-worldly, but "transcend" our reality because they are spiritual. The spirit is not supernatural because it arises from and operates within our nature; but it is more than mere nature, it is human.

And the spirit is one. Whenever we doubt that something is true, we imply that something else, though unknown, must be true, and the search for it is started. Whenever two natural laws are found to conflict with one another, a superior law must be discovered to restrict the other two and to reconcile them. Whenever an engineer builds a machine or a bridge, he trusts that the elements will fit into one another according to his calculation, that they will behave as units of a single system. That the world is a system can never be proved because nobody can measure the whole world. But in practice at least, if not in academic speculation, everybody has to rely on this monotheistic dogma, which alone enables us to think and to act in a coherent manner. With the doctrines of unity and

truth belongs the doctrine of justice. If the infinity of creation manifests itself in an infinite variety of finite beings
coexisting one with another; if each is regarded as a value
because it manifests one idea of the creative force; if they
all are endowed by their maker with the urge for self-realization and the power of achieving it, then justice is the
means of integrating God's creation and giving it peace.
Justice has to comprehend the true values of all the different individual beings and of their coexistence, it has to
allocate to them what they truly require for their self-realization and has to prevent them from taking more. That is
why creation, truth, and justice belong together. Their
seat, however, is not this world, still less another world;
their seat is symbolized as the Kingdom to come, which is
always approaching and never attained, and subjects all
human doings to its supreme judgment and criticism. This
is how religion expresses its sense of the spiritual values
which have their basis in us and are superior to and critical of us.

Conservatives and revolutionists, orthodox believers and
atheists, used to recognize the unconditional claims of
these commandments and to invoke them in support of
their diverse programs. They would admit that they might
fail before this supreme judgment and would try to defend themselves as truthful and just in any particular instance. The belief in, although by no means the obedience
to, the spiritual values, is the very criterion of occidental
civilization. It is the most precarious of all beliefs, it is
practically impossible to be lived up to by mortal beings.
Yet it alone is what makes life human and humane.

No wonder that great thinkers made such gigantic attempts to lighten man's burden. Reason appeared to permeate the life of man and society as described by the
philosophers of the Enlightenment, by Adam Smith and

his contemporaries. They taught that man could build up a world of individual and social harmony by following his reasonable interests within the limits of reasonable moral moderation. Hegel and Marx likewise tried to demonstrate that history, with all its blood and tears, is mysteriously so arranged as to lead in the direction of unity, truth, and justice, and is bound finally to realize them in this world. Nothing can be more wrong than to believe that Marx denied the existence of spiritual values. All his concepts are imbued with a passion for reason and justice which will conquer the world of lies and violence, transform "the Kingdom of Necessity into the Kingdom of Liberty," and establish the "self-realization of man" in the community of the free. Marx's idea of man is entirely in the humanistic tradition. What is peculiar to him is his confidence in the strength of the human forces; he contends that we need not appeal to the abstract commandments of reason and justice but need only describe and promote their concrete growth in the institutions of history. He trusts in the convergence and final coincidence of personal self-realization and social integration through the evolution of communal production and a communal spirit of work. This is an increasingly spiritualized reality; "reality itself urges the idea." For this reason and for this reason only, spiritual values as such are not discussed in Marx's economic and political writings, although they are dealt with in his earlier philosophical works. The spiritual concepts are included in the economic concepts and are therefore invisible to those whose eyes cannot penetrate to the human presuppositions and content of these institutional concepts.

Similarly, some modern philosophies were animated by so strong an optimism that they traced man's knowledge of Truth and Justice to experience. They held that experience teaches the indispensability of truth and justice for man's well-being, and they therefore denied the transcending character of spiritual values. (It is frequently assumed, owing to the abbreviating formulations which American pragmatism uses, that it too belongs to this group. This is a misapprehension because pragmatism assumes the humanistic concept of man as clearly and consciously as the German pragmatist Goethe.) However, the validity of the spiritual values was not only not disputed by empiricism; it appeared too obvious to demand special discussion. Whether aware of it or not, the most widely different social and philosophic movements and tendencies, in spite of all the bitterness of their strife, were dominated by these fundamental concepts of man and life—and prove thereby that they belong to a unitary occidental world.

3. The Disintegration of Humanism

This world, however, had been disintegrating for a long time. When Truth and Justice are represented as being within easy reach of man and society or as a necessary outcome of history, genuine spiritual tension becomes slack, the value of man's present or future existence becomes overrated, and attention is deflected from the things in man that are greater than himself. The consciousness of the supremacy and sublimity of Truth and Justice wanes when they appear not as values that transcend the natural world, but as naturally or historically present. Furthermore, their particular mode of existence was misunderstood; the belief in them as a matter of faith was under suspicion. The search after Truth demands the right of criticism and doubt whenever a statement is unverified. The particular existence of the spiritual values, not as things in reality, but as values belonging to and transcending reality, is not, however, demonstrable in the literal or physical sense of the word. These values are not tangible, they cannot be explained in the sense of being traceable to a cause; their peculiar existence is proved by showing that they are pre-supposed in the reality and activity of man and how they can be seized through symbols. They are therefore easily exposed to criticism and doubt—though no doubt has any meaning if the systematic nature of the world and the one-ness of truth are not assumed. As a result of all these facts, the ruling position of the spiritual values in the conscious-ness of man has been weakened.

But even more important than this is the practical side of the problem. For practical people Christian humanism is the most uncomfortable of all beliefs. It is much easier to promise, and in fact to provide for, security by the nat-ural forces of vitality and power than by a machinery de-signed to co-ordinate and reconcile the just claims of dif-ferent groups. Certainly man and society are more than mere vitality and power—they long for a direction, they seek a goal, and the merely natural organization, when suppressing the differences of directions and goals, sup-presses human nature and brings catastrophe either upon others or itself. But neither is there safety in a society based upon the fundamental recognition of the spiritual side of life because we never attain truth and justice. That these alone are capable of integrating life can never be proved by experience because they are misunderstood, im-properly invoked, and abused by finite men. Life breaks asunder again and again in either type of organization. It is not the goal but the direction, not the success but the attempt, which distinguishes a humanistic from a natural-istic foundation of life. It makes all the difference in the world whether a social order designed to realize justice violates it, or whether a social order flatly denies the idea of a justice superior to any order.

It is in the pursuit of a spiritual direction and attempt, and in the challenge to everybody to do likewise, that life appears worth living. Life is truly human when a man is not only permitted but is expected to stand up for his conviction, and if he happens to dissent, is honored for doing so. The constant need for reinterpreting truth and justice in a constantly shifting world and the relentless fight against the ever-present danger of abuse require that a humanistic society be highly intellectual and make it at the same time highly precarious. It is up to the believers in these spiritual values to make them visible and intelligible to all in concrete symbols of daily life so that everybody may put his faith and pride in them. And in the modern world this applies first of all to the institutions which shape man's social existence and work. It is they that have to convey the spirit of truth and justice and to challenge the response and participation of the people. If the will to reason and right does not speak convincingly through them, if discussion confuses the people instead of enlightening them, if the intellectual aristocracy themselves indulge in undermining the spiritual basis of humanistic society, then occidental civilization is doomed. It lives on the belief in the integrating force of Reason and Right: it cannot outlive this belief, nor can it survive unless its champions are truth-loving and just enough to comprehend the genuine nature and requirements of the people.

Although naturalism is the contrary of humanism, nature is by no means the contrary of the spirit; it is its basis. There can be no justice without a deep comprehension of that natural world which has to be organized and aided by the followers of justice into realizing its human ends. We must recognize the vital requirements of the natural world in order to give it justice and peace. The doctrines of creation, prophecy, and the gospel are not only historically, but logically one, and the doctrine of creation is fundamental to the more sublime later teachings. An utterly alarming situation, therefore, is one in which nature, which really depends on truth and justice for its integration, revolts against them. Nature and the spirit then appear as two inimical principles, whereas in reality nature must be arched over by the spiritual values which, in turn, are rooted in and based on nature. This conflict proves that nature does not feel itself sufficiently respected by those in charge of interpreting and applying the principles of truth and justice. The spirit is not strong, penetrating, and just enough, to build up a comprehensive and solid structure of life.

This situation was that of the German Republic. Its political history, as discussed above, shows that the Republic had not even attempted to form a real power by winning over those who naturally believed less in intellectual progress than in the creative forces of nature. These people represent an element of life which can be neither excluded nor destroyed. It therefore has to be included in a solid structure of the community in an appropriate way. The spirit of German democracy was not truth-loving and just enough towards the representatives of that element. It did not comprehend their particular problems and requirements, their special contribution and character, their dignity, beauty, and rights. Hence, the German Republic could not muster a real block of democratic power, and proved incapable of tackling the fundamental problems of the emergency. This ruinous political mistake concerning the lower middle class conspired with the general intellectual trend of the age in undermining the humanistic basis of civilization. All the conscious creed had been gradually weakened by decades of growing skepticism and positivism. The peasants' belief in nature, although it had found expression in old pagan myths and rites, had for more than a thousand years been incorporated in Christianity and had tacitly recognized the superiority of the spiritual values. Now, however, the peasant faced the failure of the most highly intellectualized state. The spiritual norms of Western civilization had been disintegrating for a long time in their religious form, and were now obviously refuted in their worldly application by the political failure of their advocates. The consequence was that the belief in spiritual values growing from and arching over nature broke down and that the ancient belief in the sacred spontaneity of nature gained new strength and emancipated itself. A new elemental enthusiasm for the integral power of nature arose against what seemed to be the disheartening influence of intellectualism, and appeared to warrant the use of all the natural forces in substituting a "natural" organization of society for the former intellectual disorganization. This impulse coupled with the thirst for vengeance upon those who had professed to base their political structure on truth and justice and had ignominiously missed the truth about the peasants and the justice to them. The most terrible punishment for the political and spiritual failure then took place—a punishment on the spirit, on democracy, on labor, on the Jews, on the universities, on the churches, on all the elements and carriers of a highly intellectual life and of spiritual standards.

4. German Fascism as Interpreted by Itself

This discussion of fascism as anti-humanitarian naturalism can be verified by the interpretations of German fascism given by its own spokesmen. The official pronouncement that "right is what benefits the German people" is often mistaken for an expression of political opportunism,

but it is actually the accepted maxim of German jurispru-
dence and jurisdiction today. As such it justifies the complete exemption from all legal regulations and guarantees
of many innovations regarded as beneficial by the National Socialists, such as the institution of the secret police
and its concentration camps. The same fundamental idea
on the relation of man and justice is expressed in another
official formulation: "Law and the Leader's will are one."
This means that the Leader's will may be substituted for
any written law. It is striking (and was intended to be
so) in a country where every child, under the Hohenzol-
lern Empire, had to learn the anecdote about Frederick
the Great's neighbor, the miller, who rejected the King's
angry claims and reminded him of the fact that there
were judges in Berlin established by the King but independent of him. Another noteworthy incident occurred at
a conference of law professors and judges when the most
authoritative interpreter of the new creed quoted a San-
skrit saying to the effect that "right is what Aryan men find
is right, and wrong is what they reject." This postulates
one branch of the human race as the inspired seat and
source of all higher life, ethical judgment, and conduct.
There can be no conflict between the law and justice, no
doubts on the right of the state such as are characteristic
of the humanistic countries. Right is what the men of this
state find right. There is no judge above them, either on
earth or in heaven. This doctrine is as revolutionary as it
claims to be and springs from a conscious repudiation of
the entire humanistic tradition.

Fascism likes to define itself as anti-liberalism and includes both Christianity and Marxism under the label of
liberalism because they recognize the spiritual elements in
human personality that are beyond the control of political

force. An unusual yet perfectly consistent turn to this drive against liberalism is the Academy for German Historiography's recent proclamation that fascism's rise to power marked the end of the Middle Ages. It included even communism in the principle represented by the Catholic Church—that of the spiritual significance of human life, with the consequent implications for freedom of thought and expression of individuality. The practices of both the medieval Church and communism infringe, however, upon this principle. The fascist statement rightly places the main emphasis on the potential cleavage, implied in that principle, between existing man and the independently given superior spiritual norms. Only in one item is this fascist interpretation fallacious. In its claim to be the rightful heir of the Greek all-inclusive political organization, the city-state, and of the Greek worship of natural beauty, fascism ignores the fundamental fact that Greek culture rests entirely on the values of logos and cosmos. Fascism proclaims that it has to rescue occidental civilization from barbarism. But what remains of that civilization after deducting the urge for the perfection of personal life under the lodestars of truth and justice?

Finally, the self-chosen name of anti-rationalism is another fitting expression of the new principle enunciated by fascism. It does not spurn the services of rational methods as such, but repudiates the predominant position of reasoning, and with it, the authority of the intelligentsia.

It is true that the intellectual preparation and reinterpretation of life necessary for the success of the National Socialists had been brewing for a long time. Many years before Marx optimistically predicted the triumph of labor, Goethe had expressed his grave uneasiness over the future of the spiritual life in Germany. Heinrich Heine, with appalling vision, forecast the translation of the German *Natur* philosophy into national fury, and de Tocqueville even gave sociological analyses of the specific forces that were making for the change from humanism to totalitarianism. They all, however, were completely opposed to what they foresaw. Nietzsche's transvaluation of values has often been cited by friend and foe as inaugurating the movement of rebellion against the old world of Christianity and intellectualism. But it is not sufficient to show that Nietzsche attacked these ideals. The important point is whether he passed over the line of demarcation into the camp of the anti-humanists or remained within the realm of humanistic ethics; his professedly conservative attitude in political questions and his pride in being "a good European" indicate the latter. In the case of Stefan George, whose hymns had glorified the noble blood, it is well known that he chose to die and be buried abroad. No great thinker wanted fascism.

This in a sense makes the case for fascism stronger because it demonstrates how deep the roots of the German fascist movement must go and what strong emotional forces are behind it. It certainly had intellectual precursors and availed itself of intellectual achievements, but in every case it had to adapt them to its own system of valuations. The relationship between Rousseau, Adam Smith, and Jefferson, on the one hand, and democracy on the other, or between Marx and Lenin and the socialist movement, has no analogy in fascism. In its social composition German fascism is anti-intellectual. Of all the revolutions recorded in history, this is the first without an intellectual aristocracy since it relies on the sacred spontaneity of nature and on the unitary current of life and blood through individuals and generations rather

than on the spiritual side of life. In this very strict and
consistent sense fascism is identical with anti-humanism.

5. *Fascist Socialism and Humanistic Socialism*

It is only in connection with this discussion of the spiritual issues that one of the most difficult sociological problems presented by German fascism can be adequately dealt
with. This is the proletarian problem. The social class
that has been the mainstay of fascism is the lower middle
class, with the peasant as its classical representative. Yet
fascism's rise to power was supported by millions of labor
votes, especially from among the unemployed. The strong
influence on fascism of many institutional teachings of
communism has been pointed out above. But it no longer
suffices to explain the easy shift made by these workers
from communism to fascism, now that we have indicated
the sharp contrast in human principles between fascism
and the socialist tradition.

Communism all over the world had greatly contributed
to the existing confusion, not only by focusing attention on
the institutional issues as such and neglecting their human
significance, but by ridiculing the spiritual principles instead of defending and purifying them against those who
distorted them for reactionary purposes. In the same way,
communism had misjudged the psychological obstacles it
had to overcome in order to attract adherents. Though
prolonged unemployment is certainly repugnant to people,
they do not necessarily turn communist—which would
imply adherence to an elaborate system of positive reasoning. They may choose an easier way, one which appeals
to their restless vitality without making any demands
upon their untrained intellectual forces. This does not
mean that one can become a Communist only through the-

oretic instruction; on the contrary, any theoretic instruction, even of students, easily fails if not based on rational principles which have been tested by application. The young generation of the working class, who had never seen a job, were incapable of realizing what a rationally functioning social system was like; they were driven by a revolutionary urge, but without any sense of direction, because that required a rational orientation. The strongly socialist students, who were at the opposite pole from that of the young workers, lost their faith in rational construction as they experienced the absurd contradictions in a political doctrine that was logical in theory but ignorant of reality. Although communism had attached all its hopes to the economic crisis as a practical confutation of capitalism, the crisis did more than disprove capitalism; it shook people's belief in the practicality of a rational pattern for society upon which both capitalism and communism depended. The political system of communism, with its claim to be the rational fulfillment of people's needs, requires men rationally trained through their participation in a rationally working system of life; without this moral and practical training, their reaction to critical situations becomes merely emotional. The prolonged crisis that communism welcomed undermined its humanistic basis, and thereby bred fascism even among the workers.

The same consideration applies to the present socialist or communist tendencies in German fascism. These cannot fail to produce another disillusionment if they are interpreted as a hope for an anti-fascist future. Those who continue to think in terms of two classes and two systems and identify present fascism with capitalism, necessarily view the radical wing of former communist workers and students as forces of communism. But it must be clear by now that this differentiation is neither comprehensive nor profound enough. The Fascists are again much more up-to-date. Their anti-rational ends in no wise estrange them from the use of rational means, and they use them in a very consistent way. The more the true penetration of world and life by reason is barred and man is believed to be biologically fixed, without the power to act on an independent spiritual issue of decisive significance, the more all intellectual energy is concentrated on the techniques of life in the widest sense, from racial hygiene to the techniques of administration and warfare. In this range of subjects economics may well be included, in view of its possible contribution to the aims of fascism. The institutional forms of socialism may prove most adequate for expressing and securing the amalgamation of individuals into the totalitarian organization envisaged by fascism. The purpose of fascist socialism is shown through the frequent references by the party leaders and orators to the socialization of the military company, which had originally been the captain's private enterprise with hired employees as soldiers and rented to the political powers under a booty-sharing system. In the seventeenth century the Prussian state first took over this enterprise, though its character as an enterprise with hired employees was only gradually transformed until the French Revolution proclaimed the nation-in-arms. If the state is, as the Fascists insist, to be in complete control of all activities and decisions—mainly in war since that is the supreme test, but also in peace since the nation must be trained for the "totalitarian war"—it is only logical to include the national economy under this direct control. The state will be really totalitarian only when it has a monopoly in the system of production as well as in the institutions of education, administration, jurisdiction, and warfare. Communism may become the adequate means for fascist ends.

This consistency of socialist forms with fascism does not mean that fascism must necessarily go in this direction and abandon the equally consistent scheme discussed above; still less that it would do so without a class struggle. It is certainly correct to say that the strong socialist tendencies in fascism are indicative of the continued presence of the unsolved class problem. What fascism claims to have done, however, is to have reduced the problem to a technical question of state organization, whereas in a humanistic society it represents the fundamental spiritual issues of liberty and justice. The reduction in scale of the problem is of course combined with a change in significance, as may be seen by the political connotations given to the term socialism. Socialization, in classical socialism and even in its communistic application, is destined to "restore individual property" as the basis of human realization and to lead to the dissolution of the state into a self-governing society—or at least to an approximation to that ideal. To Fascists socialism means the exact contrary: the absorption of man by the state; the supreme end is the perfection of this state.

The same economic institutions may be used in behalf of mutually contradictory ends; their significance depends on the nature of the living forces animating them. The institutional identity underlying the spiritual opposition between humanistic and fascist socialisms proves this. But fascist totalitarianism must not be regarded as a possible step to communism; its economic forms cannot be filled with different spiritual contents, as a mistaken materialism assumes. It does not depend on an arbitrary political decision whether the socialist forms shall be serviceable to one or the other of the two programs. To establish or to remove socialist forms of production is infinitely easier than to build up again a humanistic tradition of thought and sentiment once it has been interrupted; and also to interrupt this tradition is, as many historical examples show, infinitely easier than to build it up again. Communist totalitarianism, prepared to renounce its Western humanistic heritage for two or three generations as a consequence of its own despotism, is surely closer to fascist socialism than the latter is to the humanistic self-realization of man taught by classical socialism.

VI

MODERNIZED DEMOCRACY

A. The Key Position of Democracy

ANY ANALYSIS of fascism is necessarily a criticism of existing democracy, in a sense which includes communism
in democracy because of its derivation and programmatic
goal. The defects of democracy made for the rise of fascism, spiritually—through the decay of the moral and intellectual basis of democracy—and politically, through the
inadequate application of the democratic principles to the
propertied producers in Russia and Germany.

To criticize democracy is not to champion fascism. It
only means that the fascist reaction was the inevitable outcome, given the defects of democracy. The error of democracy was its narrow-mindedness and injustice to the presence of one necessary element in the social structure. This
does not mean that this element in itself is flexible and
comprehensive enough to rebuild society as a whole on a
new basis. From the standpoint of ideology, the neglected
element was the sanctity of nature as expressed in the
inflated doctrine of the sacred race and soil; in a general
sense, it was man overflowing with a vitality derived from
the direct contact with nature who revolted against intellectual misunderstanding. From the standpoint of social
classes, the neglected group was the peasantry and small
bourgeoisie who conceived of their own group character

as comprised in that symbol of vitality, and claimed to represent the true and only possible foundation of society. But this group, important as it is, is incapable of rebuilding and integrating a modern, diversified, and intellectual society as a whole. This one element cannot furnish a genuine human solution to the crucial problems of modern industry, finance, and trade, except in merely technical terms; it has no true understanding of what these other elements represent and demand in life. Nor can it even attempt to approach the problems of truth and justice and of what they signify under conditions of modern life. Democracy failed to solve the problems of this one indispensable element and thereby precipitated the emancipation of the latter from democracy. But this does not mean that the fascist attempt to build a new comprehensive structure on the basis of this particular element could be justified.

Two analogies, which are more than mere analogies, may serve to clarify the issue. The engineer who builds a machine has to calculate all the elements concerned and to combine them skillfully in the machine. If he fails to do so he risks an explosion. The task of applied science is to study the forces of nature and allocate to them their appropriate place. If properly treated, the forces of nature are wholesome; if mistreated, they turn destructive. An explosion does not prove that nature is right, but that the scientific intelligence has not lived up to its task. Such a refutation of an engineer's activities is not a refutation of the spiritual principle behind it, nor is it a justification of the blind and savage destructiveness of unspiritualized nature. The eruption of the natural element punishes him who has inadequately applied the spiritual principle and proves to him the errors of his ways, but it supplies no positive principle of its own. Thus fascism appears as a punishment of a democracy disloyal to its purport, but not as a new possibility for human life since it rejects the supreme spiritual significance and innate demands of human life. The natural element is an element in, but not a guiding principle of, life and society.

The second analogy is even more illuminating. When in the Bible the Philistines conquer the Jews, this does not prove that the Philistines were right, but that the Jews were wrong. It is not the Philistines who matter; it is the Jews. They are the chosen people, but not in the same sense that the German race claims, in fascism, to be sanctified by virtue of its very nature. The Jews are elect because God chose to reveal the spiritual character of His creation unto them and through them. This quality of being elect is far from guaranteeing that their behavior and activities will always be holy; it proves historically to be rather a curse than a privilege. It means that greater responsibility is laid upon them than upon the others and that their failure results in the disaster of mankind. Right is neither what Jews find right, nor what benefits the Jewish people; right is what helps to bring genuine harmony into the diversity of God's creation, whether or not the Jews understand that and live up to it. The heathen cannot know, but the Jews ought to know. The heathen are used as blind tools of the Divine wrath, but the Jews should be the conscious servants of Divine justice. Their righteousness makes the world prosper; but their injustice destroys the world. Their prophets are sent not to glorify but to chastise the people and to announce the invasion of the Philistines. Thus the coming of fascism proves that democracy did not give the world the justice and the peace it needs and that the believers in the spiritual principle were not equal to their task. For it is the adherents to the spiritual principle who matter, and their failure is a disaster to human life.

Two different forms of social organization had been proposed during the rise of the modern world as the means of securing liberty for man: the individualistic form, previous to the development of large-scale technology; and the socialistic form when this latter development had occurred. Apparently opposed to each other as these two forms are, their conflict can be resolved by reducing each to its particular set of conditions—the individualistic form to the realm of individual work, the collectivistic form to the realm of collective work. This correlation reveals the precise parallelism in institutions and the identity in spirit of the two programs. In both instances, liberty as an instrument of human self-realization is provided for by a correspondence between the form of ownership and the form of work that prevents any alien rule over the working people from prevailing. In each case, equality is established with liberty for all; that does not, however, preclude individual differentiation. The primary question of social integration and security is solved through liberty; individual activities under the first system are regulated by the free market, collective activities under the second system culminate in the planned economy. Both systems assume fundamentally the same type of man striving through his work for the expression of his rational and vital forces. The institutional contrast between the two systems held the attention of several generations and was considered by them to be unreconcilable; but these differences melt away as the essential identity between the two becomes visible in the light of the truly fundamental issues. Small-scale individualism and classical socialism turn out to be the two simple forms of democracy.

When the small shop, the basis of democratic individ-

ualism, vanished from many important fields, the individualistic organization lost the human effect and significance
it had had formerly, at least within the working place. The
survival of individual liberty outside the working place,
in public and private life, must not be overlooked, of
course. The application of the individualistic principle
to the sphere of communal work had a dual effect. Socially,
it destroyed that coincidence of the forms of organization
and work which makes for democratic liberty and equality, and it led to capitalistic rule. Economically, it prevented the structure of production from having the adaptability and flexibility upon which the success of a free
market depends; it thereby destroyed economic integration and security and led to the crisis. A remedy was at
hand, however. It consisted of the reorganization of the
total social structure on communal lines. The intermediary
phase of private property was to be a necessary historical
link between these two democratic systems, both of which
rested on the belief in human reason and values. But when
the economic and social structure remained diversified instead of becoming completely transformed through universal large-scale production, an exclusively collectivistic
organization became as inadequate as an exclusively individualistic one.

In this situation the Communists decided to impose by
force on the people the uniform pattern which history had
refused, but which they believed to be the only solution.
They felt that regard for individual liberty led to capitalistic domination and chaos and counted upon the people's
preference for security guaranteed by an unassailably
strong dictatorship. They supplemented the dictatorship
by the somewhat nebulous prospect of a proletarian liberty
in a remote future. Their position is doubtless more realistic than that of the true and honest democrats today who

exalt spiritual freedom but do not give much thought to physical subsistence. Yet the Communists are not realistic enough. Since they are unaware of the depths of humanity, they ignore the practical value of the liberty that they are prepared to throw away. Their error is less visible, but therefore more dangerous than that of the romanticists of liberty. The appeal of the promised proletarian security is not strong enough to entice the middle-class laggards. These have been taught by the Communists, the rightful heirs of liberalism, that universal liberty is impossible and that they should submit to a proletarian pattern for the sake of their own security. Why should they not, building on their own particular sense of liberty, set up their own system of security and impose it upon the others? Fascism is the penalty paid by the Marxists, both socialist and communist, for their betrayal of liberty. It is a punishment, not a realization.

This entire analysis has been pursued in terms of the democratic doctrines and has given factual evidence that they are capable of doing justice to the middle-class problem, which the traditional formulations of intellectual and economic progress neglect. This proves that a democratic program holds the key position if it is humanly interpreted and understood in the light of the assumptions which were considered self-evident by Smith and Marx and their successors. Those who adhere to this democratic philosophy bear the greatest responsibility, because their methods of procedure are superior to those of others and access to the truth has been revealed to them. It is up to them to make use of this and to give the world the peace that comes when justice prevails.

B. The Normative and Conditional Character
of the Democratic Program [1]

All the elements of the solution to the political crisis are comprised in the traditional liberal and socialist systems, and nothing but a slight turn of thought is required to reveal this.

Both original democracy and classical socialism make their appearance as theories of a necessarily ordained society. The superiority in competition of independent producers and the harmonious regulation of their division of labor by the operations of the market are presented by Adam Smith as natural and therefore as facts. It is true that legal freedom of personal life, property, and trade is explicitly demanded by him, since it did not exist when he wrote. But then the rest follows with logical necessity. Nevertheless, nobody doubts that the Smithian theory aims at more than a mere description of reality under certain legal conditions and that it involves an exposition of the norms of social life. The very name of the theory of harmony clearly indicates the union of objective and normative considerations. This most influential doctrine stresses the need for certain legal guarantees of liberty and shows how true human liberty and social integration will automatically arise under pre-technical conditions. This concurrence of objective and normative analyses was easily credible to a generation that could believe in the natural goodness and progress of mankind. But even when one discounts this belief, as less fortunate generations must do, the validity of Smith's normative analysis as such persists unimpaired under its assumptions.

[1] This section serves to refine and systematize the methodical approach to our problem; it adds nothing to the material and may be skipped by those who are less interested in theoretical analysis.

Disbelief in the theory of harmony casts doubt on the necessary correspondence between reality and ideality and on the automatic realization of the good. But the good, whether realized or not, still remains as desirable as ever.

The norm of individual property in individual work is certainly not applicable to the rising collective type of work, and it is more than questionable whether a man of Smith's intelligence and character would have adhered to his institutional norm when its basis was crumbling, as his successors have done and as the rising class of big plant owners was all too anxious to do. A scholar does not generalize a scientific statement beyond the sphere of its well-defined or implicit historical presuppositions and apply it where it does not belong. But despite the historical changes since Smith's day, his purely normative doctrine retains its validity within the framework of its own clean-cut assumptions: individual property belongs to individual work, whether individual work prevails everywhere as Smith assumed, or whether it is confined to a limited field.

The same mode of thinking is even more marked in classical socialism. Its central principle, historical necessity, states that the causal necessity of the historical process is identical with what a wholesome social structure requires. Where this doctrine differs from Smith's is obvious, but not relevant to the point under discussion. According to Smith, the good, simply because it is naturally present, is capable of being realized immediately once we give it the easy legal aid on which it depends. According to Marx, the full realization of the good is only the goal of the historical process, and the preceding historical phases partake in the good only through their necessary contribution toward that happy end; that contribution may, however, be concealed from uninformed contemporaries by blood and tears. The essential feature of this doctrine is,

as in Smith, the fortunate concurrence of the causally necessary and the morally desirable. Marx called his doctrine
scientific socialism because it spurns all appeals to the
moral sensibility of the ruling classes and describes the
necessary growth of the forces of good as industry under-
goes a transformation. But there is no doubt that socialism
is interested in the growth of the forces of good as such.
It not only predicts but welcomes the necessary self-realization of the workingman, the necessary "skip from the
Kingdom of Necessity to the Kingdom of Liberty," the
necessary withering away of the state which marks in this
doctrine the "end of pre-history" and the beginning of
truly human history.

Whatever the secondary grounds of Marx's personal
agnosticism and post-Marxian atheism may be, his thought
is determined by his belief in harmony as the inevitable
goal of an infallible historical process. The minor differences and the major similarities between the two democratic systems of Smith and Marx may be summarized in
two phrases: the doctrine of natural harmony, and that of
historical harmonization. Since there is no automatic realization of the good, the theory of harmony has to be
dropped in Marx as in Smith, and the coincidence of the
causally necessary with the good has to be given up. But
Marx's theory of the good, when its assumptions are rigor-
ously stated, is still tenable: the planned communal organization belongs to the communal type of work. For the
validity of this formulation it does not matter whether this
type of work prevails everywhere as Marx himself assumed
and the proletarian class interest is anxious to anticipate,
or whether it is restricted to a certain section of production.

One should distinguish the objective from the normative

approach to social problems in order to comprehend the particular structure of the latter. As long as the normative analysis seemed to be included in the objective analysis it has remained more or less invisible. This book has been guided by the principle of having the pattern of social and property organization correspond to the pattern of work. This is a normative statement because it gains significance only through its implied reference to the experiences and wants of different types of workers. The purely objective approach does not explicitly formulate this relationship because it seeks to prove that a certain condition exists and that a certain consequence will necessarily follow. By skipping the medial links in the chain of thought, a vulgar presentation directly arrives at the free play of forces taught by Smith and at the socialization of the means of production taught by Marx. Now it is true that Smith and Marx taught these doctrines, but it is also true and of far greater importance that they taught them as consequences of certain assumptions regarding the type of work and workers whose destined predominance they attempted to prove. Given certain facts about the type of work and workers, the free play of economic forces or the socialization of the means of production will be necessitated.

An accurate formulation of Smith's doctrine in purely objective terms is that the nature of society demands the free play of forces owing to the existing prevalence of individual work. In normative terms it is that an individualistic organization is most suited to individual work. This contains a conditional element and a possible limitation upon the prevalence of individual work and upon the individualistic organization appropriate to it. The complete formulation of socialism in purely objective terms is that socialization of the means of production is the goal of history because communal work will prevail. In normative terms it is that communal organization is best fitted to communal work. This contains a conditional element and a possible limitation upon the prevalence of communal work and upon the communal organization appropriate to it. When the objective approach fails owing to the invalidity of its assumptions, the advantages of the normative method become apparent, since it enables one to present the classical doctrines of liberalism and socialism in a form which indicates the conditions and limitations under which they operate. The objective approach leans on the use of positive and absolute terms, the normative method on the use of conditional terms.

The difference between the two has made world history. In the conflict between adherence to individual property in individual work and devotion to the free play of economic forces as an all-inclusive rule, capitalism decided for the latter and abandoned the principle of liberty in work while preserving civil liberties. Confronted with a choice between collective organization of collective work and wholesale socialization of all means of production, communism decided for the totalitarian state of enforced socialization. An examination of the differences between the objective and the normative approaches leads one to give up the "objective" approach as theoretically invalid and practically full of political difficulties: capitalism encounters socialism, the renewed form of democracy; communism encounters fascism, the enemy of all liberty. The normative method of making conditional statements concerning political programs and the contingencies on which they depend offers us the only way we have of steering our course clear-eyed and fully aware of all the problems.

C. DEMOCRACY IN A DIVERSIFIED WORLD

1. Liberty and Equality

The logic of our argument leads to organizational diversification for a diversified society. History has not chosen to preserve the individual type of work as the all-prevailing one and has undermined the free play of economic forces by means of the class struggle and the economic crisis. But history has also chosen not to realize the collective type of work as the all-prevailing one—particularly in farming—and has thereby provoked the fascist reaction against communism. The simple logical solution of the problem put by history is a diversified property system for a diversified structure of work; each group of workers is granted a communal or individual organization of liberty, depending upon the nature and requirements of its work. Each is to confine its particular program to its particular field without encroaching upon the others. This is the liberty that gives each individual the possibility of self-expression; this is the equality and the peace that come through justice.

At one moment during the troubles of the Great War and the post-war times this ideal seemed near realization and the world held its breath. This was when a new Russia emerged from the catastrophe of war and defeat as "the state of the workers and the peasants." Hammer and sickle became the new national emblem and symbolized the equal rights of the two groups that had fought side by side. They had united in order to end the war and overthrow the ruling classes, the feudal landlords and industrialists, who were responsible for war and defeat in foreign policy and for suppression and exploitation at home. Their aim was to build this state of the workers and peasants by giving the workers a socialist organization of industry and the peasants individual ownership in the lands they cultivated. They formed an irresistible combination; as the true champions of justice they attacked the world of injustice. But the world was able to breathe again when injustice conquered, the formidable alliance was broken from within, and the glorious program of the state of workers and peasants was dropped. The opportunity to do away with the liberty rights of the illiterate peasants was shrewdly seized, and on the ruins of the noblest dream the proletarian imperialists erected the totalitarian state of enforced proletarianization as "the first workers' state in history." This change of title symbolizes the tragic betrayal of the peasants and suggests the subsequent punishment; the first title had conveyed the entire logic of democracy in one brief phrase.

There are a number of current ideologies which attempt to cover up this weak spot by proving either that justice is not feasible for practical reasons or that justice is something other than justice. All these arguments fall to the ground upon close inspection and strict definition. Some discussion of them may therefore help to clarify the norms of democracy. The most widespread of these arguments is connected with the notion of equality, which is certainly one of the vital criteria of democracy, and which in the philosophy of socialism appears as the principle underlying the classless society. The question arises whether the side-by-side position of two or more groups impairs the condition of equality and classlessness, and particularly whether the survival of propertied peasants side by side with industrial workers does not preserve or restore the class structure. Now such groups must not be mistaken for a hierarchy of classes. Classes are groups in the same field that are related to one another, but on different levels, such as the feudal landlords and the peasant-serfs who cultivate their lands, or the capitalists and laborers in modern industry. These class relations are by definition contrary to equality and democracy. Those groups that are on the same social level, but follow different patterns in different fields, are not classes, and their coexistence is consistent with any scheme of equality. The distinction we have drawn between individual property confined to the owner's own unit of work and private property stresses the democratic nature of individual property and shows that all men could be individual owners at the same time—something which is impossible under a regime of private property. An individual's ownership in his unit of individual work certainly differs in pattern and quality from the communal ownership of industrial workers in their units of communal work, but the one is not superior to the other in rank, power, or income. Uniformity of social pattern is not required for a society to be classless.

A classless society would be socially uniform only if the spontaneous course of economic history resulted in the establishment of a uniform pattern of work in all fields. This contingency is logically possible, but to an unbiased observer of society not too probable, because the spontaneity of history is not very likely to wipe out all existing diversities in favor of only one pattern. If a plurality of types is logically the probable result for the future as it has been for the past, democratic equality will be realized through the parity of different patterns in different fields. In that case, all plans for complete uniformity of the social pattern are revealed as instruments of group imperialism, be it focused in the social-economic sphere as in communism, or in the biological sphere as in German fascism. It is very unfortunate that Marx believed in the trend toward uniformity of the economic evolution and as a consequence identified democratic equality with social uniformity. The Communists, by taking Marx's doctrine without any qualifications and forcing it upon a reluctant society, have disguised proletarian imperialism as the will to social justice and democratic equality. In a diversified social structure equality is not realized by uniformity but by parity.

The abuse of the ideal of equality for purposes of domination through a confusion between equality and uniformity is strikingly exemplified in the demand that the "contradiction between city and country" be abolished. Insofar as this simply means that rural backwardness, wherever it obtains, should be overcome by education and technical training, one cannot object. Moreover, since some differences in the social system may no longer have a functional justification and may be abused by the privileged groups, a sweeping defense of all existing differences may very well serve as the means to refuse equal rights to all groups. But just as the idea of diversity is exposed to possible abuse, so is that of equality. When the Communists proclaim that the contradiction between city and country must be resolved, they do not simply mean that an equal level of intelligence and rights should be striven for, but that the rural and urban patterns of existence should be made as nearly identical as possible. The coexistence of two different patterns in different fields is considered undesirable; a difference therefore becomes at once a "contradiction," an intolerable cleavage, and must be eliminated. They regard differences between individuals, between the sexes, between city and country, as dangerous to the integration of society; equalization is their program. In their eyes, equality prevails when all but one human possibility are prohibited and destroyed. They transform the doctrine of equality into an instrument of suppression. They do not understand the meaning of harmony. In music a unison does not make a harmony; for that different voices are required. Now diversity in itself is not sufficient to create a harmony; man's task is to make it so. A song or a marriage or a scenery may be harmonious, but not the march of a regiment of soldiers, whatever its use and merits. The world has been created diversified so that there may be not self-love, but a love for others that will make us grow beyond the limits of our narrow selves. The most beautiful poems of Goethe convey this thought, and so does the philosophy of William James.

2. *Organization and Integration*

A. ECONOMIC INTEGRATION

Again, however, the question of integration is crucial. Integration and security through liberty is a matter of life and death for democracy. It is easily attained in the case of individual property and individual work through the regulating power of the impersonal market. Under a regime of universal communal production and management, it is achieved through the unitary plan for the entire economy; this is the climax of deliberate co-operation. Can a diversified social structure provide economic integration? Since the crisis of the market is caused by the presence of big collectively operated plants, the planned economy can succeed only if it comprehends all spheres of the economic order and is not subject to interference from independent outside movements. Hence, the uniformity that was rejected as a social condition of democracy seems to be necessary as the technical condition of its economic integration. But this is an error. The free market and the plan are the instruments of economic integration in individualistic and socialistic democracies respectively; although opposed to each other logically, they are not mutually exclusive. A technically elaborate analysis of this point is beyond the scope of this book,[2] but the possibility of combining the two schemes may be suggested by two considerations—one of a factual, the other of a theoretical nature.

The first important thing to note is that the unsuspected example of Soviet Russia herself has shown that a planned economy may have many market elements. Russia's combination of the two principles has by no means been as successful as it could easily have been if the true nature of the market mechanism, apart from its social effects under capitalistic conditions, had been mastered. Despite this fact, the economic system in Russia is very remote from the popular image of communism, whether glorified or detested, as a system in which the planning authorities prescribe all individual activities and allocate all products to the consumers as they wish. The truth is that consumers buy, in many instances, according to their own preference; the producing trusts pay wages to the workers and interest to the central bank on their loans and are obliged to have an eye to making a profit on their invested capital—and so on. The result is that the familiar phenomena of the market are manifest again; their social significance is different owing to the different structure of property. Whether or not the particular Russian way of putting the market into their planned economy as a partial regulator is sound in detail, is aside from the main point. The Russians, in any case, assert that this combination is both logically sound and practically necessary.

It should be noted that the demand for a product is not compulsory nor ascertained by statistical inquiries, as popular belief would have it, but is often abandoned to the

[2] See the references given in footnote on page 194.

private decisions of customers in the market. Parallel to this is the allocation of workers to the various industries by allowing most individuals to respond to fluctuating wage rates instead of using compulsion. By far the most significant point for the present discussion, however, is the almost free market for farm products. Since the industrial trusts are state-owned, their profits belong to the state as the community of all workers. The income derived from the sale of farm products, however, goes directly to the farm collectives; and the collectives of course produce what the preferences of consumers indicate to be most profitable. What the Soviet plan docs is to estimate demand and output, to regulate finances and taxes, and in most instances to reserve materials, labor, and money for the completion or construction of additional industries. In cases where discrepancies occur between the plan and the actual result, sudden tax prices, rationing, and other administrative devices have to be used. The system as a whole is far from being consistent in theory and frictionless in practice. But its fundamental value springs from the principle behind the attempt to reconcile the economic plan and the free market through a combination of their virtues. This is not affected by the attempt proceeding more or less at random and by way of trial and error.[3]

This empirical argument of ours, based on an appeal to the authority of Russian practice, must be supplemented by some theoretical considerations. The breakdown of the market as the regulating agency of a free economy is due to the eruptive fits created by the dynamic forces in finance and technology (see page 69). Slow gradual changes of demand and technique can be digested and regulated by the

[3] The best presentation of this experimental economic system is that by Barbara Wootton, *Plan or No Plan?* 1934. It is very critical in detail but fundamentally sympathetic.

market: revolutionary changes cannot. The economic crisis, whatever its nature and roots, springs from an economy based on modern finance, industry, and transportation; a society which consisted exclusively of craftsmen and peasants would never know it. If farming today is entangled in the crisis and if the sudden changes in the methods of its production and its outputs have definitely contributed to the outbreak and intensity of the crisis, this fact only strengthens our argument. It is only under the influence of finance and industry, especially engineering, that farming is made dynamic; it is not dynamic of its own accord. The true seat of danger to the stability of the national and world market is in the domain of revolutionary progress in technique and organization, the stronghold of capitalism: finance and the heavy industries. Hence all dynamic changes in any field of production depend upon the co-operation of technology and finance. That is why a deliberate and direct regulation of their activities is needed. A plan for them conceived of in qualitative terms as well as the indispensable money terms would regulate indirectly the possible dynamic changes in all fields; the traditional flow of everyday production and consumption would be regulated by the operations of the market alone.

Now it is not by mere chance that the economic differentiation between the actively dynamic, market-breaking and the traditional, market-abiding trades coincides with the technological differentiation between large and small enterprises and with the social differentiation between propertyless workers operating capitalistic enterprises and independent producers managing their own non-capitalistic activities. The various differentiations coincide because they describe various aspects of the same fundamental phenomenon. If universal small-scale production was effectively regulated by the market, there is no reason why the remaining fields of this type, which are obviously non-dynamic, should require a direct planned control to-day. And if the big plants command a productive power that could in the past overthrow the stability of propertied producers, make them propertyless, and at the same time overthrow the stability of the market, they evidently need communal organization and planned management. The full development of our principles leads to the conclusion that the way to integrate a pluralistic democratic economy is to combine centralized planned control in the dynamic fields with a decentralized free market in the non-dynamic fields. Or, to put it differently, an all-inclusive plan embraces many large sections of free individual activities which, owing to their non-dynamic techniques, supply under given conditions a more or less known, stable, and gradually increasing output. The fact that free markets may be deliberately influenced by indirect devices such as interest rates, partial monopolies, taxes, and tariffs, is no peculiarity of a planned economy; this is a feature of any economic policy and does not affect the free-market character of the fields concerned. Thus a pluralistic democratic society can be planned which gives every worker what he needs—the workers in the fields of individual work their individual liberty and property, the workers in the fields of communal work their communal liberty and property, and all the people the security of a stable system based on the planned management of communally owned fields.

B. SOCIAL AND SPIRITUAL INTEGRATION

Of course economic integration, in the sense of undisturbed exchange and co-operation in the division of labor, does not suffice by itself. Some visible unity must pervade the whole pluralistic social structure and give its various parts the consciousness of cohesion, of belonging together despite their differences. The question arises whether individualistic and socialistic sections of the social structure would agree to live side by side and whether the institutional gap between them can be prevented from becoming a fundamental cleavage. This entire book has attempted to answer that question. In a diversified society the imposition of a uniform pattern means either the death of a particularly significant group or an explosive revolt. It is in institutional and human diversity that the spiritual unity of justice and liberty is expressed and symbolized. The conflict between the individualistic and socialistic patterns can be resolved once it is seen that they are related to the differences in technical and human patterns.

The same fundamental ideal when applied to different patterns of life demands correspondingly different forms of realization. Uniformity in a naturally diversified world is the obvious product of suppression. There is no justice without liberty, and no liberty without justice. None of the appeals to liberty, equality, justice, and peace is immune to abuse and sophistication, but nothing in the profound complexity of human life ever can be, as this book amply proves. Yet these ideals remain the polestars of human life. Political responsibility consists in realizing them through concrete institutions as the inner urge for them arises from the concrete experiences and needs of toiling men. The task of democratic statesmanship is not to utter hollow sermons on morality, but to offer concrete institutional goals that will confirm the righteous claims of the people and challenge their capabilities and their devotion to the common cause of social liberty and justice. Social liberty and justice is the foundation of democracy.

What political democracy needs first of all is a power

to build up and defend the integrated kingdom of diversified rights. The constructive task is to find out how to make the particular claims of the various groups compatible with and helpful to each other, and how to unify them through a leading principle which will embrace these different claims as partial realizations of itself and permeate them with its spirituality. The object should be to attain an integration based on the equality of the rights of the different groups in the community. Both Russia and Germany were given unique opportunities for accomplishing this, but in both cases the sponsors of justice and equality succumbed to temptation. The memory of their failure acts as a handicap to any renewed democratic attempt.

The task of renewing democracy is not made lighter by the dogmatists who insist on the scientific truth of their antiquated ideologies. We are told today, as we were ten, thirty, and fifty years ago, that independent farmers are a dying class, that they have no principle upon which to organize, etc. Even scholars repeat today as an article of faith the disastrous words of Marx: "On agriculture, big industry has the most revolutionary effect, for it destroys the bulwark of the old society, the peasant. . . . The management most lazy in its clinging to habit [4] and most irrational is replaced by deliberate technological application of science." "Small property in land creates a class of barbarians which stands half outside of society and unites

[4] The Marxian term *gewohnheitsfaul* is unfamiliar in German. Literally translated it would mean "habitually lazy." However, Marx is not very likely to have meant this, and we prefer the milder interpretation and translation above. On the other hand, the American edition of the *Kapital* by Eden and Cedar Paul (p. 546), in writing simply "old-fashioned," takes all the spice out of the passage. *Faul* means in English either "lazy" or "putrid."

all the rawness of primitive forms of social life with all the agony and misery of civilized countries." [5]

This attitude of mingled pity and contempt toward the peasants has dominated all Marxian literature from those early days on. It has been based on Marx's forecast of economic ruin for the independent farmers, who would soon be worked and starved half to death and would become too miserable to struggle for their liberation of their own accord. Hence they would need the guidance of the class-conscious workers. The transformation of the land and the other means of production into social property, as the Marxians saw it "will liberate not only the proletarians but the whole of mankind. But this transformation can be the work of the working class only," because all other classes stand for private property.[6] According to Kautsky, the peasants "have never been capable of maintaining their interests of their own accord. They are less capable of doing so today than ever." [7] In his opinion, the agrarian population "decreases in number, strength, intelligence, property, and with that the land and the farms must decay. There is no possibility for the peasant to recover." [8] "The more the capitalistic interests and forms of property conflict with the true requirements of agriculture, the less capable is agriculture of developing the necessary forces and germs of reorganization of its own accord, the more agriculture needs the impetus of the revolutionary forces of industry. . . . The proletariat cannot liberate itself without liberating the agrarian population too." [9] Lenin

[5] *Das Kapital*, Vol. I, section on "Big industry and agriculture," page 470 of the German edition, and Vol. III, part 2, summary of the chapter on ground rent, page 347 of the German edition.

[6] *Program of Erfurt*, 1891.

[7] *Commentary to the Program of Erfurt*, 1892, part 5, section 4.

[8] *Agrarfrage*, p. 294.

[9] *Ibid.*, p. 295.

says: "The poor peasantry can only emancipate itself from capitalism by joining the labor movement. . . . The industrial proletariat alone is capable of conducting a determined mass struggle." [10] The Communists today like to speak of the "liquidation of the peasantry," as they would of liquidating a bankrupt business in order to build up something else. This is a more revealing phrase than the more formal statement that the peasants can be "liberated" only by the workers. In short, the peasants are "irretrievably doomed," "decaying," "starving," incapable of sending their children to school and of organizing themselves.[11] Consequently, the workers must take care of them politically and economically. Never was there a more conceited and more pernicious ideology.[12]

Against these doctrines stand the facts. The "individualism" of the farmers is neither abstract nor irrational; it represents the liberty acquired through property-ownership of the workingman and his equality with his neighbors. They are his neighbors, not his competitors, because the ruin of one would not benefit the others; their liberty and equality directly engender the spirit of co-operation in all matters pertaining to their mutual benefit; the opportunities for co-operation range all the way from defense against the natural elements and enemies through the positive works of irrigation and drainage to entertain-

[10] "The Workers' Party and the Peasantry," *Selected Works*, Vol. I, pages 54-67.

[11] See above, page 131.

[12] The climax is reached by the foremost Marxian writer in the United States, Lewis Corey, *The Crisis of the Middle Class*, 1935, who indicates his ideas on the organization of agriculture as follows (page 268): What is imperative is "the formation of unions of farm laborers, tenants, and poorer independent farmers including industrial workers in the small towns who are in a strategic position in relation to industry and agriculture"—the farmers' unions are to include industrial workers—"and their representation in a labor party," by no means in a farmer-labor party.

ment and education and have recently been enlarged to meet the demands of modern technique. As a result, practically no farmer in an advanced country has been unorganized for many years, and the scope of their organizations and the efficiency of their farms is constantly growing. They suffer, to be sure, from the disorganization of the capitalistic market as all classes do, but this does not paralyze their ability to organize and act co-operatively. In short, their individualism means a community that defends and develops the individual independence of its members.

Kautsky had written of the reactionary sentiment which the small peasantry easily develops.[13] What are the facts? They are most impressive in the United States where Jefferson's heritage has been passed on from one insurgent generation to the next, where the great majority of all politically progressive and radical movements of practical importance have come from the western farmers, not from labor. It is true that the farmers' panaceas were often very inadequate. But their political analysis from Lincoln on of what they called the "money power" anticipated by many decades the Marxist analysis of "finance capitalism"—the amalgamation of banking capital with, and its rise above, organized industrial capital. Their attempt to build up a true farmer-labor democracy in the northern states of the West is fascinating just because it springs from practice. Of course one should not expect to find true for the old countries what has been true for American farmers in vast areas where their fathers had come as pioneers. In France, however, half the nation are small peasants to this day, extremely modest and conservative in the midst of the capitalistic world, but certainly not without cultural am-

[13] *Sozialisierung der Landwirtschaft,* page 22.

bitions and tastes and not without a stubborn loyalty to
the political ideas of the Revolution that gave them their
lands. Jaurès, the great leader and martyr of French socialism, was regularly sent to the Chamber of Deputies by
the practically unanimous vote of a constituency which
consisted half of workers and half of peasants, and more
than half of the voters of his party are peasants today as
then. This spontaneous integration of the two pillars of
democratic society in one party is the hope of democracy.
In Germany, the most highly regarded of the peasants,
those in the northwestern corner of the country between
the frontiers of Denmark and Holland, had for many decades under the Empire elected progressives as their deputies to Parliament and had made a true stronghold of
democracy before both capital and labor turned the political aggression created by the crisis against them and drove
them to fascism. But an even more impressive example
is that of the peasant democracies of Switzerland, Holland,
and Scandinavia. To call even these farmers barbarians
is a stupendous venture on the part of supposedly scientific critics. These farmers have thriven, even in the crisis,
by virtue of extreme flexibility and technical skill, and
in spite of grave uneasiness regarding the future of their
sales abroad.[14] They refuse to give the slightest indication
of moral or economic decay. Foremost of all stand the
Scandinavian states with the highest average standard of

[14] Above all, the Danish sales in the English market meet with political discrimination, which is the intended effect of the preferential
system established in the British Empire by the conference of Ottawa.
Consequently, the Danes are becoming increasingly dependent on sales
to Germany, which may eventually jeopardize their economic and political independence and the social structure interwoven with both, unless
something is done to reverse the trend. This consideration lays a grave
responsibility on the English and should be a major concern of an opposition alive to its democratic task.

education and the lowest rate of crime. Not by mere chance are they closest of all countries to the ideas of democratic humanism developed in this book. For many years they have been steadily and vigorously governed by coalitions of their workers and their peasants. They have remained immune to this day to the lure of neighboring fascism, because the workers refused to break the coalition even where they attained the absolute majority for themselves. Nobody knows what the future has in store. But the achievements of all these years in the midst of the European troubles is already a significant fact in itself. It deserves public attention all the more because a constantly growing Marxian literature, prompted by some unintelligible instinct of destruction and self-destruction, seeks to obscure it.

The leading groups of European peasants have also contributed an important institutional idea to the integration of a pluralistic democratic scheme. This institution is the co-operative. Through it individual farms partake in the advantages of large-scale trading and the use of machines wherever they would be incapable of doing so in economic isolation. The co-operatives are of course instruments of individual management and serve individual interests (see page 42). They supplement, strengthen, and preserve the individual farm by providing it with the main acquisitions available to its collective rival. Yet by doing so they form a kind of bridge to that other section of the democratic structure where for technological reasons the communal pattern prevails. They are therefore an integrating element of the first importance; they may even be a dynamic element capable of gradually effecting a reconstruction of the total economic order. Growing as they do out of the self-interest of individual farmers, they may very well bring about a shift from individual to co-operative activities if technical changes should make this desirable. Whether or not this is likely, it is certainly possible, and the possibility of a spontaneous change of pattern is what matters for democracy. The collective pattern as such is not the objectionable thing in the communist farm policy, but its application where neither the people concerned nor the technique of production require it. Even if the co-operatives were to become managing units, this would not make them communistic; for the free decisions of free people in their own affairs has nothing in common with compulsion in behalf of objectives imposed from without. It is a fortunate safeguard for democracy to have at hand institutions that will, in case of need, be helpful in reorganizing the social structure by attracting the spontaneous energies of the people.

This elasticity of the social-economic structure may be regarded as even more important than the structure itself. Nothing is more alien to the spirit of democracy than the insistence upon institutional devices as if they incorporated ultimate wisdom once for all—a dogmatism in theory which in practice is likely to serve as an ideological disguise for group imperialism. Individual property or communal property are no ends in themselves, but only institutional forms of liberty and justice under more or less temporary conditions. This conditional character of democratic institutions cannot be stressed too much. Recognition of the institutional expression of the democratic principle is of great importance; it is equally important, however, to avoid the easy confusion between the expression and that which is expressed. Therefore, the entire argument of this book, and of this chapter in particular, may best be understood as an analysis of democratic procedure under the conditions here ascertained. The ascertaining of conditions is one thing, the building up of corresponding institutions another; existing conditions are currently misinterpreted and must be restated, and the knowledge of the true democratic principle, having completely vanished, must be restored. In order to clarify this principle, the complex pattern of democracy may be described in the most universal terms by dropping, for the moment, the whole issue of how to organize industry, farming, or any other particular field. The line of demarcation between industry and farming does not matter, but that between communal technique and one-man technique does because each plays a central role in shaping human experience and aims.

Decentralized organization of farming and centralized organization of industry, much as they appear to be demanded by present conditions, contain no permanent guarantee of democracy since there is no permanent guarantee of the continuance of present conditions. Important divisions of agriculture may shift to large-scale technique, and the electromotor may effect a decentralization in important sections of industry. This would, if humanly significant enough, require a readjustment of the line of demarcation between centralized and decentralized fields. But this by no means exhausts the problem, as the centralized sphere requires the strongest possible internal decentralization in behalf of the "individual property" demanded by Marx (see page 90), and the decentralized sphere must be connected with the centralized planned sphere at strategic points. The fundamental contrast between the two spheres is mitigated by these considerations, the two types converge to a certain degree in their development. This facilitates their integration in one comprehensive scheme. The appropriate relation between decentralizing and centralizing elements and the various techniques for combining them in different fields according to their social and technical structures constitute the general problems of democratic organization. They are certainly not solved once for all by reserving centralization for industry and decentralization for farming. Only by studying and adapting one's ideas to human experience can the solution be found always anew.[15]

A final question concerning the compatibility of different patterns under the unitary principle of democracy has to do with a possible growth of individual wealth and power in the individualistic section, that might lead to the return of capitalism. A threefold answer meets the objection. First, the scheme designed in the foregoing analysis preserves the individualistic organization where history has preserved the individualistic pattern of work and life. This is by definition the non-dynamic field, where the independence of the small units has not been affected and capitalism has not found an opportunity to intrude so far. This situation may change, but it indicates the stability of the system so long as those conditions obtain. Second, and this is closely connected with the first point: it seems as though Marxian totalitarianism has revived a doctrine which was ridiculed and killed by Marx himself. This is the so-called "primer of original accumulation," the doctrine of the growth of capitalism from nothing through a combination of superior skill and thrift. Marx denounced this as a bourgeois ideology designed to demon-

[15] This reference to human experience is designed to preclude the abuse of technical and calculatory speculation in vogue among Marxians. When every Marxian, with just indignation, rejects the suggestion that the cheaper Japanese production proves the inadequacy of the Russian industrial system and the necessity for breaking it up, there is no reason why some future possibility of cheaper farm products from tropical plantations operated by Negro slaves should be regarded as impairing the validity of the Danish farming system. See also page 137.

strate the higher morality and ability of the rich and the responsibility of the poor for their plight. He himself traced the origin of capital accumulation to all sorts of violence, legal and illegal, and insisted that the gradual growth of individual shops would never have provided the capital necessary for the Industrial Revolution. His reasoning obviously applies to the present problem too, though it contains only a probability for the future and certainly no guarantee for ever or for all possible turns of history.

The third consideration is that there is in fact no guarantee for ever, and that there can be none. There is as little guarantee in communism for the continuance of uncorrupted communism as there is in democracy for the continuance of democracy. Under a communistic system the planners in time of peace, the soldiers in time of war, or the secret police in peace and war may tacitly seize more power than would be consistent with the social objectives; the coal miners or the railroaders may exploit their economic key positions by pre-empting a higher share of the available stock of goods and exerting greater influence on the drafting of the plan. There is no safety in life—life is always dangerous and always in danger, and least of all is liberty an automaton. Special dangers belong to any particular structure and have to be met in appropriate ways. Every system has to watch over its line of demarcation. Thus democracy has to prevent a dangerous growth of individual power through taxation or through prohibiting the investment of excessive wealth; in its socialistic section it has to prevent by adequate checks and balances an abusive accumulation of administrative power or the abuse of economic power by any group. It is striking to see the impotent overwhelmed with concern about the problems of their grandchildren. For those who prefer to tackle the present, the political scientist and the statesman have to offer a practicable way without promising a solution in advance of all problems to come. To operate and preserve a system of liberty in a changing world depends half on reasonably good luck and half on the courage and capacity for liberty of the people and its leaders.

C. THE CONSTITUTION

This does not mean that the legal and constitutional guarantees of democracy are negligible—they are in fact vital. It only means that, while providing as far as possible for methods of coping with the unpredictable problems of the future, they must, first of all, regulate the current of present-day life.

Any discussion of legal details would be beyond the scope of this book and its author's competence. This applies even to the methods of representation and selection. We do not propose to discuss how to ascertain and shape the will of the people, how to secure an efficient civil service that would not succumb to the dangers of bureaucracy, or how to reconcile individual responsibility and criticism with the steadiness necessary for operating the complex politico-economic system. Our presentation certainly does not exhaust the range of possible questions; it does not even touch upon the technical particulars of political integration.

Two things, simple in themselves, but important practically because they are buried under a heap of disastrous misconceptions today, need to be said, however. First, democracy is not anarchy but a form of government; and second, democracy is not unfettered majority rule, but rule under definite constitutional limitations.

The idea that democracy permits absolute and unrestricted liberty to do as anybody pleases is absurd, whether

in existing democracies or in the future society we
discussed. Democracy is one form of state. In contradis-
tinction to other forms of the state, democracy and the
laws enacted by it may be discussed and criticized; but
as any other state it must be obeyed and protected against
dangers. Democratic liberty can never include the liberty
of destroying democracy by organized slander or armed
force. This fact ought to have been clear even before it
was driven home by the disastrous German experiment of
tolerating the organization of opposition on a military
basis owing to the Republic's lack of self-reliance and definite standards. What distinguishes the practice of democracy from that of fascism and other forcible forms of
government is not the renunciation of force in the face of
insurrection but the reduction to the attainable minimum
of such occasions through such an administration of justice to the people that they need not be suppressed to make
them comply with the law. The more people's willingness
to co-operate is used as a force to animate the body politic,
the less anyone can complain of the actual use of armed
power in case of need: Justice needs power and must not
abandon its power to injustice.

Tragic conflicts are certainly not eliminated by democracy; they may be said to become more tragic not as brute
force stands against brute force but as one interpretation
of justice stands against another. Revolt against the established government may be just, as its defenders may be
lacking in insight and good will; or suppression of a
revolt may be a public duty although we are aware of
our opponent's personal sincerity and our own shortcom-
ings. No present or future democracy can escape the tragic
possibilities inherent in political life as such. What matters for the political choice we all have to make, however,
is not the traits common to all political forms but the

differences between them. Once again it makes all the difference in the world whether or not we try to follow the lodestar of justice, are free to invoke its authority, and are enabled to invite public support.

The function of organized violence and the limitations upon its use have been discussed in connection with the Marxian doctrine of dictatorship. In the original version of this doctrine (page 75) the dictatorship was invoked for purely defensive purposes: protection against the anticipated resistance of the capitalists, aggressive as the recommended strategy of this battle might be. The positive reconstruction of the economic and social order needed no violence but followed only the spontaneous urge of a people supposedly united in communal work by capitalism. It is only in the later version of the doctrine (page 141) that violence organized by the dictatorship assumes a positive productive function: it is used to change the nature of a hundred million non-proletarian Russians so that they may fit into the proletarian scheme. The principle embodied in the first version of Marxism is a truism: any state, whether old or new, needs power to secure its existence; the graver the anticipated danger, the more power is needed. What the second version contains in excess of the first is the glorification of proletarian lust for power and imperialism. The extreme emphasis put upon the entire doctrine of dictatorship by the Communists is due not to the truism of the first version, but to the satisfaction of very undemocratic desires by the second version. Unfortunately, those opposed to the abuse of the doctrine are in danger of rejecting the truth in it just because those with a lust for power try to use the truism as a justification for their arbitrary actions. In this way the real issue is missed. Since a truly democratic regime is a government that is responsible for preserving the democratic order, it needs power to defend itself. What distinguishes democracy is the objective and direction of its rule, not the absence of any rule.

If the democratic goal is to be achieved, pluralism has to be made secure by being put into the constitution. The popular notion that democracy consists in acting as the majority desires is obviously very wrong if it is not confined to secondary decisions. No majority, unless it abrogates democracy, can decide to kill the members of the minority, to abdicate from its position of responsibility, to repeal the rights of national or religious groups, or to prohibit the free and dignified expression of independent and possibly non-conformist opinions. It is only within certain constitutional limits that a majority can act and that a change in the majority controlling the government may affect the course of policy. It is these limits first of all which characterize any democracy, incomplete though it may be, and prevent it from being a majority tyranny or a majority totalitarianism. They remind the majority that its will is not absolute but finite and that the different patterns, natures, and opinions possess inalienable rights because they have human value and possibly more human value in them.

Constitutional limitations are not by themselves sufficient to insure democracy. They may protect hierarchical privileges as well as the rights of men including that of equality. Everything depends on the content of these constitutional rights and restrictions, written and unwritten. In the traditional democracies political rights and civil liberties are rooted in the constitution. In the kingdom of social liberty and justice the fundamental pluralism of social patterns likewise needs to be incorporated in the constitution as the accepted interpretation of the rights of men under existing conditions. Politically this means the endorsement of parity and co-operation by the groups that establish the new order. By consenting to this stipulation they forego the possibility of ever attacking each other's pattern of life; they recognize each other's rights, and the limitation and particularity of their individual patterns and desires.

Whether there are two or more of such constitutionally recognized patterns makes no difference to the principle; whether there is one or two constitutes the difference between totalitarianism and liberty. There is an obligation to recognize human diversity as a value and to stop setting oneself up as a yardstick with which to measure mankind. Fairness to and love for other human beings and an incorruptible appreciation of human quality are the cardinal virtues of a spiritual life, and they are embodied to the greatest possible degree in a pluralistic constitution of democracy. That is why the democratic form of government has so precarious an existence. It requires more inner strength and poise to do justice to another than to oneself, to despise an impotent critic and to learn from an honest adversary than to persecute them, to relax from a pose of dignity and enjoy a joke on oneself than to display heroic gravity. All this is included in the distinction between pluralistic democracy and the totalitarian pattern imposed by a particular group. We should prize our liberty for all that it makes precious, but still be aware that there are different patterns of life that possess equally genuine significance for others. That thought leads us to a spiritual sense of human life and to a concrete although limited realization of the infinite spiritual values.

D. THE PROBLEM OF INTERNATIONAL INTEGRATION

This approach is the only one that can solve the problem of peace. No international social-economic pattern can ever secure peace: this was the conclusion we arrived at in our discussion of internationalism. There is much more cause for real pessimism here than in the analysis of the domestic patterns. A very distinct and simple principle exists by means of which liberty and integration within a given state may be achieved, though that principle may be easily overlooked or, if found, abused. Nothing of the kind exists in the international field. It is only as an independent state that any people may hope to institute a planned democratic basis for its life. The best it may expect in the international field is parallel endeavors in other countries and friendly exchange of advice with them as a moral and intellectual help. A plan such as is required for a minimum of security in any country, democratic or not, is a political act, and therefore presupposes a sovereign political body. Exchange of goods between countries is wholesome for all and may be indispensable for some of them, but does not make them into one unified body because it does not equalize their very different levels of wealth. This is certainly a precarious situation and becomes increasingly so the more their population rates vary. What can be said from the social-economic angle is only that there is less danger of conflict if everybody is well settled at home and sees prospects and tasks ahead. What remains is a question of political intelligence and morality, and that is eventually a question of constitutions. Wide historical experience certainly does not support the belief that democracy guarantees peace. Still it remains true that that same spirit of self-restraint for the sake of liberty which results at home in genuine democracy, works for peace abroad. Totalitarianism, devoted as it is to the worship of its own inflated self, has in itself no principle for peacefully organizing a certainly diversified world. It may behave peacefully for practical reasons dur-

ing domestic reconstruction or because of military considerations, but nothing in its philosophy compels it to
do so. A pluralistic philosophy recognizes the values and
claims to liberty that others have and is not confined to
any political or national borderline. It might therefore
lead to an organization of justice on an international
scale and thereby attain real peace.

3. The Applicability of the Doctrine

This leads to the final question, what is the use of
discussing such a scheme of democracy as we have proposed? What are its prospects and chances? Is its realization possible? If by possibility one means the inner consistency and logical coherence of institutions and their
harmony with existing tendencies in occidental life, the
realization of the program is unquestionably possible. This
even understates the strength of our case. The realization
of the proposed political order is historically necessary in
exactly the sense that classical socialism claimed for its
own scheme. The true elements in the notion of historical
necessity were used to build up our notion of democracy.
Democracy corresponds to the true interests in liberty and
security of the groups that establish it, as classical socialism corresponds to the true interests of the workers under
a supposed system of universal large-scale production. The
workers would not only follow their own interests as assumed in that older scheme, but would realize that there
is a most indispensable and powerful section of production
outside their own sphere and that it is to their interest
to limit their claims to their own sphere and give way to
the claims of those working in the other spheres. The
farmers would be freed from the menace of suppression
by the industrial workers and would join forces with them
under the impact of another capitalistic crisis in order to

acquire that security from creditors and the crisis which they have always desired. It is true that the farmers could nearly always decide for fascism if they wanted to. But it is difficult to see why they should prefer it to democracy since democracy also offers them a ruling position and their whole energy in the event of a crisis could be turned against the representatives of the system responsible for the crisis. It would be foolish for them to attack the workers needlessly when they are not attacked by them. Democracy offers them a more simple and logical solution than fascism. It enables them to free themselves of the imminent danger with comparative certainty and ease. If they were to turn against both capital and labor their task would be decidedly more complicated and could not lead to greater economic success. All these considerations are borne out by the growth of democratic movements in several leading countries. Democracy is the most simple, most logical, and least revolutionary solution in terms of actual conflict.

Recent events have deprived the democratic program of that triumphal certitude so characteristic of the older doctrines; these, however, have been frustrated by history. We contemporaries of communism and fascism can no longer believe that the rational force behind well-understood and well-balanced interests inevitably rules history. We are left with the doctrine of the political norms themselves and the earnest hope that a positive elaboration of their spiritual significance and institutional logic may be helpful after so much confusion and sophistication.

If the rational norms truly represent something like the inner logic of those existing tendencies that are striving for liberty in an integrated order, it may serve as a basis for evaluating the course of political events. These events could then be judged according to their deviation from the standard. The overt and hidden suppressions and the disturbances in social cohesion could thus be recognized, and the amount of avoidable destruction which men choose to accept or to achieve would become conspicuous. Any true understanding of political movements would have to be attained through a use of the principles formulated in the system of rational norms.

But this system must not be used merely as a gauge for academic measurement. Realization and preservation of the rational order is far from being certain, yet it is still within the range of possibility. If men's faith in and desire for liberty and peace are violated and abused without end, they are still among the driving forces of history as surely as a spiritual existence is among the potentialities of man. Therefore we ought to know what is the true way out of the deep entanglement of our political troubles and what is the actual form of peace and justice in this world of ours. It is needless to invoke justice and peace unless we attempt to implant them in the world through coherent and working institutions. This book tries to demonstrate that an approach to this true task of political humanism is practically possible because even under the most precarious conditions it is theoretically conceivable. It is an entirely realistic approach; forceful movements in various countries point in its direction. And we need not believe in the necessary realization of justice to pronounce justice.

INDEX

absolutism, 18, 71, 122, 145, 222
Abyssinian war, 233 ff.
agriculture,
see also: co-operatives; defeated in Russia, 115 ff.; democratic farmers, 216, 268 ff.; development under communism, 126 ff.; as economic foundation, 118 ff., 152 ff.; German farmers, 210 ff.; individual farming, 33, 40 ff.; and socialism, 130 ff., 158 ff.; in western countries, 133 ff., 151 ff.
America, 30, 31, 87, 208, 269; democracy in, 32 f., 269
American revolution, 21 f., 26, 58, 146, 167, 175
anarchism,
distinguished from democracy, 53, 59, 276; syndicalism as, 164
Anglo-Saxon countries, 171 ff., 187, 204
anticipation of development as center of communist theory, 111 ff., 122, 127, 137 f., 142, 148, 150
anti-Semitism, 221 f., 236
aristocracy, 29, 57 n., 106, 193
Aristotle, 147 n.
armament, 58, 171
army, 18, 74, 164, 210, 242
Athens, 147
Austria, 162, 203; downfall of democracy, 212
autarchy, 196 ff.
authoritarian system, 47 ff., 59 n., 80, 93, 180, 213

Bauer, O., 161 f.
Bavaria, 164
Belgium, 197
Berlin, 163; traffic strike in, 189
Bingham, Alfred, 207 n., 218 n.
blood and soil, 215 ff., 236, 245
bourgeoisie, 23 ff., 71, 145 ff.
Brady, R. A., 182 n.
Brentano, Lujo, 86

British, 56, 87; Empire, 166, 172, 224, 270 n.; Guild socialism, 104
Bryce, J., 147 n.
Bukharin, N., 141
bureaucracy, 22 f., 29 f., 102 f., 145, 185, 276

capital, 25, 27, 69, 90, 133 ff., 143
capitalism,
communist theory of, 109 ff.; free, 22 ff., 29 ff.; socialist theory of, 66 ff.; under mercantilism, 17 ff.
cartel, 45, 81
Catholicism, 209 ff., 226, 238
Chinese labor, 208 n.
Christianity, 78, 124 f., 228 ff.
civil servants, 163 f., 174, 185
classes in capitalism, 29 ff., 65 ff.; require state, 77; classes and groups, 257 ff.
Cohen, Morris R., 218 n.
collective and individual ownership, passim
collectivization of farming, 126 ff., 137, 156, 162, 174
communism,
and agriculture, 115 ff., 268; anticipates the development, 112 ff.; as applied Marxism, 109 ff.; character of dictatorship, 138 ff.; conditions of Russian victory, 116 ff.; defeat in western countries, 164 ff.; and equality, 259; and fascism, 188 ff.; German, 160, 189 n., 210 ff.; heritage of syndicalism, 105 ff.; Strachey on, 171 ff.
Communist Manifesto, 76, 131
constitution, 47, 54 f., 147; in pluralistic democracy, 276 ff.; Russian, 169 ff.
co-operatives, farmers', 42 ff., 64 n., 71, 90 f., 132 ff., 162 n.; and pluralistic democracy, 268 ff.

285

Requisites of civil liberty

(a) agreement on fundamentals e.g.
   religious freedom, right to own
   property

(b) Order & reasonable prosperity.

Requisites of civil liberty

(a) agreement on fundamentals e.g.
religious freedom, right to own
property

(b) Order & reasonable prosperity.